Tokyo Calling:

Japanese Overseas Radio Broadcasting 1937-1945

Jane M. J. Robbins

EUROPEAN PRESS ACADEMIC PUBLISHING

2001

Japanese Studies Series

directed by Yone Sugita

This series deals with various aspects of Japanese studies, including history, politics, diplomacy, security, economics, literature, cultural studies, comparative studies, and other fields. There are many concepts, ways of thinking, lifestyles, traditions, and ideas widely accepted in Japan that are not familiar to people outside Japan. The major purpose of this series is to introduce diverse viewpoints on Japan and to precipitate constructive discussion to have better understanding this country.

This series is unique because it includes research monographs not only by scholars and researchers in the academic community, but also by professionals (such as doctors, lawyers, business executives, etc.) and practitioners (such as NGO representatives, volunteer groups organizers, etc.). The common thread among the series authors is that they are all respected individuals who offer new perspectives on Japanese studies.

Other books of the Japanese Studies Series

Timothy Iles, *Abe Kôbô: an Exploration of his Prose, Drama, and Theatre*

Ryuji Mukae, *Japan's Refugee Policy: To be of the World*

Cover design by Biz Stone

ISBN 88-8398-013-1

Via Valle Bantini,4 – Fucecchio, Firenze, Italy

www.e-p-a-p.com

TABLE OF CONTENTS

List of Maps and Figures

INTRODUCTION

From the 1920s, there were parallel developments in the separate but inter-linked fields of propaganda and radio, both of which had been used experimentally during World War One. During the 1930s overseas broadcasting became one of the principal means by which one state sought to influence the thought or behaviour of the population in another. In most economically advanced countries the development of broadcasting was under state control. It was, thus, natural that states developed broadcasting for state purposes. In the inter-war years, notions of mass psychology and the manipulation of public emotion also developed in both democratic and totalitarian states and these ideas increased the perceived importance of both domestic and overseas broadcasting. By the start of World War Two all the major powers had established regular short-wave broadcasting schedules, along with official monitoring posts, which sought to determine the potential threat of incoming transmissions. Japan was a member of this group of international broadcasters and Japan's overseas radio broadcasting during the China and Pacific Wars (1937-45) was an ambitious and far-reaching operation.

Despite this, some European scholars seem to have implicitly dismissed the Pacific aspect of World War Two as secondary to the European theatre, and the efforts of Japanese propagandists as secondary and inferior to those of Germany. The propaganda activities of Italy have often been treated in the same way. Charles Rolo, writing in 1944, described Italian overseas radio as "Berlin's Branch Office" which "became but an echo of its German lord and master after Italy's entry into the war." Japan's "Penny Whistles from the Far East" were similarly described as "a crude imitation of Berlin's." (Rolo, 1943:105 & 170)

This attitude, however, generally reflects the lack of research undertaken by Western scholars into Japan's propaganda activities, and into its overseas broadcasting in particular. Much has been written in both German and English regarding the activities of Josef Goebbels and all facets of the Nazi propaganda machine. However, the only major study to analyse Japan's wartime radio operations is Kitayama Setsurō's three volume work in Japanese, *Rajio Tōkyō* which was published in 1988. So far, this work has been neglected by both Japanese and Western scholars.

The objective of this study is to bring Japan's overseas radio propaganda into a more central position in World War Two historical debates. In so doing it seeks to assess whether Japanese propaganda was generally inferior to that of the other belligerents, as is frequently assumed. Did it have any distinctive features? Or did it merely follow patterns developed by Nazi Germany? This follows an important trend in Pacific War studies, studying the issue in broad terms. It does not concentrate on one region, period or theme, but spans the whole course of the war and compares it to developments in other countries. In so doing it is necessary to trace the development of the changing political and military situation in the Pacific War, in order to assess the reliability and significance of Japanese propaganda in its complex content.

Apart from Kitayama's work, there are few studies which examine Japanese radio broadcasting, either domestic or international. The Japan Broadcasting Corporation, NHK, published two histories to celebrate its fiftieth anniversary in 1975, one in Japanese and one in English. The Japanese version is more detailed than the English language one, but their very nature, 50-Year General Histories, limits their detailed treatment of any one period. In addition, they did not draw upon material from archives in the United States, Britain and Australia, being based exclusively on material in NHK and Japanese Government sources, which are extremely limited.

The only major work in English on Japanese overseas broadcasting is L.D. Meo's *Japan's Radio War on Australia*. Published in 1968, this deals exclusively with Japanese broadcasts to Australia and is based on material contained in the monitoring reports of the Melbourne Listening Post. This is a very detailed and immensely valuable monograph. However, as a result of its narrow regional focus, it does not assess Japan's radio propaganda activity in broad terms and thus cannot attempt to set Japanese broadcasting into the overall picture of World War Two propaganda.

In this current study much of the detailed content of broadcasts is drawn from the BBC's Monitoring Reports, daily records of all foreign broadcasts picked up by the monitoring station, which date back to 1939. Despite some limitations, which are described in Appendix 1, the *Summary of World Broadcasts* offers a daily account of world-wide short-wave broadcasting which is unique and of immense value.

Much other material has been drawn from the vast volume of material relating to wartime radio broadcasting, which is held in the United States' National Archives in Washington D.C. Along with the NHK archive this was one of the principal sources used by Kitayama in preparing his work. However, Kitayama knew nothing of the BBC material, which does not appear to have been consulted previously by scholars.

A further major source of information for this study was Mr. Kitayama Setsurō, the author of *Rajio Tōkyō*. He also kindly provided copies of material from his private collection of broadcasting memorabilia, acquired from people he had interviewed during the course of his own research.

Some historians may assume that there have been few studies of Japan's overseas broadcasting in World War Two because there is insufficient material on which to base such a study. However, this is not the case. There exists an abundance of material. The aim of this study is to provide an overview of the whole of Japanese overseas broadcasting during World War Two in an attempt to fill an important gap in scholarship on the Pacific War. It will seek to examine the views and values expressed by Japanese broadcasts to different regions, their relation to each other and to views expressed within Japan. It will also consider the Japanese approach to overseas broadcasting in comparison to that of other belligerents, both Japan's Axis partners and the Western Allies. Finally, this study will attempt to assess the effectiveness of Japanese overseas radio propaganda in achieving the results Japanese propagandists sought to achieve.

CHAPTER 1
THE DEVELOPMENT OF SHORT-WAVE BROADCASTING IN JAPAN

1. INTERNATIONAL SHORT-WAVE BROADCASTING: A QUICK SURVEY

Radio was first used for propaganda in the later stages of World War One. The potential of a medium which, unlike the press, was not confined by national borders, was recognised but radio was not a major means of disseminating propaganda amongst the population at large. However, the significance of its potential meant that the Treaty of Versailles included a three-month ban on broadcasting from certain German stations, and on the German government constructing any new radio stations. (Taylor, 1983:29)

One of the reasons the Allies feared the use of radio for propaganda was that they had witnessed Soviet experiments with radio as a tool of the Comintern, following the Russian Revolution of 1917. Bolshevik ideology held that class revolution in Europe was the inevitable next stage of world history and the Comintern was established to aid this. During the turmoil of the closing stages of World War One Soviet radio had urged the proletariat, regardless of for whom they fought, to rise up and fulfil their revolutionary destiny. Later it urged on British workers on to success during the 1926 General Strike and continually encouraged German workers to revolt between 1930 and 1933.

Figure 1 clearly indicates that, with the exception of the Soviet Union, the states which made the first short-wave broadcasts were those with colonial Empires spanning the globe. The Dutch and the British began experiments in the use of long-wave frequencies in broadcasting in 1927. However, research switched to the use of short-wave when it became clear that long-wave transmissions were proving unsatisfactory. Dutch short-wave broadcasts proper began on 24 December 1928. These were in Dutch, principally directed at Dutch people living or travelling overseas.

1928	Holland
1929	Soviet Union
1931	France: "Radio Colonial"
1932	League of Nations: "Radio Nations" Great Britain: "Empire Service"
1933	Germany
1934	Italy, Belgium
1935	Japan
1936	Yugoslavia, Iceland, Czechoslovakia
1937	Denmark, United States: NBC and CBS

Figure 1. Dates when regular short-wave broadcasting began in different countries (Ono, 1982:2)

The British experienced some technical problems and so did not begin their regular short-wave service until much later. In the meantime the French "Radio Colonial" (later "Paris Mondial") began regular broadcasts to French colonies in Asia, Africa and the West Indies on 1 May 1931. Unlike other mother countries France adopted a policy of broadcasting in languages other than the mother tongue from the beginning. Broadcasts were thus on topics of general and cultural interest and avoided political issues, so as to promote a gradual process of cultural assimilation.

The BBC's short-wave service, the "Empire Service," began regular broadcasts from Daventry on 19 December 1932. Like the Dutch, the British broadcasts were directed at British people living in the colonies, so there was a strict policy of broadcasting solely in English. This continued until world events forced the British Government to reassess this policy in 1938. From the beginning the BBC divided its broadcasting into five geographical transmission regions centred on Australia, the Far East, India, South Africa and Canada. (Briggs, 1965b:381) It negotiated with the national broadcasting corporations in Australia and Canada, to have the Daventry broadcasts inserted into their regular schedules. These corporations then relayed the BBC's short-wave broadcasts across the national network on medium-wave so that more listeners could hear them. (Ono, 1982:10)

Experiments in short-wave broadcasting were carried out in Germany from 1929, but there was no regular short-wave service until 1 April 1933, after the Nazis had come to power. Significantly, this service was placed under the directorship of the Minister for Propaganda, Josef Goebbels, as was all radio broadcasting.

In general, German overseas broadcasts were shaped to suit the culture, language and educational background of their listeners. Programmes were skilfully adapted to suit the expected audience. Consequently, on separate occasions they appealed to workers or the upper classes, the majorities or minorities. When Germany began broadcasting in Afrikaans in 1938, it became very popular amongst the Afrikaners in South Africa, who abandoned the BBC's "Empire Service," which was still only broadcasting in English. (Ono, 1982:13) In addition, German radio made a point of researching and celebrating the local festivals of the region to which it was broadcasting, and also paid homage to local heroes.

Intensive German radio campaigns towards an area usually preceded diplomatic or military action. The case of propaganda towards Austria prior to the entry of the German army in March 1938 is a good example. Between 1933 and 1935 German radio had attempted to cause riots in Austria in order to bring down the Dolfuss government, using Austrian Nazis in Germany to produce and present the broadcasts.

While major powers stepped up national and international radio propaganda, the League of Nations established a station transmitting on short-wave in February 1932. Named "Radio Nations," it broadcast from Geneva principally in order to keep League officials working in difficult situations around the world in touch with the League's headquarters. However, Radio Nations may also be considered a propaganda station, in that it deliberately advertised the ideals and aims of the League in an increasingly turbulent decade.

At the World Disarmament Conference between 1932 and 1934, the Polish delegation called for "moral disarmament" with regard to radio propaganda. The League of Nations' response was to call on all countries to use radio "to create better mutual understanding between peoples." (Taylor, 1983:31) There had been previous agreements not to transmit propaganda, such as a *Union Internationale de Radiodiffusion* (UIR) resolution passed in 1926, to prevent nations making broadcasts which might have a political religious or spiritual content damaging to international relations. There were also "gentlemen's agreements" on similar lines, such as one between Germany and Poland in 1931, but these were rendered virtually ineffective by 1933. Indeed, at the Madrid Telecommunications Conference in 1932, the Italian delegation asked for a resolution to be passed which would allow a state to jam "unfavourable broadcasts" made by a foreign power. There was, however, little support for the resolution and it progressed no further.

In 1936, twenty-eight countries signed a League of Nations convention entitled "Concerning the use of International Broadcasting in the cause of Peace." By signing it they agreed to "prohibit the radiation from their territories of broadcasts detrimental to good international understanding, of warlike and subversive propaganda and of false news" and to promote cultural and peaceful relations with other countries. (Mance,1944:37-8) The details of the convention were, however, imprecise and only extremely serious infringements were punishable. The convention expressed a spirit of co-operation rather than a series of concrete laws. It came into effect on 1 April 1938, having been ratified by nineteen of the twenty-eight signatories. It was, however, never a serious obstacle to the worsening propaganda war of the late 1930s, for whilst Britain, France and the Soviet Union had signed the convention, Germany and Italy had not, and this rendered the agreement virtually impotent.

In the 1930s the Middle East was the scene of the first full-scale "war" between democratic and fascist short-wave radio stations. This was initiated by the Italian station at Bari, which expanded its services from seven to fourteen languages during the build up to the Abyssinian war in October 1935. Italian broadcasts to Britain were conciliatory, but those to the Arab world were vehemently anti-British. Broadcasts to Egypt and Palestine, in particular, portrayed Britain as the imperialistic oppressor and Italy as the defender of Islam. Radio receivers locked into Italian stations were distributed free to cafés and other places where people gathered. These programmes included popular Arab singers and poetry, which were interspersed between propaganda items.

British officials were, initially, unconcerned by these broadcasts, and only occasionally broadcast very late replies to Italian accusations from the BBC's station in Jerusalem. By the autumn of 1937, it was clear that this response was insufficient, and on 24 October the Postmaster General, G.C. Tyron, announced to parliament that the BBC would begin an "Arabic Service," abandoning its policy of only broadcasting in English. The "Arabic Service" became operational on 3 January 1938. It failed to respond directly to Italian accusations, however, instead broadcasting talks by friendly Muslim leaders, and readings from the Koran. Indeed, it was referred to by critics as objectivity turned to extreme dullness. The Italian station at Bari ridiculed the BBC's attempts at foreign broadcasting, but following a "gentleman's agreement" between the two countries later the same year Italian attacks died down.

Another important battleground of the "radio war" between the democracies and fascists was Latin America. Germany and Italy were in an advantageous position, as there were large numbers of expatriate Germans and Italians in several South American states. Germany began a co-ordinated radio campaign on South America in February 1934, and broadcasts to Central America began in May 1935. By 1938 Zeesen was broadcasting twelve hours a day to South and Central America and in 1939 a separate transmission was established solely for broadcasts to Brazil.

There were few short-wave receivers in Latin American states, so the Germans developed several ways to disseminate their message. Like the Italians in the Middle East, they distributed radios locked into their own station. They also had their programme schedules printed in local newspapers. Visitors to Germany broadcast greetings home in special programmes, and when other countries attempted to broadcast to South America the station at Zeesen jammed their frequencies.

As the problem of minimal numbers of short-wave radios in Latin America persisted, Nazi propagandists began another tactic. Local South American stations were allowed to fill their airtime by relaying German short-wave broadcasts on medium-wave at no cost. In addition, the German broadcasters produced pre-recorded and canned programmes which were sent out for use by these stations which could often not afford to produce many of their own programmes. To strengthen Latin American ties with Germany, exchange broadcasts were also encouraged.

The British response to fascist propaganda directed at Latin America was slow. It was not until March 1938 that the BBC began its second foreign overseas service, the "Latin American Service," which broadcast for three hours a day and included two sections in Spanish and one in Portuguese. These sections were generally news bulletins and the remaining programmes and talks were usually in English. In addition, the BBC failed to provide free services in order to advertise its ideas. News from the BBC was copyrighted and so could not be freely used by local newspapers. Although British government intervention later released a free news service, the BBC continued to charge for its advance programme schedules. The combined effect of these policies was that British broadcasts were considerably less popular than German ones.

French broadcasts to Latin America were even less well organised. "Radio Colonial" had always included some broadcasts in Portuguese, but these were intended for French colonial possessions and were not broadcast specifically for South America. With the establishment of a new short-wave station, "Paris Mondial", in the spring of 1938, South America became one of four zones to which special programmes were broadcast. Bad organisation, however, placed Central America in the North American zone, which received broadcasts in English, German, Italian and French, but not in Spanish.

During the Munich Crisis in 1938, the BBC began broadcasting news bulletins and translations of talks by British politicians in German and Italian. After the Crisis, these became regular broadcasts and formed the "European Service," which was added to the three existing services. By 1939, the BBC was transmitting in sixteen languages but its broadcasts were always characterised by the unemotional presentation of the information. British schedules were also inflexible, so that broadcasts usually went ahead on time, even if they clashed with a speech by Hitler or Mussolini.

The French also began broadcasts in German and Italian, although there was a general lack of organisation in much French short-wave broadcasting. In addition, French radio was at times further hindered by broadcasts being banned at the last minute by politicians, following a policy of appeasement towards Nazi Germany.

The one major Western power absent from the 1930s "radio war" was the United States. American policy towards much of the world remained detached. Americans often felt far removed from events in Europe, and the political focus was on domestic events and conditions. The nature of radio ownership and organisation in the United States also played a role. American radio stations were private companies and they relied on advertising for their income. There was no centralised organisation capable of arranging programmes for transmission abroad, as a centralised government station conflicted with the strongly held American ideal of private enterprise.

American companies were granted short-wave licences in 1929, but before 1936 overseas broadcasting consisted of merely transmitting domestic broadcasts simultaneously on the home network and to Latin America. The programmes were not adapted for the foreign audience, nor were languages other than English used. Furthermore, no effort was made to persuade local stations to relay American broadcasts on medium-wave and no research was carried out by the American companies into the conditions and tastes of the audience, as research was expensive, and not economically viable for a commercial station. The aim of broadcasting American programmes to South America was to familiarise Latin Americans with North American radio, in order to encourage sponsorship, which would fund research into broadcasting specifically for South America, and later Europe.

After Japan's attack on Pearl Harbor on 7 December 1941 the need for United States' Government control over short-wave broadcasting was recognised, and in November 1942, following its establishment the previous June, the Office of War Information (OWI) took over supervision of the broadcasting companies and all propaganda. In February 1941, the Government had established its own short-wave station, the Voice of America (VOA) and later established other stations such as the Armed Forces Radio and Television Service (AFRS) and the World Wide Broadcasting System (WWBS).

As a result, short-wave propaganda broadcasting in English and foreign languages developed rapidly. (Ono, 1982:16)

2. THE START OF OVERSEAS BROADCASTING

Domestic radio broadcasting in Japan began in March 1925. That autumn NHK received a letter from Wrangell, Alaska, stating that a Japanese station had been picked up there. Almost a year later, on 30 August 1926, the Japanese Ministry of Communications Electric Laboratory picked up its first foreign broadcast from KGO in Oakland, California, which was beginning to make experimental medium-wave broadcasts to Japan. (Kitayama, 1988a:14-16) From this time Japanese interest in international broadcasting grew, as it was growing in advanced countries in Europe and the United States.

NHK began two types of research into international broadcasting. The first was an investigation into experimental broadcasts already made by European broadcasting organisations. In addition, from February 1926 JOAK (Tokyo Central Broadcasting) received Ministry of Communications permission to make monthly short-wave transmissions for one year. It transmitted a request to amateur radio hams overseas, asking them to write in if they had received the transmissions, which were made on 30 and 35 metres short-wave. These transmissions were principally directed towards Australia and the West Coast of the United States and would probably have been in both Japanese and English in order to receive as many responses as possible.

In 1928 NHK's domestic radio stations were formed into a national network and their power was increased to five kilowatts. (Kitayama, 1988a:19) Following this Japanese stations were frequently audible on the West Coast of Canada and the United States and in Australia where the Sendai Central Broadcasting's signal was often clearly audible. Indeed, when the Sendai station became aware that its domestic broadcasts were often audible on the Pacific Coast of the United States it began to quote a San Francisco Japanese newspaper, *Shinsekai* (*New World)* as one of its regular news sources.

Interest in broadcasting to Europe followed. The first planned Japanese short-wave broadcast to Europe was in August 1929, when the German airship, *Graf Zeppelin*, reached Japan on its journey around the world. A broadcast of greetings to Germany by diplomatic officials and the airship pilots was planned, but the quality of Japanese equipment proved inadequate and the transmission failed. (NHK 1977c:63)

Plans for another overseas broadcast were made in an ambitious project to broadcast from the Naval Arms Limitation Talks in London in 1930. The opening ceremony and a later conversation between the Japanese Ambassador Matsudaira Tsuneo (as an English speaking representative of Prime Minister Hamaguchi), President Hoover and Prime Minister MacDonald were to be broadcast to Japan by the BBC. NHK was to relay them on its medium-wave network whilst the American station KGO, which was involved in a joint development venture with NHK, was to use the Japanese experimental short-wave station to boost the transmission signal in order to transmit the broadcasts to the United States. Transmission of the opening ceremony on 8 February failed due to problems at the British end. The first KGO transmission to America also failed, as the output of the Japanese-made equipment proved inadequate. Following adjustments by KGO engineers, however, the conversation between the three national leaders was successfully transmitted to the United States. This was the first overseas short-wave broadcast to be made from Japan. However, the Wall Street Crash the previous year and subsequent recession had already weakened the position of KGO which was forced to relinquish its share in research at the Japanese experimental station and further joint development plans were abandoned. (Kitayama, 1988a:25-8)

In the period following this first successful transmission to the United States Japanese-American exchange broadcasts flourished. On Christmas Day 1930 songs and greetings from San Francisco were broadcast to Japan and these were returned in a Japanese transmission starting at 12.30pm the next day. The President of NHK, Iwahara Kenzō, acknowledged these broadcasts in his New Year speech and called for further development in international broadcasting in the New Year.

However, the development of Japanese-American broadcasting relations suffered significantly after 18 September 1931, when Japanese forces began the conquest of Manchuria.

The Manchurian Incident [*Manshū Jiken*] changed the direction of Japanese broadcasting development. Hitherto overseas broadcasting had lacked a strong political mission, and was principally concerned with maintaining links with Japanese abroad, and raising Japanese technical prestige to the level of that of major Western powers. From this time, the Japanese government saw it as a means of defending Japanese actions in Manchuria in the face of international criticism. Radio was also considered essential in the attempt to establish the puppet state of Manchukuo [*Manshūkoku*]. In the early stages of the Manchurian Incident NHK staff and transmission equipment were sent to assist the Kwantung Army. The army used the equipment to establish radio exchanges between Tokyo and the capital of Manchuria, Hsinking. (Kitayama, 1988a:41) The aim of these broadcasts was to encourage the colonisation of Manchuria by Japanese. Broadcasts from Hsinking, which defended Japan's presence in Manchuria, were also made to the United States, Europe, China and the Soviet Union.

Following the outbreak of the Manchurian Incident, radio became increasingly important to the Japanese in the dissemination of propaganda, for in the face of League of Nations criticism of Japanese action in Manchuria, overseas radio became one of Japan's primary tools to inform the world of Tokyo's views.[1] As a result tighter government control over broadcasting became a priority. A meeting of government officials established the basis for the formation, in September 1932, of the "Information Committee" (*Jōhō Iinkai*) which was to "guide" the output of radio propaganda.

In early January 1932 the League of Nations established the Lytton Commission to investigate the situation in Manchuria, and on 7 January the United States announced its adoption of the Stimson Doctrine. Naturally, this was a criticism of Japanese operations in Manchuria. A week later an American journalist, Floyd Gibbons, was permitted to broadcast to the United States on short-wave from Kwantung Army Headquarters in Manchuria. This broadcast was an example of Japan's new use for short-wave broadcasts. During the course of the broadcast Gibbons said,

> *I ate and slept with the Japanese Army for three weeks prior to its triumphal entry into the Kum region and I respect and admire the rigour of its military discipline and the strength of its sense of righteousness. Having seen the plunder, rape and insatiable atrocities of the rebels I consider it natural that the Japanese Army subjugate them. (Kitayama, 1988a:43)*

The *New York Times* described the report as the first clear war broadcast from Manchuria.

Japanese broadcasts to American and Britain, were highly critical of the Lytton Report, and the criticism increased throughout the latter part of 1932 and 1933. The League of Nations accepted the Lytton report on 24 February 1933 whereupon Japan withdrew from the organisation. Japan's increasing isolation from the international community in 1932 and 1933 necessitated the use of radio to express the Japan's viewpoint to the rest of the world. On 1 June 1932, NHK began broadcasting a weekly English language programme on short-wave entitled "Current Topics." Its aim was to present current affairs to the English speaking world from a Japanese perspective, at a time when Japan was the object of widespread international suspicion.

After September 1932 all radio output was scrutinised by the government's Information Committee, which met weekly as part of Japan's aim to increase overseas transmissions. The Committee decided that news reports from the established news agencies gave the news from a British or American perspective. In the past Japanese news had always been handled by Reuters as part of Asia. There had been previous attempts by the Japanese authorities to break the Reuters' hold on news in Japan, such as the establishment of the Kokusai agency in 1914 and its successor, Rengō, (The Japan Newspaper Association) formed in 1926 in conjunction with AP, but Reuters maintained a strong influence. In an attempt to rectify this situation the Japanese government formed its own news agency, Dōmei, to provide news from a Japanese perspective. It was formed in 1936 by merging Rengō and its counterpart for telegraphic messages, Dentsu, at a time when Reuters' influence was greatly diminished following a long battle with AP. It began operations on 1 January 1936, becoming the first real Japanese news agency. (Purdy, 1992)

In 1933 Germany also withdrew from the League of Nations, and to many Japanese, Germany increasingly appeared a natural ally. To encourage links with Germany, NHK began exchange broadcasts with the German short-wave station at Zeesen in November 1933. These were usually musical exchanges, such as live broadcasts of concerts, and they proved to be popular in Japan. In contrast, however, broadcast links with America became less popular with the Japanese authorities. On 18 November 1933, NHK was permitted to participate in an international musical celebration of the opening of the new NBC Radio Centre by transmitting music to the Rockefeller Center in New York. However, the Japanese government refused to allow the broadcast of the programme on the domestic Japanese network. (Kitayama, 1988a:66-7) This was the first indication of a policy whereby German culture had governmental approval, and was encouraged, but that of the democracies (particularly America) was restricted in Japan. (The transmission made to New York reflected a desire to maintain Japan's international image.)

Despite the growing political attraction of Germany, exchanges between Japan and America did not cease. In April 1934 a very ambitious broadcast was planned for the Emperor's Birthday, which aimed to create a radio link across the Pacific, involving stations in San Francisco, Manila, Bandung, Bangkok, Hsinking and Tokyo. Following its success, there were other broadcasts involving several stations, which aimed to forge "links across the Pacific."

In 1934 the government decided that the BBC would be given the honour of the Christmas exchange. The Japanese government decided on this so as to promote Japanese political, economic and cultural ideas to a wider audience than Germany and America. A Federation of British Industries Mission led by Lord Barnby had visited Japan and Manchuria the previous

September. It was officially an unofficial trade mission which the government allowed under pressure from British exporters who feared that the continued non-recognition of Manchuria would result in the loss of a potentially valuable market. The mission was unofficial as the British government had to consider the political repercussions surrounding trade with a country whose recognition was forbidden by the League of Nations. During the trip, however, members of the mission had received an audience with the Japanese Emperor, an honour incompatible with the unofficial status of the mission. The report issued by the mission after it's visit stated, "We expect and hope Britain to export capital goods to Manchurian cities, which are developing rapidly" and concluded that there were good prospects for Anglo-Japanese co-operation in the development of cities in Manchuria. (Kitayama, 1988a:101) It is a reasonable supposition that the Christmas good-will exchange broadcast was part of the Japanese policy of improving ties between Japan and Britain to encourage Britain to recognise, and trade with, Manchuria.

During this period of increasing overseas radio activity there were several changes in political attitudes towards broadcasting in Japan. In October 1934, the Army Ministry published a pamphlet regarding national defence based on their new policy, which stated that "A battlefield is the Father of Creation and the Mother of Culture." (Kitayama, 1988a:95) This dealt principally with propaganda concerning the role of Manchuria in Japanese policy, and the Japanese role in developing Manchuria. It was published at the same time that talks were being held in London over the limitation of naval armaments in October and November 1934.

From the end of October 1934, there was much discussion about the repeal of the 1922 Washington Naval Arms Limitation Treaty, which had set the level of British, American and Japanese capital warships at a ratio of 5:5:3. On 3 December the Cabinet decided to repeal the treaty. This was a significant step which led to deteriorating relations between Japan and the United States.

Research into short-wave broadcasting continued in late 1934 and early 1935, and on 3 March 1935 NHK applied to the government for permission to broadcast a regular short-wave overseas service. The specified aims of the service were "to communicate truly authentic news, and all cultural truth to concerned Japanese abroad and to other peoples." (Kitayama, 1982:115) 23 March marked the tenth anniversary of NHK broadcasting and its President, Iwahara Kenzō, announced the establishment of an overseas service to celebrate the event.[2] Following detailed planning and consultations with representatives from the Ministry of Foreign Affairs (although there were none with representatives of the Ministry of Communications which became responsible for radio output) official governmental permission to establish the overseas service was granted on 4 May.

At 10.30am on 1 June the NHK overseas service opened, a month after its planned opening, according to a letter dated 15 April 1935 from the Head of the Overseas Section to Mr. J. D. Benzie of the BBC's Foreign and Overseas Department,[3] with the words, "*Toku kaigai Minasama! Kochira wa Nihon Hōsō Kyōkai, Tōkyō Atagoyama no sutajio de-arimasu.*" [Greetings everyone in far off lands! This is the NHK studion at Atagoyama, Tokyo.] (Kitayama, 1988a:111) Broadcasting on 14,600 kilocycles per second (kc/s) with a call sign of JVH, the service's 50kw transmitter was second only to the BBC's Empire Service in output power.

The initial broadcasts of one hour per day were directed at the Pacific Coast of America and Hawaii, where at 40% overseas

Japanese accounted for a larger percentage of the total population than anywhere else. (Stephan,1984:23) On 21 June these transmissions were moved to 2.00-3.00pm, which was considered a much more convenient time for the listeners, being 6.00-7.00pm in Hawaii and 9.00-10.00pm on the Pacific Coast. Other transmissions were also soon begun, beginning on 21 June with broadcasts to the Eastern United States and South America.[4] A European service began on 4 September with transmissions on Tuesdays and Saturdays from 4.00 to 5.00am, and at the beginning of 1937 a transmission to Java and the Straits Settlements (Singapore and Malaya) was added.

During the first few weeks of broadcasting there was one feature or radio play per day in the transmission. These included an interview with a touring American baseball team and a "Radio Review" from the Moulin Rouge, in Paris. Scheduling, however, was learnt through trial and error, as precise scheduling had not been necessary for exchange broadcasts when the two halves of the exchange had been on different days. On 9 June the feature ran over time by two minutes and the news in Japanese had to be shortened at the last minute. The next day the schedulers were careful to ensure that everything ran to time.

From the beginning, censorship was an integral element of overseas broadcasting. This was understandable as the impetus to begin short-wave broadcasting derived from the need to improve Japan's international image following the Manchurian Incident. Thus the government had an important role in scrutinising broadcasting output from a very early stage.

The formal permission to broadcast overseas, issued on 4 May, contained clauses relating to government censorship of the broadcasts. All programme outlines were to be passed to the Department of Communications in the Ministry of

Communications for approval seven days prior to transmission. The contents of scripts not under the direct jurisdiction of the Department of Communications were then to be resubmitted to the Heads of the Departments of Communications and Electrical Affairs two days before going on air. In addition, NHK was required to submit a monthly report to the Head of the Department of Communications via the Head of Electrical Affairs.

From December 1926 NHK's domestic transmitting stations had been equipped with circuit breakers which allowed Ministry of Communications censors to interrupt a programme for as long as material strayed from the approved script, (Kasza, 1988:89) and these were also installed in the overseas broadcasting studios. In addition, on 8 May, after the licence was issued to NHK, a direct line telephone was installed in Atagoyama to the Ministry of Communications for the purpose of programme surveillance. The Ministry had the power to shut-down a transmission at any point if it was not considered suitable. Thus a comedy transmitted on 15 July was cut because it was considered to dishonour Japanese troops in Korea.

At this time several broadcasts by prominent academics were censored. A speech entitled "The Japanese Spirit and World Peace" by a leading Tokyo Imperial University Professor, Shioya Atsushi, on 26 June had a passage removed which criticised Mussolini, Hitler, the Soviets, the British, the French and the Americans. (Kitayama, 1988a:115) Presumably the government was unwilling to offend all the leading nations simultaneously. In addition, the first attempted simultaneous domestic and overseas radio broadcast, of a film drama, "Breakthrough Wireless," was dropped because it dealt with the Ministry of Communications' cable boats, which carried out repairs to undersea cables in Japanese coastal waters. It was considered that the image of the boats' operations given by the programme revealed too much about the Japanese emergency first line of defence, so the domestic broadcast was made, but it was dropped from the overseas schedules.

NHK broadcasters had admired the impartiality of the BBC's "Empire Service" from its establishment in 1932, and had hoped to emulate it in their own short-wave broadcasts. However, the importance of censorship and propaganda to Japanese international broadcasting was incompatible with a BBC-style approach. From its very beginnings the Japanese governement saw NHK's role as to present a positive Japanese image in the face of much international criticism.

3. THE DEVELOPMENT OF OVERSEAS BROADCASTING

Criticism of the American government was an important element in Japanese broadcasts from soon after regular overseas broadcasting began. In August 1935, the first broadcasts appeared which discussed the issue of possible war with America resulting from American policy in the Pacific. However, it was recognised that Japanese Americans were generally loyal to the United States and that it was important not to alienate them. Under the title of "Observations and Studies of the Fatherland," NHK began a series of broadcasts, which aimed to increase the awareness of Japanese in America of "things Japanese."

On 1 October 1935, the frequency and call sign of NHK's overseas service were changed from JVH on 14600kc/s to JUN broadcasting on 10660kc/s, 28.14m (Kitayama, 1988a:122) and this coincided with a change in the tone of output from Atagoyama. The portrayal and exaltation of the "Japanese Spirit," and its uniqueness became a dominant theme. Takashima Heisaburō summed it up for overseas listeners on 11

October, in a talk entitled "Concerning the Japanese Spirit," which defined the Spirit in terms of

A Clear Heart	*[Aki Kokoro]*
A Pure Heart	*[Kiyoki Kokoro]*
A Just Heart	*[Tadashiki Kokoro]*
An Honest Heart	*[Jiki Kokoro]*

(Kitayama, 1988a:122-3)

Growing hostility to the West in overseas broadcasts did not, however, prevent exchange broadcasts taking place, and music broadcasts from other countries were still relayed on the Japanese domestic network. These exchanges included a broadcast to the United States to celebrate American Independence Day. In August 1935, there was an exchange with Germany which discussed the preparations for the Berlin Olympics to be held the following year, and on 28 October the German station at Zeesen relayed a Japanese broadcast to Germany across Europe for the first time. A further exchange, with France, included a relay of Saint Saens' opera *Samson and Delilah* on the Japanese network.

In domestic broadcasts NHK emphasised the Shinto nature of Japan, in line with government policies to restrict western influences in Japan by emphasising the native state religion, which presented the Emperor as a living God to be followed unquestioningly by his subjects. Christianity was discouraged because it was not only a western import but its followers' allegience was to a God external to the Japanese regime. However, the Japanese maintained an international Christmas broadcast on the overseas service in 1935, as they had done in previous years. On 20 December, a speech on the national network denounced the celebration of Christmas, but on 22nd a

Bach Christmas Concert was relayed from Leipzig. (Kitayama, 1988a:132) A choral broadcast to Italy had been planned by NHK for midnight on Christmas Eve, but it was finally cancelled after a three-hour delay due to technical faults in the transmitting equipment. (Kitayama, 1988a:133-4) At the end of 1935, NHK had by no means perfected its overseas broadcasting technology.

Soon after the beginning of 1936, on 28 January, King George V broadcast to Japan on the BBC following the conclusion of the Naval Arms Limitation Talks in London. However, throughout his two broadcasts, music by Beethoven was played by Tokyo Central Broadcasting on the same frequency. It is not unreasonable to presume that this was an organised attempt to mask the King's voice and prevent his speeches being audible in Japan, rather than a coincidental clash of frequencies, and was probably the first occasion on which the Japanese authorities attempted to jam a foreign transmission.

On 26 February 1936, an attempted coup d'état by a radical military faction (the 26 February Incident) occurred in Tokyo. The overseas broadcasting station at Atagoyama was not overrun[5] and the broadcasters there tried to maintain the usual schedules, although the government imposed a news blackout regarding the incident. A brief statement, in the form of a short announcement by the War Ministry, was made in Japanese language reports on both domestic and overseas broadcasts late on 26 February. It stated that early that morning, "junior officers" had attacked and killed or wounded the Prime Minister, the Finance Minister, and other government officials. However, this item was not inserted into the English language schedules until the following day. Generally, coverage of the situation in English did increase as the situation unfolded. Reports in Japanese also increased, and besides the usual news reports, these included messages to Japanese diplomats abroad, who, caught by surprise, had no other means of obtaining information or instructions from Japan, as the situation was so confused. The International Department tried to adhere to its approved schedules, but some allowance was made for the increase in news coverage, and songs were omitted in order to make room for it. The attempted coup was eventually put down and the 26 February Incident came to an end at 2.00pm on 29 February, following a radio appeal to the rebel troops which pointed out that the troops had not realised that their actions were treasonous when they joined the rebellion, but that they were now in direct rebellion agianst the Emperor, and should respect his orders and surrender. (NHK:1977c:66-7)

Subsequently, Japanese overseas broadcasting's treatment of the incident was criticised by two sides. The Ministry of Communications was extremely unhappy at the detailed information, which had been broadcast abroad about a domestic situation, and it began research into the standard of censorship at NHK. Criticism from outside Japan, however, was directed at the slowness of NHK to report that a serious incident was occurring. Western journalists had transmitted reports regarding the attempted coup as the story had broken, and maintained a steady stream of transmissions to the West throughout the three-day period. Besides the brief statement in Japanese on 26 February, NHK did not report the situation until the following day, and even then the reports remained very brief for a further day. In addition, foreign broadcasters outside Japan were critical of the programme schedules, which they claimed had been too inflexible in not allowing sufficient news reports to be inserted. The International Department was caught between these two opposing criticisms, and whilst seeking not to damage its image abroad, as a serious journalistic broadcasting station, it could do little except bow to the pressure of its own government and agree to an increased level of censorship.[6]

Fearing further trouble the Okada government subsequently mounted a "Tranquility Campaign," in order to bring calm, and this was reflected in both domestic and overseas radio schedules. This media campaign stressed the qualities of Japan and the Japanese, and coincided with the flowering of the cherry blossoms, the symbol of Japan. In addition, overseas radio broadcast programmes sought to repair the damage caused by the 26 February Incident, and improve Japan's image abroad. One such programme was "An Introduction to Japan" a thirty minute "D.J.-style" programme, which was broadcast weekly for seven episodes. It attempted to describe "Japaneseness" to foreigners and dealt with such topics as "Summer in Japan," "Kamakura" and "Summer Holidays." The need to repair the image of Japan was considered urgent, as Japan was eager to be approved as host for the 1940 Olympics.

The Italian occupation of Addis Ababa, in Abyssinia (Ethiopia) on 5 May 1936 provided an early example of the dual nature of Japanese broadcasting with different perspectives marking domestic and overseas transmissions. Within Japan the public position of the government was that Italy had recognised the Japanese position in Manchuria, and that of Germany in the Rhineland, so Japan would naturally recognise Italian gains in Abyssinia. This position was also expressed in broadcasts aimed at Germany and Italy. However, the Emperor expressed his wish to Japan's political leaders that good relations with Britain should also be cultivated, and quite differing sentiments about Abyssinia were expressed in broadcasts intended for British listeners.

The Berlin Olympics dominated the summer of 1936 on the radio. In June the Director of the Overseas Section and two assistants flew to Berlin and in July there were broadcasts from various places in Germany on both domestic and overseas radio.

Japanese commentators at the Olympics used both the Japanese-made, carbon microphones, which they had taken with them, and more advanced German-made crystal microphones, which they brought back to Japan after the Olympics, in order to assist NHK's research into radio equipment. (Kitayama, 1988a:161)

Following the 26 February Incident the political value of broadcasting was increasingly recognised. During the incident the rebels had paralysed other communications systems, but broadcasting operations had continued almost without change. However, following criticism that NHK was too liberal, on 2 May the cabinet agreed to establish a new body to oversee the media, the Cabinet Information Committee. Its establishment on 1 July removed responsibility for censorship from the Ministry of Communications. The Information Committee consisted of representatives of each of the ministries, Dōmei, (representing the press) and NHK. It was claimed that a body with a single task would be more effective in censorship of the media than the previous system of circulating material around several departments in the Ministry of Communications. The expansion of NHK and other communications networks had rendered this an enormous burden on the Ministry. The Cabinet Information Committee removed this burden and meeting daily, it reported directly to the Cabinet. Scripts continued to be submitted a week in advance for the approval of subject matter, and two days in advance of transmission for approval of details. However, the daily discussions between representatives of the Ministries, who had previously not met when considering the censorship of a script, meant that government control over NHK broadcasting was greatly strengthened, as the possibility of the Department of Communications misinterpreting the censorship comments of other bodies was removed.

The Cabinet Information Committee became increasingly important. In September 1937 it was expanded and elevated to the status of "Division." It was further expanded in 1940 to "Bureau" status, and remained the body in charge of media censorship until the end of the war.

After the 1936 Olympics, NHK's Overseas Section began an autumn series of broadcasts which, it claimed, was to build on the feelings of international goodwill generated by the Berlin Olympics. These broadcasts began in September with a programme introducing the Japanese poetic form, *haiku*, to an American audience. In this the announcer encouraged the audience to write *haiku* and send them in. In October the presenters of the sequel programme read out some of the *haiku* by Americans, and English translations of some famous Japanese *haiku*. The aim of the programmes was to introduce Japanese culture to foreigners and thus spread foreign acceptance of "things Japanese."

The Autumn schedules were not, however, based solely on exporting Japanese culture, but also on demonstrating that Japan accepted other cultures. As part of this, on 21 September a broadcast was relayed by NHK, which surveyed different musical styles and backgrounds across America. In October, a programme entitled "Radio Cabaret" began. As an experiment in attracting foreign listeners, it included jazz records and songs as part of the promotion of a good image of Japan, although jazz was rare on domestic radio broadcasts as it was considered an evil of the "decadent West."

On 15 November 1936 NHK joined NBC and other broadcasting companies in a world broadcast of cultural items to celebrate the anniversary of the founding of NBC. NHK relayed both the Chinese and Australian sections of the broadcast on the domestic network, as well as broadcasting the Japanese section on short-wave. The broadcast involved many of the world's leading broadcasting companies and corporations, and according to Kitayama Setsurō was the final "goodwill" broadcast involving Japan, Germany and the United States, before the beginning of World War Two. (Kitayama, 1988a:169)

The unstable situation in China deteriorated further in the summer of 1936, and in August two Japanese journalists were killed in Chengdu. There were other anti-Japanese incidents in China, and on 28 September, as tension mounted, the Cabinet Information Committee issued a report on the situation. It condemned the actions of the Chinese in attacking Japanese nationals and issued a policy statement, which called for propaganda to promote the Japanese view of events, particularly within China. As NHK's Overseas Section was well placed to promote the Japanese case abroad it was given this task. The strict radio censorship begun in the autumn of 1936 was the forerunner of the censorship system which became standard in foreign propaganda after the outbreak of fighting with China in July 1937.

With the conclusion of the Japanese-German Anti-Comintern Pact in Berlin on 25 November 1936, the Cabinet Information Committee was faced with the need for a propaganda line to justify the Pact to the rest of the world. On 21st, in preparation for the signing, the Committee announced to NHK and Dōmei that the Pact was to be presented as a treaty to confound the activities of the Comintern. They were still faced with the problem that Japan was seen to be allied to fascism, but the strong promotion of the anti-Communist line was intended to overshadow this, and radio news stressed this point at every opportunity.

On 13 December 1936, all the Japanese morning newspapers carried reports of a coup in China, and the arrest of Chiang Kai-shek. The first reports concerning the Xian Incident[7] were made to the rest of the world over NHK's overseas radio service, and this increased the international prestige of NHK. In line with Cabinet Information Committee propaganda, the coup was attributed to the Comintern, which, it was claimed, had initiated the coup solely as part of its plan to overrun Japan.

In mid-December the Vice-Chairman of the House of Representatives, Okada Tadahiko, broadcast a summary of the year's events for overseas listeners. In it he commented on the Comintern rallying left-wing elements against the peaceful Germans and Japanese, but he did not dwell on this as he recognised that it was damaging to Japanese relations with both the Soviet Union and China. Regarding the Xian Incident specifically, he stated that Japan was the defender of peace in the Far East, and would maintain that peace by all means, by opposing any extremist groups.

On 1 January 1937 the Overseas Section was expanded, in accordance with plans approved the previous June and broadcasting time was increased to four hours daily. The broadcasting day began with a transmission to Europe at 4.30am. Newscasts were in English and were ten minutes long. They were followed by a record and it was announced that items in French and German would soon be added to the schedules, when a second 50kw transmitter came into operation. From 6.00 to 7.00am the transmission was directed at the Eastern United States and South America, consisting of ten minutes of news in Japanese, records and news in English. The transmission to Hawaii and the Western United States continued at the same time, 2.00 to 3.00pm, including on New Years Day a relay of the celebrations for the "10,000 Year Anniversary" of the high-ranking Atsuta Shrine in Nagoya, which followed the news in both Japanese and English. Between 11.00pm and 12.00am NHK began a transmission to the Straits Settlements and Java.

Generally, all the features broadcast during the following weeks were based around promoting Japanese culture and the "Japanese Spirit." "Japan Invites You" and "World Radio," both broadcast to Europe in January 1937 are examples of this type of programme, which attempted to increase interest in Japanese culture, whilst playing jazz records to persuade Europeans to listen in.

4. THE PRELUDE TO WAR IN CHINA

On 27 January 1937 the "News of the Japanese Homeland," a round up of news for Japanese in the United States, reported the fall of the Japanese cabinet on 23rd. On 11 February the new Prime Minister, Hayashi Senjūrō spoke to the overseas audience from NHK. His speech emphasised that the "completion of military preparations for national defence [was] necessary for the realisation of national policy." The March edition of *Hōsō*, NHK's monthly magazine, said that this was the first time a new Prime Minister had presented the policies of his cabinet primarily by radio. (Kitayama, 1988a:178)

In February a joint Japanese and German film was released, "which it was hoped would show 'the unity of the Nazi group spirit and the racial spirit of the Japanese as opposed to the weak spirit of the democracies.'" Entitled *Atarashiki Tsuchi* [New Earth] and given the English title *Daughter of the Samurai*, it was publicised heavily on Japanese overseas radio. The aim of the film was to "'praise the Japanese family system and particularly stress the volcano-like sacrificing spirit of Japan' by portraying the conversion of the Japanese hero from democracy back to a belief in the Japanese family system,"[8] in order to familiarise Germans with their new ally. On 11 February the director, Arnold Fank and the Japanese female star, Hara Setsuko, were interviewed during the morning broadcast to Europe and the theme song was introduced. A special broadcast in German reviewed the film in more detail and the broadcast was simultaneously relayed across the German domestic network as German-Japanese co-operation in producing the film was considered extremely important.

On 1 April the French and German language programmes which had been promised in the New Year expansion of the Overseas Section finally began. However, the upgrading of the 20kw Nazaki transmitter, which had been planned to accompany this did not occur until 10 May. French broadcasts were transmitted on Tuesdays and Thursdays for ten minutes following a shortened ¾ hour broadcast in English. German broadcasts occupied the same place in the schedule on Mondays, Wednesdays and Fridays. Both broadcasts were presented by a Japanese presenter and a native speaker. With the increase in output after 10 May, the schedules again changed slightly as the power of the transmitters was increased and the range of transmissions to the Straits Settlements and Java was extended to include Australia and New Zealand. The growth of overseas broadcasting resulted in the Overseas Section being upgraded and renamed the International Department on 26 May, with an increased staff of twenty. The size of the staff continued to rise as the International Department played an increasingly important role in Japanese political propaganda.

During the Spring and Summer of 1937 the political situation in Manchuria became increasingly tense. Japanese and Soviet troops clashed several times along the Manchurian-Soviet and Manchurian-Mongolian borders. In June, Soviet troops landed on an island in the Amur River border at Kanchasu. The first report from the scene was broadcast in the transmission to the Straits Settlements, Java and Australia in Japanese and English on 30 June. The news was considered too important to delay its broadcast in French until the regular French language broadcast the following day, and reports on the situation in English, German and French were made during the transmission to Europe. However, as the regular schedule called for a German-language news programme, the length of the French report was carefully monitored. Once NHK had received permission to report on the incident, information about the situation in Kanchasu dominated the news on overseas broadcasting, with forty-eight reports made between 30 June and 3 July.

On the evening of 7 July 1937 Japanese troops on the outskirts of Peking clashed with Chinese forces and seized control of the Marco Polo Bridge. The Marco Polo Bridge Incident signalled the end of skirmishes in China and the outbreak of a full-scale, though undeclared, Sino-Japanese war, which contributed to a serious worsening of relations with the United States.

In the 1930s Western visitors to Japan were often highly critical of Japanese broadcasting. In 1943, John Morris a Briton who had lived in Japan from 1938 to 1942, wrote of his experience of Japanese broadcasting, "Little attention had hitherto been paid to microphone technique, with the result that nearly every talk opens with a burst of thunder, the speaker, clearing his throat. This is followed by frequent coughing and the crackle of pages being turned over." He was also critical of the NHK studios at Atagoyama which, "were situated in a converted mansion, and there were none of the faculties one finds in a modern studio. Not one of the rooms was soundproof and loose wires trailed all over the floor. I talked once or twice to America from this building . . . and before I got to the end I nearly always heard the gentleman in the next room clearing his throat and warming up . . ." (Morris, 1943:135-9) However, contrary to this contemporary view, by 1937 the overseas broadcasting operation of the Japanese was not primitive. Although, like other broadcasting companies, many of the techniques of timing and programming were learnt by trial and error, the rapid rate at which the Japanese caught up with European overseas broadcasting displayed a significant advance in technical capability. This continued after the outbreak of war in China and enabled Japan to participate fully in the world "radio war," which began during the "China Incident" and developed into a wider conflict with the Western powers after Japan's attack on Pearl Harbor.

CHAPTER 2
FROM WAR IN CHINA TO WAR IN THE PACIFIC

1 THE WAR IN CHINA

On the night of 7 July 1937, Japanese troops conducting manoeuvres near the Marco Polo Bridge, south-west of Peking, engaged in a skirmish with Chinese forces, after hearing shots. Details regarding the start of the "China Incident" still remain unclear. However the "Incident" was first reported on Japanese overseas radio during the transmission to the Western United States on 8 July 1937. The report consisted of a translation of a military communiqué which appeared in a similar format in the *Japan Times and Mail*:

> *The Japanese military authorities at Peking made the following announcement at 7 o'clock this morning. About 10 o'clock last night, while detached Japanese troops were engaged in night manoeuvres about 1,000 metres north of Lukouchiao, a sudden attack was made by Chinese soldiers under the cover of several guns. (Kitayama:1988a:197)*

The Information Committee directed NHK to explain the "Incident" in terms of the Japanese people making a sacrifice to stop Chinese aggression, in order to keep the peace in East Asia and oppose Communism in Asia. The International Department was instructed to increase the length of news reports in overseas broadcasts, to tighten the censorship of them and to double the number of political speeches broadcast. Hence French and German news reports became daily broadcasts in the European transmission. (Kitayama:1988a:202)

Broadcasts were strictly regulated, not only to prevent sensitive material from being broadcast, but also in order that the language used was not overtly anti-Chinese. It was considered that such language would not appeal to potential foreign listeners and, combined with media reports in their own countries, would turn them against the Japanese view. Instead, the need to protect Manchuria, now stable under Japanese control, from China, and the need for stability in Asia were stressed, and the military language used more frequently in domestic broadcasts, was toned down or omitted.

In August 1937, newscasts in Spanish and Chinese were added to the overseas schedules. Newscasts in Spanish were inserted into the transmission for the Eastern United States and South America. The first newscast in Chinese[9] consisted of three news items read in very faltering Chinese, by an announcer with a heavy Japanese accent. It was in retaliation to the Chinese station XGOA which broadcast on short-wave in Japanese and indicated the start of the "radio war" in China. This was recognised by the Tokyo *Asahi Shinbun* which called it "AK's (Tokyo Central Broadcasting's) sound-wave bombing." (Kitayama:1988a:205)

In the 1930s and 1940s the Japanese Empire was considered to fall into two parts, the *naichi* (internal region) and the *gaichi* (external region). The *naichi* consisted of the four Japanese mainland islands, the Ryūkyū Islands and Karafuto (Sakhalin) and the *gaichi*, the South Sea Islands and other areas of Asia under Japanese administration. The co-operation of the *gaichi* radio stations with those in the *naichi* had been discussed at conferences in Tokyo and Seoul in 1936.[10] These conferences resulted in the establishment of a Broadcasting Liaison Council [*Hōsō Renraku Kaigi*] to ensure co-operation on policy between the Japanese government and the broadcasting stations in Japan, Manchuria, Korea and Taiwan.

At the time of the China Incident, the Japanese *gaichi* radio stations were included in the plan to explain the Japanese position to foreign audiences. The 10kw Dairen station in Manchuria began broadcasting news reports in English and Manchu for China and the Straits Settlements on 13 July. In addition to the regular broadcasts, following the opening of the Tientsin station on August 1937, weekly North China - Manchuria radio exchanges took place. These concentrated on current affairs, and discussed political developments and important speeches made during the week. The Hsinking station also began broadcasting in English, Manchu and Japanese on 1 September, and by the end of the year the Manchurian Cable and Telegraph Company received 174 listener reports from overseas, 147 of which were in the United States. (Kitayama:1988a:209-10)

Map 1: *Gaichi* radio stations, which began overseas broadcasting following the start of the China Incident

The 10kw station in Taipei was employed to counter the broadcasts of the Nanking (Nanjing) station to Southern China. In July it began two daily news broadcasts in the Fukien (Fujian) dialect and a third in the Peking (Beijing) dialect. By the end of the month a further newscast, in English, was inserted into the Taipei schedule, bringing the total daily overseas broadcasting time of the station to one-and-a-quarter hours. (Kitayama:1988a:210)

The Peking Radio Station, itself, which the Japanese had been keen to restore to operation, was re-opened on 17 October 1937 with an increased power of 500w. It was to be "engaged in the important task of enlightening the local public by the distribution of news, cultural matters, and means of recreation." (*Japan Times & Mail* 19 October 1937)

In Korea, the Seoul station's powerful 50kw transmitter began broadcasting a daily five-minute newscast in Russian in December 1937. This was picked up and relayed by the smaller transmitter at Chongjin, in north-west Korea, to explain Japanese actions to the USSR, the most powerful neighbour to the north of Japanese occupied territory.

In his annual New Year broadcast for 1938 Kōmori Shichirō, the Head of NHK, stressed the important role of international broadcasting in the current political climate, and officially announced an expansion and re-structuring of the International Department. The four transmission regions were increased to five, South America and the Eastern United States being separated. As the South American transmission no longer included the Eastern United States, English language items were dropped from the schedules and replaced by newscasts in Spanish and Portuguese on alternate days.

The transmission to the Eastern United States was further divided into two half-hour transmissions, one in English and the other in Japanese, although this arrangement remained experimental until 1 July 1939. Both the European and the Java, Straits Settlements and Australia transmissions were increased by thirty minutes. In addition, the latter began newscasts in

French, Dutch and Spanish, for people in French Indo-China, (Cambodia, Laos and Vietnam) the Netherlands East Indies (Indonesia) and the Philippines. From January 1938 the daily schedule for the International Department was as in figure 2 below.

04.30 - 06.00	to Europe	Japanese; English; French; German
06.30 - 07.30	to South America	Japanese; Portuguese; Spanish
08.00 - 08.30	to the Eastern United States	English
09.00 - 09.30	to the Eastern United States	Japanese
14.00 - 15.30	to Hawaii and the Western United States	Japanese; English
22.00 - 23.30	to Java, Australia and the Straits Settlements	Japanese; English; French; Dutch; Spanish

Figure 2: The International Department schedule from January 1938

During the spring of 1938 programme planners at NHK decided that more entertainment was needed in the overseas schedules, particularly in the broadcasts to Europe and America. Generally, Japanese radio was very serious in content, and overseas broadcasting had followed the same pattern. However, it was noted that American and European broadcasting was based on a greater proportion of entertainment programmes, and in order to coax listeners to tune in to Japanese broadcasts, it was decided that NHK's schedules should reflect the Western stations more closely. Entertainment focused on the classical music of Japanese composers living abroad, such as Hayasaka Fumio, and Germanic and Italian composers, such as Mozart and Rossini.

Time	Signal 1	Signal 2
22.00	Opening statements in Japanese and English	
22.05	News in Japanese	
22.15	Two folk songs (records)	
Chimes - Start of Split Transmission		
22.25	News in English	News in English
22.35	Continuing News in English	Talk in Chinese: "Ending Dependence on the Europeans and the Americans."
22.45	Continuing News in English	News in Chinese
Chimes - End of Split Transmission		
22.55	Chinese records	
Chimes - Start of Split Transmission		
23.05	News in Dutch with Wilhelm Josias Van Dienst[11] and Kumakura Miyasu	News in French
Chimes - End of Split Transmission		
23.15	Talk in Japanese: "The August edition of News of the Mother Country"	
23.25	Closing statements in Japanese and English.	
23.30	Close down	

Figure 3: The transmission schedule for "China and the South Seas," 15 August 1938, the first day the new "split transmission" came into operation.
(Kitayama, 1988a:252-3)

At the end of July 1938 the structure of the International Department of NHK was again re-organised. In August, *Hōsō* Magazine, described the extension of the target audience from Java, the Straits Settlements and Australia to those who felt "the waves of the Japan Current . . . (and) . . . its great ripples in the Southern Regions," (*op cit*. Kitayama, 1988a:252) and on 15 August it was renamed the transmission for "China and the South Seas." New technology meant that this service could use two transmitters simultaneously. This allowed for greater diversity in the languages, which could be transmitted or the areas which could receive a broadcast. Figure 3, shows the transmission schedule for 15 August 1938, the first day that the new system operated. This expansion programme was completed on 18 August when NHK announced it was to introduce broadcasts in Dutch as part of the broadcast to the Netherlands East Indies and the South Seas, as it was "aiming at the presentation of correct facts and news concerning Japan and things Japanese." (*Japan Times and Mail*, 5 August 1938)

The start of direct short-wave broadcasts to China precipitated a series entitled "Chinese Dispatch," which examined various issues relating to China including "The Fallacies of the National Government's Propaganda." (Kitayama:1988a:253)

Besides the expanded short-wave broadcasting to China, the "Propaganda Plan and Outline for Strategic Propaganda" also made provision for the opening of medium-wave stations in occupied China, ideally no more than 10km apart, to ensure clear reception for everyone. The first of these stations to go into operation was the one in Japanese occupied Nanking, which began broadcasting on 10 September 1938. Previously a National Government station, it was rebuilt and refurbished by the Japanese and was given a 10kw transmitter by Tokyo Central Broadcasting.

The "new" station went into operation using its former Chinese call sign of XGOA. The Japanese deliberately planned this, because when the National Government had abandoned Nanking for Chungking (Chonqing) it had begun broadcasting from there, with the same call sign, as it was recognisable to listeners as the National Government station. By using the same call sign the Japanese hoped to trick listeners into tuning into the Japanese station instead of the Chinese one.

In the latter half of 1938, most exchange broadcasts were with the Axis nations. A group from the Hitler Youth Movement visited Japan in August and September, and a broadcast of greetings from them entitled "A Present to our Anti-Communist Ally, Germany" was transmitted to Europe on 23 September. A visit of Japanese students to Italy in August prompted a Japanese-Italian radio exchange on 8 August, and a Manchurian Economic Mission trip to Italy in September produced a Manchurian-Italian exchange, which was also broadcast on the Japanese overseas network.

2. STRUCTURAL CHANGES

The New Year, 1939, began with a campaign in the International Section of NHK which incorporated two key themes; "The Japanese Spirit" and "The New Order in East Asia." This reflected Nazi claims to be establishing a "New Order in Europe" free from the influence of the democracies. Japan's claim was that she sought to establish a "New Order" whereby East Asia was free from Western domination. It included a new series of broadcasts, the "Japan Culture Series." The initial talk in the series described the essence of the "Modern Japanese Spirit" as a "Spirit of patriotism and loyalty to the country."

The start of a campaign to stress that the task of the Japanese was to build a New Order in East Asia, was hailed by a broadcast by Tokyo Imperial University Professor Rōyama Masamichi entitled, "The Intention to Build a New Order in East Asia." In it Professor Rōyama stressed that although intellectuals supported the Japanese effort, the prospects for the establishment of the New Order were fraught with difficulties and Japan would have to tread a "careful path through the rose bushes." (Kitayama:1988a:270)

A campaign, which also began in early 1939, was aimed at *nisei*, second generation Japanese immigrants, particularly on the Pacific Coast of America. It began with a talk in Japanese, "The Education of the Second Generation," which claimed that American society failed to accept the *nisei*. Other broadcasts included an examination of the importance of having Japanese blood, even for those born abroad, and stressed that *nisei* needed access to Japanese culture, by radio.

On 10 April 1939 NHK, the Korean Broadcasting Corporation, the Taiwan Broadcasting Corporation and the Manchurian Cable and Telephone Company jointly established the East Asia Broadcasting Corporation to relay broadcasts to Chungking. This was a direct response to the opening on 6 February of a 35kw station in Chungking by the Chinese National Government, which was to broadcast on short-wave. The May edition of *Hōsō* magazine explained,

> *While we have been prosecuting our Holy War to establish a New East Asian Order in the Orient, China has put all her energies into a skilful radio propaganda war and broadcast convenient and exaggerated news, regardless of whether it was truth or lie, in order to attract the sympathy of Chinese abroad, and to inspire in them feelings for the Chinese in China. (Kitayama:1988a:277)*

In Spring 1939, NHK began a campaign entitled, "Creating Culture for China." The aim of the broadcasts was to reverse the Chinese view of Japan by exerting 'correct' cultural influences on the population. One of the themes seized upon in this series was that Chinese antagonism towards Japan stemmed from the large proportion of anti-Japanese music in China. It was, thus, considered necessary to "match the anti-Japanese [songs] by writing a lot of pro-Japanese songs about interesting things, and making them popular with the Chinese youth." (Kitayama:1988a:279) Music broadcasts, of songs using Chinese history and Sino-Japanese relations as their themes, became more important in NHK broadcasts to China.

On 13 May 1939, NHK moved from its Atagoyama studios to a new larger headquarters at Uchisaiwaichō. An article by Kōmori Shichirō, Head of NHK, in the *Japan Times and Mail* on 31 March 1939 detailed the role of overseas broadcasting:

> *Programmes for the overseas broadcasts are selected with care and designed to appeal to all our listeners. Material covers, besides news reports of the day . . . musical entertainments, talks and commentaries on various subjects and occasions. In short, we are making an effort to present to the listener a complete picture of Japan, the melting pot of the Orient and the Occident, of its present as well as its past.*

The opening of the new site was celebrated on the domestic network with musical relays from abroad on 13th, 14th and 15th. On the 13th, ten-minute broadcasts were transmitted to Japan from Germany and Italy. The following day it was the turn of the American stations, NBC and CBS.

On 15 May the BBC's congratulatory broadcast was made to Japan. This consisted of greetings and music: Elgar's Pomp and Circumstance March No.1 in D, played by the BBC Empire Orchestra. From the BBC's files it appears that NHK had contacted the BBC on 22 April in preparation for this broadcast, and had suggested that the broadcast include a Handel Oratorio. The BBC, it appears, had made a recording of a performance of the orchestra playing the Elgar March on a recent Empire Service broadcast and hence sent a return telegram suggesting that this be played in preference to the Handel work. Recording was fairly unsual at the time, as most orchestral pieces played on air tended to be live performances. A telegram from NHK confirmed that this was acceptable, and the ten-minute transmission to Japan was incorporated into the BBC schedules at 12.30pm on 15 May. On 1 May a letter was also sent to the Press Attaché of the Japanese Embassy in London to obtain a translation of the greetings for the broadcast.[12]

On 1 July NHK's International Section was further enlarged, to fifty-five people, and elevated in status. The International Section became the International Department which was headed by Tanomogi Shinroku, and was divided into Sections One and Two. The work of Section One was concerned primarily with the technical aspects of broadcasting and was also responsible for carrying out checks into the clarity of NHK overseas broadcasts. Section Two was responsible for the content of the news, announcements in the broadcasts, and for translating items for the different transmissions. It was also agreed that an increase in broadcasting time should accompany the elevation of the International Section to Department status. The five broadcast regions remained the same, but the total broadcasting time was increased to eight hours a day and an Italian news service was inaugurated, bringing the total number of languages used to nine: Japanese, English, Chinese, German, Italian, French, Dutch, Spanish and Portuguese. (Kitayama, 1988a:282-3)

Overseas broadcasting incorporated several different themes during the summer of 1939. News editor, Yokoyama Sei, described the first of these in the May edition of *Hōsō*. He wrote that the aim of Japanese language news was to bring Japanese who were living abroad up to date on events in and concerning Japan; that of Chinese language news was to pacify China and to reconstruct Chinese culture, and that of the English language news was to build friendly relations with the United States and Great Britain. (Kitayama, 1988a:284)

Music played a vital role in attracting listeners to the station, so that the news and reports could serve their purpose. Playing gramophone records had been part of programming since the start of overseas broadcasting in 1935, but the songs were almost exclusively Japanese. In order to include different music in the schedules some Hawaiian bands had been featured from February 1939, but the entertainment part of any broadcast was really aimed at Japanese living in the target country. As previously, it was decided that jazz music, which was considered decadent and corrupt in Japan, should lead the way, and several programmes were added to the schedules of the American transmissions, such as "Musical Variety." It had its own resident band, the "Japanese Swing Singers," which sang up-beat swing and jazz during the programme. The songs were, however, were still in Japanese and whilst they included songs such as "Birthday Afternoon", [*Tanjōbi no Gogo*] a large number of the songs were on Japanese themes, such as "Nihonbashi in the Edo Period"[*O-Edo Nihonbashi*] which were not popular with American audiences. Other programmes, such as "Rhythm Cocktail", which included medleys of hit records such as "Japanese Sandman" and "Tiger Rag" would probably have had a wider appeal in America.

A further experiment began on 2 July. National domestic broadcasts were simultaneously transmitted to the Western United States between 3.00 and 3.25 on a Saturday afternoon. This made use of the system of transmitting two programmes at the same time in two different directions so that whilst domestic listeners heard a Japanese announcer, a second announcer was making an announcement in English via the transmitter directed to America. As it was primarily a domestic Japanese broadcast, the music was generally classical, with some Japanese songs and did not include any of the jazz and swing music, which was included in other broadcasts to the United States, but it was hoped that the programme would appeal to Japanese Americans. This dual broadcast on Saturday afternoons continued until just prior to the outbreak of war in the Pacific in late 1941.

An anti-British radio campaign was sparked by the "Tientsin Incident" on 9 April 1939, when a Japanese Maritime Customs Inspector was killed in the British concession in Tientsin. Although the local British authorities initially promised to surrender the four suspected assassins for trial by the Chinese puppet court, the British Foreign Office refused. After two months of fruitless discussion, the Japanese Army imposed a stringent blockade of the British Concession in mid-June.

Despite using strong language in domestic broadcasts, NHK was directed to avoid using military language in its overseas broadcasts. News reports and commentaries on the overseas service thus concentrated on Japanese and British attempts to find a solution to the crisis. Hence on 22 July a speech in English to the Western United States by Uno Ichimaro, the Japanese-American Relations correspondent of the *Rafu Hōshin*, [*Los Angeles News*] was entitled "Consideration of Peace between Japan and Britain." (Kitayama, 1988a:288)

In May 1939, a clash began between Japanese and Soviet backed troops at Nomonhan on the Manchurian/Mongolian border. This developed into a full-scale border war, with both sides mobilising aircraft and armoured units. In late August the Japanese Kwantung army was completely routed. Along with the signing of the non-aggression pact between Germany and the Soviet Union on 23 August, this defeat prompted Japan to sue for a cease-fire, which came into operation on 15 September.

Overseas radio played a central role in presenting the Japanese case during the four months of the crisis. Both Mongolian and Russian were added to the list of languages used in broadcasts from Tokyo, and in June a lecture series was begun in Mongolian regarding the situation in East Asia. The station at Hsinking was heavily employed in the radio campaign, using both medium- and short-wave transmitters to broadcast news in Mongolian, Manchu and Russian, and a daily "North Manchuria Hour" which was aimed directly at the border region. In order to diversify the range of transmissions Hsinking also began broadcasts on short-wave frequencies to Europe and America and the South Seas.

The Japanese cabinet under Prime Minister Konoye, which was formed on 30 August, was faced with a critical situation in Europe when Germany invaded Poland on 1 September 1939. At 10am that day Hitler's speech from Berlin was received by NHK and relayed live across the domestic network, as was Chamberlain's speech declaring war on Germany, two days later. (Kitayama, 1988a:296-7) In Japan, it was announced that

> *Although this present war has broken out in Europe, Japan will not intervene, but will press on towards a conclusion of the China Incident. (Kitayama, 1988a:297)*

Japanese overseas broadcasting, then, maintained strict Japanese neutrality with regard to the war in Europe, and continued the campaign to stress the 're-building' of Chinese culture and the establishment of a New Order in East Asia. Typical broadcasts were programmes such as "This is the Mission of the People of East Asia" [*Tōa Minzoku kore Shinmei*] which were broadcast to Asia and the Pacific during September 1939. (Kitayama, 1988a:299) On 25 September the German military attaché in Tokyo made a speech regarding German successes in Poland during the transmission to Europe.

Apart from this, there was little reference to the European war in broadcasts to Europe, and most programmes concerned events in China, and on the Manchurian-Mongolian border where the cease-fire agreement between Japan and the Soviet Union came into operation on 15 September.

In his 1940 New Year speech, which was broadcast to all the transmission regions, Kōmori Shichirō, Head of NHK, stated that radio was the most important of the media in increasing the consciousness of people abroad as to the greatness of the Japanese Empire. He also stated that radio was helping to strengthen reverence towards the Emperor in Manchuria and China. Thus, the International Department of NHK received instructions in January that it was to be a "Guiding Spirit in Asian Development" and the "Developing Countries' Guide in *Hakkō-Ichiu*." (Kitayama, 1988a:308)[13]

On 14 February 1940, the International Department at NHK began its first correspondence course for foreigners wanting to learn Japanese. Aimed at English speakers, it was transmitted to the Western United States and to Europe. The broadcast lessons continued into the summer and were presented by the Italian linguist, Oreste Vaccari. Later, the course was adapted for native Spanish speakers and re-broadcast to South America and Europe during the late summer and autumn of 1940. After the war, "*Nihongo no Kōza*," as the course was known, became a regular and popular programme on the NHK Overseas Service, but in 1940 according to the May edition of *Hōsō* Magazine, its aims were to,

> *Accompany the development of a New Order in East Asia, . . . to plan large scale training of Japanese teachers for the continent, . . . (and to) give short-term, three month, positive assistance to the cultural sectors of both the Ministry of*

Foreign Affairs and the Asian Development Institution. (Kitayama, 1988a:311)

Between April and July 1940 the German army swept through Europe in its historic *blitzkrieg*. However, Germany's military achievements events had little effect on Japanese broadcasting, and news reports to Europe continued to report Japanese victories in China and the crisis in the Chinese Nationalist Government. In particular, broadcasts focussed on the collapse of the Chinese dollar and the Chinese Government's pleas to the United States and Britain for financial aid to stabilise its currency.[14]

On 1 June 1940, the fifth anniversary of Overseas Broadcasting proper, the International Department of NHK was once again re-organised, and expanded. Because of static interference in broadcasts to Hawaii and the Western United States, the transmission was split and a separate Hawaiian transmission was established. In addition, the Ministry of Communications considered it essential to keep Asian broadcasting separate from broadcasts to the West, because of the special "Asian Spirit" being cultivated by Japan. Thus a transmission for "South-west Asia" was established to transmit one hour a day specifically to the countries of South- and South-east Asia. As part of this transmission, Thai, Burmese, and Hindi news reports were incorporated in to the schedules, bringing the total broadcast operation of the International Department to ten hours a day, for seven broadcast regions using a total of eleven languages. In addition, the Ministry of Communications established a Monitoring Service of foreign radio broadcasts in June 1940.

The *gaichi* stations, too, were increasingly involved in overseas broadcasting. In February 1940 the Korean Army Information Section began broadcasts in Russian the

"Propaganda Emphasis" of which was said to be, "Military Operations within Mongolia," "The Intensification of the Dispute between the Countries," and the "Development of a Movement to Establish the New Central Chinese Administration." (Kitayama, 1988a:323) What relation the radio operations of the Korean Army Information Section bore to the Korean Broadcasting Corporation is unclear, but it is probable that the Army broadcasted from the Corporation's Chongjin station, in north-west Korea.

The Taiwan Broadcasting Corporation had been broadcasting to Mainland China from the start of the China Incident. In July 1937 it began newscasts in the Fukien dialect, and between then and the start of December 1939 added reports in English, Peking dialect, Cantonese, Malay and Vietnamese. In the far north of Japanese-controlled territory, the short-wave broadcasts of the Manchuria Cable and Telephone Company were transmitted daily to four regions by June 1940. The first was a transmission to Europe in English. Transmission Two was to the Western United States also in English and Transmission Three was to "All East Asia" in Mongolian and Russian. The final transmission was in Chinese and English and was directed at Southern China and the South Seas. By the third anniversary of the China Incident on 7 July 1940 there was, therefore, a complete radio network across East Asia, which served to promote Japanese ideas on both medium- and short-wave.

During the Summer of 1940 the slogan "New Order in East Asia" was officially revised by a cabinet policy decision to "New Order in Greater East Asia" so as to include a larger area of possible Japanese operations. With the scope of Japanese interests in Asia widened to "Greater East Asia," on 8 August the International Department in Tokyo began a daily service of news in Cantonese for South China and Hong Kong. (Kitayama, 1988a:328)

The Japanese-German-Italian Tripartite Pact for mutual defence was signed in Berlin on 27 September 1940. The following day the first half of the Japanese broadcast to Europe was conducted mainly in German, though it did include one address in Italian. The usual schedule was abandoned and recent news was omitted completely, in favour of opinion and commentary regarding the new agreement. The second half of the transmission was in English and French and this stressed the special relationships, which now existed between Japan and Germany and Japan and Italy.

1940 was the official 2,600th anniversary of the mythical first Emperor, Jimmu's, ascent to the Japanese throne. Official celebrations to mark the event began in February and reached their climax in the latter three months of the year. Exchanges with Berlin on 17 November and 30 December concentrated on these celebrations and the regular schedules of the International Department also included recordings of rallies throughout Japan and concert performances by the specially created "2,600 Years Celebration Symphony Orchestra." These were performed solely for the overseas audience and included music by French, Italian, German and Hungarian composers.

Germany and sometimes Italy continued to be the usual exchange countries. A rare exchange was the "Exchange of Music and Addresses regarding Japanese-Australian Friendship" which was planned for on 27 September following the exchange of ambassadors between Japan and Australia. This ambassadorial exchange was an indication of Japan's growing commercial and political importance to Australia. 27 September was the day the signing of the Tripartite Pact was announced. The first part of the broadcast went ahead as planned from

Japan, but the Australian half was cancelled after news of the pact was received. (Kitayama, 1988a:331)

To further strengthen the integration of propaganda broadcasting, the Third East Asia Broadcasting Conference took place in Taipei at the end of November 1940. It was attended by representatives of NHK, the International Department, the Korea Broadcasting Corporation, the Manchuria Cable and Telephone Company, the North China Broadcasting Corporation, the Mongolian Posts and Communications Bureau, the Taiwanese Broadcasting Corporation, and the China Broadcasting Section as well as the Japanese Minister of Communications and other political officials. Despite the Conference's name, however, with the exception of the Head of the North China Broadcasting Corporation, Zhou Tai-wen, the delegates were exclusively Japanese. Overseas broadcasting was the principle topic of discussion at the conference and the resolutions, which it passed dealt in large part with the expansion of the International Department, which took effect from January 1941. This was the first time that the term "Radio Tokyo" was coined to describe the overseas broadcasting operations based in Tokyo, and from this time the Overseas Service became known as "Radio Tokyo" until the end of the Pacific War.

On 6 December 1940 the Cabinet Information Bureau (CIB) was established. It was in fact a larger version of the Cabinet Information Department, and was responsible for general surveillance of the media. 29% of the total bureau personnel was military, and in certain sections this figure rose to a third. For radio the new Bureau created a complicated series of relationships between NHK, the CIB, and the Ministry of Communications. The new Bureau took over the guidance and surveillance of most of NHK's activities, but matters relating to the censorship of individual programmes, and surveillance of broadcasts remained under the jurisdiction of the Ministry of Communications. Under a Cabinet decision, also effective from 26 December 1940, corporate surveillance of NHK itself was the joint responsibility of the CIB and the Ministry of Communications.

The expansion of NHK's International Department discussed at the East Asia Broadcasting Conference was announced by Komori Shichirō, the Head of NHK on 1 January 1941. This expansion was, he said, to "Build the Nation and the National Defence State" and to "Establish the Greater East Asia Co-Prosperity Sphere." As part of this expansion the total broadcasting time of the International Department was increased from ten hours to twenty-five hours twenty minutes daily, (Kitayama, 1988a:344) transmitting to twelve transmission regions as shown in Figure 4.

The February 1941 edition of *Hōsō* magazine outlined the aims of the new broadcasting system. In broadcasts to America the aim was to portray the situation from a new angle and to explain the New Order and the Co-prosperity Sphere to the American audience. This was in addition to the earlier aim of cultivating the pro-Japanese feeling of Japanese Americans. In broadcasts to China, the importance of employing the Fukien and Cantonese dialects, alongside Mandarin was stressed, and scriptwriters were encouraged to use both of these dialects more frequently.

French language broadcasts were extended to include French exiles in Britain, and broadcasts were begun to South-east Asia for French speakers in Indo-China. The use of the Dutch and Malay languages was also increased in broadcasts to South-east Asia and the South Seas in order to counter Western propaganda, and to reassure local inhabitants of the value of the Co-Prosperity Sphere.

Transmission 1	00.00-01.55	South-east Asia	Japanese, English, Thai, French, Malay, Chinese
Transmission 2	02.00-03.30	Middle East	Japanese, English, Arabic
Transmission 3	04.00-07.30	Europe	Japanese, English, French, German, Russian, Italian
Transmission 4	08.00-09.30	South & Central America	Japanese, Spanish, Portuguese
Transmission 5	10.00-12.00	Eastern United States	Japanese, English
Transmission 6	12.30-15.00	Western United States	Japanese, English
Transmission 7	15.30-17.30	Hawaii	Japanese, English
Transmission 8	18.00-19.00	South & Central America	Japanese, Spanish, Portuguese
Transmission 9	18.00-20.00	Imperial Troops (renamed Front-line Broadcasting after 1 February 1941)	Japanese
Transmission 10	19.30-20.25	Australia & New Zealand	Japanese, English
Transmission 11	20.00-23.30	China & the South Seas (the broadcast to China was also transmitted on medium-wave)	Japanese, English, Dutch, Chinese
Transmission 12	20.30-23.30	South Seas	Japanese, English, Dutch, Chinese

Figure 4: Total broadcast operation of NHK's International Department as of 1 January 1941 (Kitayama, 1988a:344-5)

3. PRELUDE TO WORLD WAR

For five months from the end of July 1940, two NHK employees carried out a "Grand Tour" of countries on the Pacific rim in order to monitor the reception quality and clarity of broadcasts from Japan. Their findings were published in *Hōsō* magazine in early 1941. Anazawa Tadahira, Head of the NHK Engineering Department, visited Australia, New Zealand and South-east Asia, and in his report he noted that in general the signals of overseas broadcasts seemed haphazard and indistinct. He wrote that in Asia he was treated with suspicion in every radio station he visited to enquire about Japanese broadcasts, because as an NHK official asking about Japanese strategic broadcasting he was considered a spy. He reported that his attempts at research in South-east Asia were, thus, hampered by the prejudices of those he visited, and the results, he claimed, could not be regarded as conclusive. In the English speaking countries, however, he stated, that people who listened to short-wave broadcasts considered NHK broadcasts inferior to those of the BBC in both reception and content. As a result Radio Tokyo's audience was very small. (Kitayama, 1988a:351)

The second investigator, Satō Taiichirō, Head of Section One of the International Department, visited North America and reported in the March 1941 edition of *Hōsō* magazine that there was a huge audience for NHK short-wave broadcasts in the regions of the United States and Canada bordering the Pacific. Presumably this was among the Japanese community, although he did not state this. However, his report stated that it was very difficult for the average family receiver on the eastern side of North America to pick up Japanese transmissions, as the signal appeared to be insufficiently strong. In general, he added, Japanese announcers needed to be allowed more freedom to ad lib between items, as American presenters did. In contrast, the

Japanese presenters sounded stiff, as though they were merely reading from a prepared script (which, of course, they were.) Satō was also critical of speeches made in foreign languages by the Japanese, which he said were unpopular for similar reasons. They were stiff in comparison to speeches made on Radio Tokyo by native speakers. He concluded that Japan faced formidable enemies in the "radio war" and needed to improve its overseas service. (Kitayama, 1988a:351) These reports, particularly the criticism contained in the latter, were extremely influential in improving the monitoring service in Japan and in encouraging experimentation in some of the programme formats used in foreign broadcasts.

The issue of jazz versus classical music in overseas broadcasts was further discussed in March and April 1941, after an article had appeared in the *New York Times* criticising Japanese broadcasts for being dominated by classical music. A review of the music played in the first three months of 1941 showed that classical, orchestral performances had been broadcast eight times a week, in various transmissions, and the inclusion of more jazz music in the overseas schedules was once again made a priority. A 4-piece jazz group NORO (New Order Rhythm Orchestra) was introduced into the regular schedules. It had been performing irregularly in NHK transmissions since October 1940, but from the spring of 1941, it became part of the new drive to diversify the types of music played in overseas broadcasts.

Programmes and music regarding Japan and Japanese traditions also continued to be important in the spring schedules in 1941. Broadcasts were made which presented both traditional and modern Japan to the outside world. Broadcasts in Japanese and English were most frequent, including "The Life of the People under the New System," by Ogata Taketora a representative of the Imperial Rule Assistance Association

(IRAA). (Kitayama, 1988a:357) The IRAA was a single mass political party, established in 1940 which replaced all the other parties. It was headed by the Prime Minister and operated throught local branches throughout Japan. However, it became little more that a national bureaucratic control tool and took over some responsibilities from the ministries, and absorbed many independent organisations. It was disbanded in June 1945.

There were addresses made to virtually all the transmission regions in most languages, including "From New System Japan," in French by Robert De Bière, Head of the Japanese-French Cultural Association. In addition, a "Japan History Series" was broadcast to all the broadcast regions, as the emphasis on popularising Japanese culture continued. Speeches in languages other than the usual Japanese, English, German and French became increasingly frequent during the summer of 1941, as it was felt that there was a need to widen appreciation of the Co-Prosperity Sphere and explain its meaning to a much wider audience. "What is the Greater East Asia Co-Prosperity Sphere?" was an Arabic address made in a broadcast to the Middle East and "Japan and the South Sea Islands" was an address in Burmese, which aimed to explain the mutually beneficial relationship between Japan and her colonies.

Diplomatic events in the spring and summer of 1941 played a dominant role in the news reports on both the domestic network and the overseas service. Border skirmishes between Thailand and French Indo-China in January had ended with a cease-fire negotiated by the Japanese on 31 January. Throughout February and March news reports to all the broadcast regions covered the peace negotiations and stressed Japan's role as the peacemaker.[15] Broadcasts to South-east Asia also sought to explain the "New Order in East Asia" and the "Greater East Asia Co-Prosperity Sphere" to the inhabitants of the Thailand-

Indo-China region, and presented them with a favourable picture of what benefits would accrue from formal links with Japan. All overseas broadcasts emphasised that the Japanese troops stationed in French Indo-China were a mutually agreed and mutually beneficial defence force, not an occupation army.

On 12 March 1941 the Japanese Minister of Foreign Affairs, Matsuoka Yōsuke, left for an official visit to Europe. Over the following month, there were regular broadcasts between Europe and Japan regarding Matsuoka's progress. An address in German on 25 March stressed that the visit was a significant indication of the close collaboration between the three Axis powers, as Japanese Foreign Ministers rarely travelled abroad, and this was the first visit by a Foreign Minister to Europe since 1905.[16] There was also a broadcast from Europe of greetings by Matsuoka and the Italian Foreign Minister, Ciano, on 2 April, which was relayed across the domestic and East Asian Relay Networks. (*Asahi Shinbun* 03-05-41)

During his tour, in May 1941, Matsuoka signed a Neutrality Pact with the Soviet Union. This meant that when war broke out between Germany and the Soviet Union in June, the Japanese, having treaties with both sides, had to devise a plan regarding their presentation of the war. On 2 July, an "Outline of Imperial Policy concerning the Change in the Situation" was issued. It instructed NHK to use overseas broadcasts to explain fully the situation in Asia, the New Order in East Asia and the Greater East Asia Co-Prosperity Sphere. Overseas broadcasts thus neatly side-stepped the problem of war between two Japanese allies for they rarely mentioned it.

During the last week of September 1941 the International Department was once more re-organised, and a new schedule, which increased the total transmission time to thirty-two hours fifty-five minutes a day, became effective from October.

(Kitayama, 1988a:377) The twelve former regional transmissions were reduced to seven new transmissions to allow for more overlapping in the time schedules and to prevent interference between transmissions. Each of the seven transmissions was broadcast on two different wavelengths so that if there was interference, from other Radio Tokyo transmissions, or from local stations, the broadcasts would usually be audible on another wave-length. The frequency of English language news reports was increased in each transmission. Figure 5 shows the new schedule.

Transmission 1	London, Paris, Berlin, Rome, Moscow	03.55-07.30	3 hours 35 minutes
Transmission 2	New York, Chicago, Bayliss, Rio	07.55-11.30	3 hours 35 minutes
Transmission 3	Mexico, San Fransisco, Hawaii	12.25-17.00 (with a close down from 15.25-15.30)	4 hours 30 minutes
Transmission 4	Front-line, Peking, Nanking, and Canton (Guangzhou)	17.55-19.00	(1 hour 5 minutes)
(Split Transmission)	Sydney, Singapore, Saigon (Ho Chi Minh City) Bangkok, Nanking, Canton	19.00-21.55	2 hours 55 minutes
Transmission 5	Saigon, Bangkok, Canton, Rangoon (Yangon)	21.55-00.00	2 hours 5 minutes
Transmission 6	Batavia (Jakarta) Singapore	21.55-00.00	2 hours 5 minutes
Transmission 7	India and Tehran	00.25-03.30	3 hours 5 minutes

Figure 5: The schedule of NHK's International Department from 1 October 1941

(Kitayama, 1988a:377)

At the start of the week of re-organisation in the NHK International Department, a new NHK station on the Pacific Island of Palau was opened. In February 1940, it had been planned that the station would open in January 1941, (*Japan Times & Mail* 24 February 1940) but it finally became operational on 24 September, opening with a twenty-minute broadcast of greetings to the South Sea Islands, which was relayed across the Tokyo domestic network. (*Japan Times and Advertiser*, Morning Edition, 8 September 1941) The inhabitants of the South Sea Islands had previously been the only inhabitants of Japanese-controlled territory who were encouraged to own short-wave receivers and listen to short-wave broadcasts because short-wave had been the only means of broadcasting Japanese programmes to the South Sea Islands. Elsewhere in the area controlled by Japan owning a short-wave receiver was illegal.

The new transmitter overcame this by allowing the islands to participate in the East Asia Relay Network. The station also transmitted on short-wave to Hawaii and to China and the South Pacific. The aim of these broadcasts was to convince the inhabitants of the Philippines, Netherlands East Indies and New Guinea that Japan was the nation to lead them into overthrowing the oppression of the Americans, Dutch and British, and to liberate them into full participation in the Greater East Asia Co-Prosperity Sphere.

During 1941 relations between Japan and the United States worsened steadily. Japan was criticised for moving troops into French Indo-China, although she claimed this had been mutually agreed between the two governments. As a response to Japanese expansion, which caused concern for the safety of the oil-rich territories of the Pacific, in July and August 1941 the United States placed economic sanctions on Japan, including an embargo on oil exports, and froze Japanese assets. Diplomatic negotiations continued throughout the autumn with a forlorn hope that the United States might make concessions before Japanese stockpiles dwindled too far, but by November few members of the Japanese government thought there was any alternative to a pre-emptive strike on America.

Amid this diplomatic crisis, the cabinet of Tōjō Hideki came to power in Japan in October 1941. One of the initial consequences of the formation of the new cabinet was an alteration in the emphasis of newscasts in broadcasts overseas. News programmes and commentaries contained fewer news items, and placed greater emphasis on the Japanese standpoint in the negotiations with the United States.

During November 1941, Liaison Conferences between the cabinet and the Emperor came to view war as increasingly inevitable. At the 69th Liaison Conference on 15 November it was agreed that,

> *Strategic propaganda against the United States will be stepped up; emphasis will be placed on enticing the American main fleet to come to the Far East, persuading Americans to reconsider their Far Eastern policy, and pointing out the uselessness of a Japanese-American war; American public opinion will be directed towards opposition to war.*

It continued, "Attempts will be made to break the ties between the United States and Australia." (*op cit*. Nobutaka, 1967:248) At other meetings it was also decided to increase the emphasis and energy put into overseas broadcasts to South America.

During November 1941, the Navy also began using overseas broadcasts to send coded messages. On 19 November it was first revealed to Japanese diplomats abroad in coded messages during newscasts, that information regarding the outbreak of war, if war became inevitable, would be given during the regular transmissions in the form of a weather forecast. (Weather reports were not usually given out on an international broadcast.) The weather forecast message, coming both in the middle and at the end of a regular transmission, would be decoded as follows: (Kitayama, 1988a:384-5)

East wind; Rain [*Higashi no kaze; Ame*]	War has begun between Japan and the **United States**. Burn all important documents.
North wind; Cloudy [*Kita no kaze; Kumo*]	War has begun between Japan and the **Soviet Union**. Burn all important documents.
West wind; Fair [*Nishi no kaze; Hare*]	War has begun between Japan and **Britain**. Burn all important documents.

On 5 December, this code was replaced with another and these codes became obsolete. (Kitayama, 1988a:399) Despite this, however, "West wind; Fair" was read on overseas transmissions on the night of 7-8 December 1941 as Japanese forces prepared to attack Pearl Harbor and Hong Kong. The signal for the Navy to start the attack on Pearl Harbor, "Go

Climb Mount Niitaka," also to be given out over short-wave radio, was similarly decided at the beginning of December.

On 7 December 1941, short-wave newscasts indicated only that Japanese raids on Lushih, near the Yellow River in China on 6th, had been successful, and that the Thai government had increased the number of troops on the border with Malaya owing to a build-up of Australian troops on the other side of the border.[17] At 01.30 on 8 December (Japanese time – 06.00 and 11.30 on 7 December in Hawaii and Washington respectively) Japanese troops and aircraft moved into action, as short-wave radio transmitted the weather forecast "West wind, Fair." By 02.15 the Japanese forces were approaching Hawaii and landing in Malaya, and at 03.22 the Japanese pilots over Hawaii radioed back "*Tora! Tora! Tora!*" [Tiger! Tiger! Tiger!] the signal that the attack on Pearl Harbor had been successfully carried out. War had brokent out in the Pacific.

CHAPTER 3
PEARL HARBOR AND THE DEVELOPMENT OF GREATER EAST ASIA

1. THE OUTBREAK OF WAR

There is some confusion concerning when the announcement of Japan's Declaration of War on the United States and Britain was made on overseas radio. It centres, principally, on whether the broadcast to the United States was made before or after the attack on Hong Kong. What is clear, however, is that following the announcement of the Declaration of War within Japan at 7am on 8 December 1941, translations were broadcast on a general transmission to all overseas regions, starting with a statement in Japanese, continuing with the Axis languages and ending with the translation in English. The English and Italian translations were made directly from the Japanese, but the German who produced the German translation was unable to speak Japanese, and his translation was made from the previously prepared English version. (Kitayama, 1988b:17-24)

From immediately prior to the outbreak of the war a new body, the Overseas Broadcasting Liaison Council [*Kaigai Hōsō*

Renryaku Kyōgai] was established to unify all overseas broadcasting. Consisting of representatives from the Cabinet Information Bureau (CIB), the War, Navy, and Communications Ministries, Dōmei and NHK, it met daily with the CIB. The meeting of 8 December agreed a series of five points, which outlined the information and propaganda policy to be employed in the war against Britain and the United States. Issued by the CIB, Point 1 of the "Outline of Information Propaganda Policy towards Japan's War with Britain and America" dealt with domestic broadcasts and the other four were as follows:

> *Radio is –*
>
> *to ensure the co-operation of the Axis countries and the indivisible link to both Manchuria and China.*
>
> *to obstruct enemy collaboration, resulting in the loss of their war aims, and to produce a split between the enemy countries.*
>
> *to bring the peoples of the Southern Regions into co-operation and alignment with us.*
>
> *to prevent neutral countries moving towards the enemy, and to bring them in line with us. (op cit. Kitayama, 1988b: 27)*

Within ten days of the outbreak of the "War for Greater East Asia," a plan for propaganda to be broadcast to different regions was produced. It was the result of high level discussions on propaganda themes between the CIB, the Navy and War Ministries, the Ministry for Foreign Affairs and NHK. Within Asia, the main aim of broadcasting was to turn the native inhabitants against Britain and the United States, so a strong anti-British campaign was waged in broadcasts for Malaya and Burma.[18] In Hong Kong and India, too, anti-British feeling was encouraged. On 26 December 1941, the Nanking Ambassador to Japan, Hsu Liang, made a broadcast to Hong Kong in which he claimed that Japan would soon rescue Hong Kong from British "exploitation and ruthless plunder." (*Japan Times and Advertiser*, 27 December 1941) In addition, the attraction of Japanese policies to the inhabitants of China proper was emphasised in broadcasts to Hong Kong, and British cruelty in the campaigns in Malaya (and later Burma) was stressed in broadcasts to both Hong Kong and India. The broadcasts frequently declared that British troops committed "every kind of atrocity"[19] claiming "Thousands of Indians and Malays have already been sacrificed."[20]

As part of the same strategy, the inhabitants of the Philippines and Indonesia were to be persuaded that co-operation in the Greater East Asia Co-Prosperity Sphere was advantageous to them, and thus prised away from the Western powers.[21] In addition, both Burma and the Philippines were to be tempted with the prospect of independence.[22] Broadcasts to Thailand and French Indo-China were to encourage the inhabitants of that region to strengthen their existing co-operation with Japan in the name of Asian unity.[23]

The Japanese also aimed to break the ties between the United States and Latin America, and between Britain and Australia. Plans were made to ridicule the United States' "Good Neighbour" policy in broadcasts to Latin America,[24] whilst Pan-Asian unity was stressed to portray Japan in a favourable light to Australians. Broadcasts suggested that as Australia was geographically closer to Asia, its future was inextricably linked to Asia and Japan, not to a former colonial power in remote Europe. To Britain and the United States broadcasts were to criticise Anglo-Saxon aggression in the Far East and they emphasised weak points in the American economy, such as the production surplus. (Kitayama, 1988b:28) In addition, all enemy nations were to be told of the weakness of enemy strategies and the decadence of the West, illustrated by the love of jazz among prisoners-of-war. These were compared unfavourably with the physical and moral superiority of the Imperial Japanese army and navy.

The stations which had already been opened in the Japanese occupied areas, were also to play an important role. The Korean and Manchurian stations called for the maintenance of East Asian security and stressed the need for continued co-operation with Japan. The stations of the Central China Broadcasting Corporation were involved in transmitting propaganda to Chungking, consolidating the Japanese position in the region. In November 1941, the proportion of propaganda broadcasts to the Chinese Nationalist capital from Radio Peking was increased, and after the outbreak of war in the Pacific, it also began broadcasting regularly to San Francisco, Sydney and London.

The Japanese also established an "Emergency Broadcasting Planning Committee" [*Rinji Hōsō Kikaku I'inkai*] in Peking, which met every morning to review all enemy broadcasts to China made the previous day, concentrating particularly on those made by the Nationalist Chungking station. Discussion of these broadcasts produced "guidance policies" for Radio Peking broadcasts on both short- and medium-wave. The victories of the Japanese army and the improved stability and lifestyle of people in occupied Northern China were emphasised in broadcasts to China, along with speeches urging the Chinese to resist the Chiang Kai-shek regime. In broadcasts to Chinese living outside China, particularly to those in Malaya and Singapore, the news was to concentrate on the strength and discipline of the Imperial army, whilst seeking to damage the image of the Chungking government.

The committee also considered transmissions to Indonesia and decided that in all broadcasts, the script-writers were to make a point of using the term "Indonesia" not the "Netherlands East Indies," as the "Free Netherlanders" had become an allies of Britain and the United States following the invasion of their homeland by Germany in 1940. Broadcasts from Japan were to hold up independence as a temptation, whilst damaging the image of Britain and the United States amongst the native population in a strongly news-based schedule. As a result, the North China Broadcasting Corporation was permitted to begin broadcasting to Indonesia in 1942, under the strict supervision of the Japanese Army in China.

The Japanese attacks on Pearl Harbor, Hong Kong and Malaya on 8 December 1941 were celebrated as great victories on all the transmissions throughout December. In news reports, as well as features, Radio Tokyo revelled in the attacks and the continuing advances of the Imperial army. A report on 20 December claimed that "Secretary Knox (American Secretary for the Navy, Frank Knox) had told the graduating class at the U.S. Naval Academy that the Japanese navy and airforce 'were so powerful that they succeeded in knocking out the American fleet stationed at Pearl Harbor.'"[25] Two days later there was a lengthy report claiming that the British blamed the attack on U.S. negligence.[26] Britain, which benefited immensely from America's entry into the war, was very unlikely to have made such a statement and this seems to have been one of Radio Tokyo's wilder accusations.

On 20 December, NHK's International Department was expanded, as broadcasting to the Southern Regions became increasingly important. Broadcasts on Transmission Four to Japanese troops on the front-line increased by thirty minutes daily. In addition, two new services were established; one (Transmission Six) to Indonesia and the Philippines in Malay,

Dutch, Tagalog, English and Fukien dialect began broadcasting from 20 December. The other (Transmission Five), to French Indo-China, began broadcasting in Burmese, Malay, Thai, Vietnamese, Cantonese, English and Spanish. Following the conquest of the Malay peninsula, Japanese language newscasts were added to the latter in February 1942, and after 1 August 1942, the English and Spanish languages were dropped in favour of Hindi and increased coverage in Malay. (Kitayama, 1988b:45-50)

The surrender of Hong Kong on 25 December 1941 was immediately announced in news flashes to all the transmission regions, announcers for all the seventeen broadcast languages being rushed to the Tokyo studios to make the announcements.[27] Japanese broadcasts stressed the significance of 100 years of British tyranny in Hong Kong and the potential power of the East Asian Co-Prosperity Sphere, following the eradication of British influence from Asia. "The Meaning of the Capture of Hong Kong" was explained to several of the transmission regions, this message being broadcast in Vietnamese, Fukien dialect, Cantonese, Mandarin, English and Arabic. (Kitayama, 1988b:52-55)

After the fall of the colony, reports citing British atrocities against the Chinese in Hong Kong were broadcast. The atrocity theme was also used in broadcasts regarding United States' action on Mindanao. "The Slaughter of Chinese on Mindanao: the Responsibility of the American-Philippine Army" was a talk in English which claimed that American Soldiers slaughtered Chinese women and children there. (Kitayama, 1988b:57) Japanese troops were said to be discovering feelings of anger towards the United States in all regions of the island.

It is not clear what the Japanese intended by citing the mistreatment of Chinese in Mindanao, rather than making a general accusation of atrocities committed against the local population, as was the case in broadcasts regarding Malaya and Hong Kong. It is probable that these broadcasts were aimed directly at overseas Chinese, who were generally sympathetic to the Chungking government, an ally of Britain and America. Perhaps the intention was to disillusion overseas Chinese in order to cut off this potential revenue supply for the Chungking government.

As the Battle for the Philippines intensified in late December 1941 and January 1942, the emphasis of overseas broadcasts switched. America was increasingly accused of cultural atrocities and cultural imperialism against the Philippines. Broadcasts charged America with supplanting Filipino culture with that of the United States. In addition, broadcasts to South and Central America concentrated on the common Catholic heritage of the Philippines and Latin America, and denounced American bombings of churches in raids on Manila.

Broadcasts to the Philippines itself were largely appeals to the native population to throw off American oppression. Programmes entitled "A Plea to Filipino Soldiers" and "The Filipinos have become the Americans' Human Sacrifices" claimed that American troops were only concerned for their own safety. In turn the example of Filipinos was held up to the rest of Asia to inspire the overthrow of Western oppression, and a programme entitled "The Rising of All Filipinos" was broadcast to Indonesia.

At the end of December 1941, the Japanese authorities in Tokyo decided that overseas broadcasts should not be permitted to mention the "Liberation of the Peoples of East Asia," as it was felt that this would inspire the peoples of East Asia to fight for freedom from the Japanese. The phrase agreed was the "Liberation of East Asia," to emphasise that it was Greater East

Asia (not a series of independent states) that was to be created by the overthrow of the Western powers. As Japan was the leader of the Greater East Asia Co-Prosperity Sphere it was hoped that this would ensure that the initial pro-Japanese feeling of native revolutionaries would not be dispelled. The agitation of nationalist movements was encouraged, and announcers on the Indonesian language programmes were permitted to play the Indonesian national anthem which had been banned by the Dutch authorities. However, local independence sentiment was not encouraged, and nationalist movements were encouraged to act only within the framework of the "Liberation of East Asia." Hence a meeting of the Imperial Headquarters and Government Liaison Committee on 3 March opposed proposals to encourage Javanese nationalists to think in terms of independence. (Kitayama, 1988b:62-3)

In broadcasts to the Pacific region in January 1942 Australia was portrayed as the "Orphan of the Pacific." Overseas radio waged a campaign to arouse Australian fears of isolation as Japanese troops advanced southwards across the Pacific, landing on New Britain, New Guinea and British Borneo on 24 and 25 January 1942. Broadcasts frequently cited English and Australian newspapers which, it was claimed, showed that the English cared little for Australia. They reported that British troops were being pulled back from the front line in North Africa, whilst Australians were forced to stay and fight for them. On 29 January Radio Tokyo reported that Britain had completely withdrawn her own forces from Libya leaving only the inhabitants of her colonies to fight.[28] It is now known that Australia was unhappy at having her forces deployed in the Middle East and this was, then, an occasion where Japanese propaganda accurately reflected the mood of its target. However, whether it acquired more regular listeners is impossible to determine. The context of reports and the quality of radio reception are important to listeners, before they accept a propaganda message. These reports may have reflected the prevailing Australian feeling, but most Australians would probably have needed more than one such example of Japanese empathy to overcome their suspicion of an enemy radio station.

America, it was claimed, was interested in Australia, but only in order to be able to use Darwin as a naval base. In order to divide Australia from the "mercenary" and "arrogant"[29] Americans, Radio Tokyo promised Australia co-operation in the Greater East Asia Co-Prosperity Sphere, and aid in securing Australian independence from Britain, in return for her withdrawal from the anti-Japanese forces.

Japanese radio directed at South and Central America attempted to separate the countries of Latin America from the United States, and the "Good Neighbour Policy" of the United States was frequently derided in broadcasts. A CIB policy for "Information Propaganda concerning the Greater East Asian War," established immediately prior to the outbreak of war, stated that neutral countries in South America were to be enticed away from America by emphasising the historical, cultural, ideological and linguistic differences between them and the United States. When Nicaragua, Honduras, Guatemala, El Salvador, Panama and Cuba declared war on Japan and Mexico, Columbia, Costa Rica and Venezuela broke off diplomatic ties with her in December 1941, a policy of inducing fear though broadcasts was planned. In December a feature on Radio Tokyo warned that these countries were to be sacrificed for the United States. The language was similar in tone to that used to Australia regarding the sacrifice of Australian troops by the British. In addition, Spanish language newscasts suggested that the "crafty strategy of the Americans in South America" was to destabilise South American governments by introducing Communist elements into the countries, in order to increase their dependence on the United States. There were also programmes such as, "We Hope South American Politicians Use Discretion," broadcast in English, Spanish and Portuguese, which questioned the diplomatic stance of South American countries. The reassurance that Japan had no quarrel with Latin America was also reported in Spanish and Portuguese to those republics that remained neutral. (Kitayama, 1988b:95)

As Japanese troops advanced in Malaya, Radio Tokyo regularly announced their victories. News reports to all the transmission regions at the end of January and the beginning of February 1942 concentrated on the situation in Malaya and Singapore. This was probably a deliberate policy to deflect attention from the situation in Bataan, in the Philippines, where the military campaign had reached a stalemate.

On 11February a broadcast to Italy stated:

Tonight we cannot talk of anything else . . . the hoisting of the Rising Sun [over Singapore] means the end of the Union Jack . . . From the suburbs the Malayan and Indian populations have flooded into the street to watch the passage of our glorious infantry, waving improvised flags of the rising sun and shouting: "Banzai!"[30]

Continuing the theme that the British never fought themselves but deserted the battlefield to let the people of the colonies fight for them, which had first been used first in broadcasts to Australia, the same broadcast claimed one quarter of the troops fighting in Malaya were British, the rest being Australians, Malays and Indians: "Thus the British government confirms the English habit of fighting with the blood of others."[31] The figure of one quarter British troops to three quarters Empire troops in the Malaya campaign was, in fact a fairly accurate one, although naturally the British did not draw the same conclusion from the figures that the Japanese radio reports did.[32] The same theme reappeared later in the war in broadcasts to India and to Indian troops in Africa, where the Japanese aimed to disillusion Indians with British rule.

On 14 February 1942 after Japan's complete occupation of Singapore, it was renamed '*Shōnantō*', and the port '*Shōnanko.*' The United States Records of the FBIS records that Radio Tokyo explained to its listeners;

> *The root words of both names are 'Shōwa,' which is the name of the present Imperial era, and 'nan' which means self. . . . 'Shōnan' symbolizes the supreme ideal of Japan for the establishment of a new order in the world and especially in Greater East Asia.*[33]

However, the characters for 'Shōnan' are the character for 'light' or 'bright,' which is indeed the first character of 'Shōwa,' and that for 'south,' not 'self.' The Imperial Headquarters-Government Liaison Committee meeting which agreed the name, chose these characters to symbolise the light being spread through South and East Asia by the extension of the rule of the Shōwa emperor. (Kitayama, 1988b:104) It was not unusual for Radio Tokyo to provide a different version to an enemy audience, from that given by radio stations to domestic or East Asian audiences. However, given that the renaming of Singapore, the former prized centre of British rule in South-east Asia, was a propaganda device in itself, in this case this is unlikely. It must be assumed, therefore, that the confusion caused by the FBIS report is merely a case of the monitor having misheard 'self' for 'south' during the course of the programme.

Radio Tokyo celebrated the Fall of Singapore with a series of programmes to all the transmission regions on the day of "The

First Congratulatory Party to Celebrate Victory in Greater East Asia." (Kitayama, 1988b:107) To Britain, a talk entitled "Let Them Speak" claimed that in a change "from the usual, confident, bellicose Churchill" the British Prime Minister "admitted that Britain did not have the slightest chance against the Japanese even if she had been prepared." The speech also aimed to produce discord between the British and the Americans, accusing the United States of drawing Britain unnecessarily into a war in the Pacific, and then abandoning her when help was needed asking;

> *What does Churchill really think about his Ally, who pulled him along in a reckless policy against Japan only to leave him in the hour of need?*[34]

Alongside the Malaya campaign Radio Tokyo also gave broadcasting time to discussion of the situation of Chiang Kai-shek in China, particularly after the Fall of Moulmein in Burma on 31 January 1942. Overseas Chinese were urged to stop sending aid to Chiang's Government, as it was claimed his position would be hopeless following the inevitable fall of Rangoon and the closure of the Burma Road, the Allied supply route from India and Burma to Chiang Kai Shek's government in China.

In February 1942 the role of Radio Peking was reviewed, and an increase in budget was agreed in order to increase pressure on the Chinese Government. In addition, news services to Chungking from the stations in Nanking and Hankow were established. This review agreed several propaganda themes to be used by these stations; the main ones were to emphasise Chungking's isolation when the Burma Road was cut, and to drive a wedge between Chiang Kai-shek's Nationalist troops and their allies the Chinese Communists. Ideologically, the two groups had little in common besides opposition to Japanese occupation. Indeed after the end of the Pacific war in 1945, the Nationalist Government which was formed, was thrown almost immediately into Civil War against the Communists, which ended in the establishment of Mao Tse Tung's Communist Government in 1949. Hence alongside appeals such as "Ladies and Gentlemen of Chungking! Volunteer for the Spirit of East Asia!" which resembled those made to people in other areas of Asia outside Japanese control, there were talks such as, "The Chinese Communist Offensive against Chungking." This claimed that the Communists had deliberately caused the isolation of Chiang Kai-shek, through their control of the Burma frontier region.[35]

2. RADIO BATTLE ACROSS THE PACIFIC

At the outbreak of war in the Pacific, America mobilised its piece-meal short-wave broadcasting and in February 1942, established a government short-wave station, the Voice of America. The San Francisco station, KGEI, was expanded and upgraded under this reorganisation, in order to broadcast to Asia and the Pacific nations. The programme schedule was expanded to include broadcasts in Mandarin, Cantonese and Fukien dialect, and contained news and speeches in Japanese. However, these programmes would only have been heard by the Japanese radio monitors as listeners in Japan and occupied Asia were forbidden to own short-wave receivers. It is unclear when precisely they were banned in Japan, but from BBC documents it is clear that orders banning ownership of short-wave receivers were issued in all Japanese administered territories.[36]

In January 1942, KGEI made a broadcast claiming that the Japanese had not in fact sunk the United States aircraft carrier *USS Lexington*, as Japanese broadcasts had claimed, and that, although it had been damaged, repairs were being carried out to restore it to full service. It was reports such as this, which prompted the Japanese government to respond directly to KGEI's Asian broadcasts.

On 11 February 1942, NHK began a programme, "Answering to KGEI." (Kitayama, 1988b:111)[37] Many of these broadcasts followed a pattern of announcing "War Results," as Radio Tokyo did on other transmissions. These consisted of lists of the numbers of troops and machinery killed or destroyed and captured. In "Answering to KGEI," however, the figures conflicted directly with figures claimed by American stations in recent broadcasts, the American figures being quoted and directly refuted. Thus the first reply broadcast took issue with a KGEI broadcast which, it claimed, had stated on 5 February that there had been 6,082,500 Japanese killed in China. The first edition of "Answering to KGEI" stated,

> *This figure bears no relation to the number of people who have died in the China Incident. Just over 100,000 Japanese have been killed in the action in China." (Kitayama, 1988b:112)*

It would appear that the radio battle did not progress to anything more than a conflict over the "truth" of figures, and that the broadcasts took on the nature of haggling rather than achieving any noticeable propaganda aims.

"Answering to KGEI" and programmes which made direct reference to the broadcasts of other nations continued throughout the war and the regular round up of "War Results" was a feature on all Japanese transmissions in the "Radio War" over figures. Japanese and American broadcasters were not the only ones to quote from specific enemy broadcasts. The BBC employed George Orwell to make weekly commentaries on the war situation to India between December 1941 and March 1943.

Many of these were clearly answers to Axis broadcasts to India. On 25 July 1942 part of Orwell's review refuted the "World picture presented by Axis propagandists," which stated that the Axis nations were "fighting the unjust [British and American] oppression" of the rest of the world "not in any way for their own interests, but simply in order to set the enslaved peoples free." Orwell continued his commentary as follows:

> *Thus the Japanese assure the Indians if they invade India, it would be with no intention of settling there, but merely in order to drive the British out after which they will retire again. Simultaneously, the Germans and Italians are assuring the Egyptians that they have no desire whatever upon Egyptian territory, but are merely invading Egypt in order to expel the British, after which they, too, will retire to their own territories. (West, 1985:121)*

This was certainly a direct response to a "Message to Indians" broadcast by Subhas Chandra Bose on Azad Hind on 20 July, in which he had described the British Empire as having two lungs, Egypt and India. He had claimed that one lung had collapsed after the Axis powers had declared the independence of Egypt, and that only the Indian "lung" needed to collapse for the British Empire to die completely. (West, 1985:225) Azad Hind was a Free Indian station broadcasting from Berlin, which began operations on 19 January 1942 under Indian Nationalist, Subhas Chandra Bose. After Bose's escape to the Far East (he arrived in Tokyo on 13 June 1943) following a six-month journey, the Azad Hind was given air-time in the Shonan transmitter schedule by the Japanese authorities. Azad Hind broadcasts to India continued for an hour a day from Shonan until the end of the war.

2.1 The Radio Attack on the Netherlands East Indies

Following the occupation of Singapore on 14 February 1942, Japanese radio attention turned to the Netherlands East Indies. There was a steady stream of news items in Dutch, English and Malay indicating the inevitability of a Dutch capitulation, which included such items as "Brothers and Sisters in Indonesia, Stand-up for yourselves right now!" (Kitayama, 1988b:115) In addition, the station in Saigon played an important role in the radio war on the NEI. Under the joint control of NHK and the Japanese military authorities, a special team gathered there to prepare broadcasts to the NEI. Broadcasting from the Saigon station as "Radio Bandung," the team of ten (four NHK personnel, an accountant from the Japanese forces, a Dutch announcer, two Malay-speaking prisoners-of-war, and Dutch and Malay translators) began transmissions on 3 March 1942, claiming that the station was broadcasting from within the NEI. For the first few days broadcasts were intermittent and this was explained as being on account of the difficult war conditions. On 5 March the station claimed that the Japanese military authorities had launched a full-scale attack around Batavia, and that they were officially changing the name of Batavia to Djakarta. To give Radio Bandung credibility on 6 March the Dutch announcer, Kreufel, broadcast over the recognised station, Radio Saigon, an appeal to the Dutch urging them to throw down their arms. This allowed Radio Bandung to "reply officially" the following day that the Dutch administration in Batavia was considering starting negotiations with the Japanese, as Britain, America and Australia were providing little support.

Radio Saigon proper announced the fall of Rangoon on 8 March and the same evening, "Radio Bandung" announced that negotiations for the surrender of Indonesia had begun. The

Japanese authorities announced the complete surrender of Indonesia at the following day, and "Radio Bandung" was "forced" off the air with the words "Long live Queen Wilhelmina!" (Kitayama, 1988b:116-19)

The key to this sort of black propaganda[38] is that the listener believes that the station is what it purports to be, and in the NEI this does seem to have been the case. It appears that the station had a large influence on the attitude of the civilian Indonesian population, particularly those in the more remote areas who had little idea of the true situation around Batavia. However, NEI troops also responded to "Radio Bandung." This may be because the Japanese had swept through Malaya so quickly, and had already captured the "impregnable British fortress" of Singapore with comparative ease. It seems possible that belief in inevitable collapse, by a force already thought to be weakened by the fall of the mother country in 1940, was perhaps less surprising than it at first appears. The resigned defeatism of a "Dutch" station seemed to hasten the surrender by confirming the inevitability of a Japanese victory.

2.2 The Radio War on Australia

An article the March 1942 issue of *Denshin Kyōkai Kaishi* [*Communications Corporation Magazine*] entitled "War Becomes the Mother of Culture," described the role of Japanese radio as being to build and strengthen an "Asian Culture" whilst discrediting that of the West. It claimed that an "Asian Culture" had existed in the nineteenth century, before Western influence in Asia had become strong, and stated that radio's role was to recreate this. The article claimed that if radio started with art and music, the whole ideology and culture of Asia would eventually revert to its natural "Asian Culture." (Kitayama, 1988b:124-5)

As it was felt that Western languages necessarily promoted Western culture, in February and March 1942 the use of English loan words in Japanese language broadcasts to occupied Asia was reduced dramatically. (*Hōsō Kenkyū* 05-42:118) Thus, the term '*Anaonsaa*' [Announcer], a broadcasting term borrowed from English, was dropped, and radio presenters became '*Hōsōin*' [Broadcasters]. (Kitayama, 1988b:125) In the same way '*Nyūsu*' [News] became '*Hōdō*' [Information] although '*Rajio*' [Radio], deemed a Latin word, was permitted to stay. At the same time the Japan Alps became '*Chūbu Sangaku*' [Central Mountains] and the name of the *Japan Times and Advertiser* was changed to the *Nippon Times*. (Shillony, 1981:148)

Also in March 1942, Prime Minister Tōjō issued a statement that Australia and India were to be the next targets in the Japanese propaganda war, and announced a large increase in the budget of NHK's International Department. In the propaganda war against Australia, the broadcasts of prisoners-of-war played a major role and letters from Australian troops captured by the Japanese were read out by the presenter during transmissions. The first prisoner letter had been made in the transmission to Australia on 19 December 1941 and it was introduced as follows:

> *Calling 1st Lieutenant Borden's Mother, Mrs. F. Borden. Are you listening to this broadcast from Tokyo Japan? Are you listening to this broadcast of a letter from your most important and beloved son in the world? Your important son 1st Lieutenant Borden is safely with the Japanese Army after receiving hospitable nursing he said there's no need to worry. (Kitayama, 1988b:16-7)*

However, following Tōjō's statement the prisoner letters campaign intensified.

Initially, letters were inserted into the schedules between other broadcasts, to entice Australians to listen regularly to Radio Tokyo. Hence, "The reading of news was customarily interrupted merely by an announcement, . . . that the messages would begin. Thus continued listening was necessary or the messages would be missed." (Meo 1968:163)

The stations in the NEI were particularly important to the Japanese radio assault on Australia and prisoner letters were an integral part of the transmissions from the summer of 1942. On 5 June, Radio Bandung made the following announcement, which was followed by a list of prisoners' names:

> *. . . The best thing for you to do is to listen to our radio service from Batavia. Just turn on the radio and listen in. . . . The information you eagerly wish to know about Australian officers and men now interned by the Nippon Army comes to you at 12.15 midday and again at 9.15 in the night . . . .*[39]

Letters written by prisoners themselves were also incorporated into programmes from early in June 1942. The first one was picked up by monitors at the BBC on 14 June although reception was bad and the name of the prisoner was inaudible. It was written by a medical officer who stated that he was fine, although missing his wife in Melbourne, was learning Japanese and bridge at the camp, and was enjoying the warmer climate of Indonesia. He begged people not to judge the Japanese harshly, but claimed that many were nice and had a good sense of humour.[40] This was not the first prisoner letter broadcast from Batavia, but the reception of the previous ones had been too indistinct for the monitors to be able to record what had been said.

Many of the prisoner letters gave the names of two or three of their companions and asked the addressee of the letter to pass on details to their relatives. Most described similar scenes of camp life, a prisoner vegetable garden was common, as were classes set up by the prisoners themselves, and church services on Sundays. Problems with obtaining money and clothing were also frequently mentioned in early broadcasts, although the statement that there were problems was usually qualified with one that the Japanese had promised to pay prisoners. Most of the letters expressed gratitude to the Japanese for their good treatment of the letter writer. From the end of June 1942, the Prisoner Letters became a regular feature of Radio Batavia broadcasts to Australia and New Zealand, which became known as "Australia Home News Hour." Usually one or two letters were read followed by a list of prisoners' names.

Broadcasts of prisoner letters were also made by Radio Tokyo in transmissions to North America. It was announced on 1 January 1942, that

> *. . . fully aware of this universal sentiment, [the desire for news of missing loved ones] the Japanese military authorities now are planning to broadcast the names or whereabouts of those American and British soldiers and sailors who have either been killed or made prisoner.*[41]

The United States Department of Transport Monitoring Station at Point Grey in Vancouver monitored the broadcasts and sent the details to the Federal Communications Commission (FCC) in Washington.

Generally the letters broadcast in these "Postman Calls" programme were much shorter than those kept by the BBC, and they tended not to contain details of camp life. For example, a message from Alvard Lucy Davis on 27 October 1944, read:

Hello Mother and the rest of the folks back there. I am well. I would like to take this opportunity to wish you all a Merry Christmas and a Happy New Year.[42]

There were also longer reports, sometimes recordings of the prisoners' voices, which were broadcast under the title of "Humanity Calls." One from Private Ralph Knox in Tokyo Camp, gave details of a hospital for prisoners-of-war he had visited "where our own doctors, working under the direction of the Japanese doctors, . . . have ----- supply of drugs and equipment."[43] Many of the messages in both the programmes aimed at America mentioned the prisoners' financial provision for their families at home, or the fact that letters and parcels from home had reach them. However, descriptions of life in the camps were absent, as these tended only to feature in transmissions from Radio Batavia, which broadcast to Australia.

It is difficult to ascertain the effect of the broadcast of prisoner letters on the populations of Australia and North America. The prisoners genuinely wrote much of the material contained in the letters, as they contained personal details. This ensured that the audience remained interested. However, the Japanese authorities tampered with the letters and

It was noticed, especially from Batavia, that stock phrases would appear time and again about the good food and living conditions, the excellent treatment of prisoners and the strength of the Japanese forces. (Meo, 1968:164)

According to an official survey carried out by the AIF Women's Association in November 1942, for the Australian Government's Sub-Committee on Enemy Propaganda, generally the few people who had both leisure time during the day and a short-wave receiver did listen in to Radio Batavia, as did unofficial monitoring organisations such as the Prisoner-of-War Relatives Association.

The response of the Australian Government to these findings was two-fold. Firstly, it refuted the claims of Japanese kindness to prisoners citing Japanese atrocities. It did this over the national broadcasting network to ensure that the number of people who heard the response was far greater than the number who had heard any of the Japanese broadcasts. Secondly, in January 1943, it formed a body to ensure that the full text of letters monitored was sent to the addressees in order to negate the Australian public's need to listen to Japanese broadcasts. (Meo, 1968:169-71)

2.3 The Radio Battle for India

The second radio offensive of 1942 was on India. Anti-British feeling had been mounting in India since the outbreak of the European war in 1939, when Britain had postponed India's promised dominion status until the end of the war. Unrest intensified during 1942, following the fall of Rangoon and climaxed in the outbreak of the "Quit India" campaign of civil disobedience in July.

Japan's radio war on India was signalled by an increase in broadcast time to the sub-continent in March 1942. Transmission Seven to India and the Middle East broadcast in Japanese, English, French, Hindi and Arabic. A broadcast in "Indian Languages" was inserted into the schedules to include news and features in Urdu, Bengali, Tamil and Punjabi. Unfortunately, Radio Tokyo did not have announcers who could speak all of these languages so broadcasts began in Punjabi only until a Tamil announcer began broadcasting in April. Urdu was added in December 1942 and Bengali broadcasts did not begin until March 1943. (Kitayama, 1988b:137)

Rash Behari Bose, leader of the Indian Independence League (IIL) had been resident in Japan since escaping the British police in Calcutta in 1915. The IIL was encouraged by the Japanese authorities, which allowed an IIL Conference to be held in Tokyo in March 1942. Following the fall of Singapore, Japanese radio appealed to Indians across Asia to join the Japanese in throwing off the oppressive regime of the British, and these broadcasts continued as Britain's position in Malaya and Burma worsened.

The radio station in Singapore, which was re-opened by the Japanese on 28 March 1942, became the second most important Japanese overseas radio station after Tokyo. It was the centre of Indian Independence broadcasting, and on its opening day it included transmissions in Tamil and Hindi besides English, Japanese, Thai, Malay, Fukien dialect and Cantonese. The Hsinking station in Manchuria also began broadcasts for India at this time, as did captured stations in Burma, which were "patched up" sufficiently to be able begin broadcasting to India as soon as the fighting allowed.

This increasing broadcasting activity coincided with the failure of the British government's mission to India lead by Sir Stafford Cripps and the heightening of Gandhi's campaign of Civil Disobedience. The Cripps Mission itself was the subject of frequent derision in broadcasts to most regions. A commentary to Italy in March claimed that Indians had previously been frequently fooled, and questioned if the British could dupe them again through Cripps.[44] Another talk in Italian claimed that the tricks used by the British in their chicanery in deceiving Indians were well known.[45] The British offer to India of dominion status at a later date was ridiculed as a mere "sweetener" offered only to keep Indians as enemies of Japan by Britain which was unable to resist her without Indian resources and manpower.

Broadcasts by George Orwell in the weeks prior to the arrival of the mission, on the other hand, stressed Cripps' good character, "a man of great personal austerity, a vegetarian, a teetotaller and a devout Christian" (West, 1985:61) countering derisive Japanese broadcasts describing him as a British stooge. Following the break-down of negotiations British broadcasts to India referred frequently to Japanese broadcasts, refuting their claims directly. A commentary described as "a direct lie" Axis attempts to "represent the breakdown as a refusal on the part of India to defend herself and an actual Indian desire to pass under Japanese rule." (West, 1985:77) In contrast, Japanese broadcasts used the break-down of negotiations to point to India's refusal to be bribed with promises of American money, without immediate independence and described the situation as "the beginning of the end of the British Empire."[46]

As part of a new policy in broadcasting to India, plans were made to strengthen the stations in Saigon, Bangkok and Bandung and for them to become the basis of a radio onslaught on India, although the overall base for broadcasts to India was to remain in Tokyo. Links between these outlying stations and the major Japanese newspapers were also strengthened in order to improve the perceived credibility of news reporting to India.

3. FIRST JAPANESE SETBACKS

3.1 The Doolittle Raid

A broadcast from Tokyo on 16 April dismissed a Reuters' claim that three American 'planes had bombed Tokyo as "idiotic" and "laughable" fiction, which did not worry the Japanese. (Kitayama, 1988b:144) On 18 April, however, sixteen American B-25s from the USS Hornet carried out air raids on Tokyo, Osaka, Nagoya and Kobe.[47] The aircraft involved in the so-called "Doolittle Raid," named after its commander, then flew on to bases in China.

The Japanese authorities decided that it would be impossible to make no admission of the raid, so it was agreed that overseas radio would explain the "real situation" regarding the raid. The raid was admitted in a news report broadcast to the Pacific coast of the United States. This news report was subsequently translated into all the broadcast languages and re-broadcast during each of the transmissions over the next twenty-four hours. The report closely followed guidelines set out by the authorities, and admitted a raid had occurred, but stressed it had been inhuman, targeting hospitals, schools, residential areas and temples. It emphasised that the bombs had fallen in suburban areas killing only the innocent, as others were at work in the city centres. The only result of the inhuman raid, it claimed, was to increase Japanese patriotism and to deepen the Japanese desire for victory over the inhuman enemy. Broadcasts using similar language continued in subsequent days. A further broadcast to the United States described the American airmen deliberately directing their machine-gun fire at children in a school playground in Tokyo, killing thirty of them.[48]

Of the American airmen that flew on to bases in China, three died when their parachutes failed to open, and a further eight were arrested when they landed in Japanese-occupied China. They were transported back to Tokyo on 21 April to stand trial and it was reported on 27th that airmen who surrendered themselves having bombed Japan would be shown no mercy. All eight of those captured were eventually sentenced to death in August 1942, but five had their sentences communted as a demonstration of the Emperor's benevolence a month later. The remaining three were executed on 10 October. The trial became the basis for an important American propaganda film, *The Purple Heart.*

During the Summer of 1942, occasional references were made in Japanese overseas broadcasts to the fact that the American public had no knowledge that four-fifths of those who took part in the raid had not returned, but the trial did not take place until October 1942. On 21 October, Radio Tokyo reported that officials had hinted that the airmen would be sentenced to death[49] and a day later it reported that they had confessed to bombing non-military targets.[50] Reports concerning the trial were accompanied by further reports that the United States' government had withheld news of the capture of the American flyers, but news of the trial and the fate of the airmen disappeared from the news schedules before the end of October 1942.

3.2 The Battle of the Coral Sea

The Fifth Conference of the East Asian Broadcasting Corporations took place in Tokyo in April 1942. Representatives of the Broadcasting Corporations in Korea, Taiwan, Manchuria, North and Central China attended along with delegates from the Japanese military authorities, the CIB, the Ministry of Communications, the Asia Development Institute and the Manchurian Government. Representatives from the Mongolian Broadcasting Corporation also attended as observers. The Head of NHK, Kōmori Shichirō attended, although there were no representatives of the International Section. This was largely as it coincided with Tanomogi Shinroku's announcement that he was intending to resign in order to stand in local Tokyo elections. On his resignation the leadership of the International Section was taken up by the Head of the Operations Bureau, Seki Masao, who held the two posts concurrently.

The Broadcasting Conference itself discussed the role of the smaller stations in Asia in broadcasting to the enemy. A list of which stations broadcast to whom and in which language was compiled (Appendix 2) and it was agreed that there should be several medium-wave and 2-3 short-wave stations in each area producing programmes for broadcast overseas. (Kitayama, 1988b:151)

In May 1942, the military situation in the Pacific was the main topic of Radio Tokyo news broadcasts. Reports in German said that Corregidor, in the Philippenes, had been shelled heavily by the Japanese[51] and a Japanese military communiqué was issued on 7th, following the island's complete occupation. This was broadcast first to China and Australia, and then to the other transmission regions.[52]

In April 1942, the Japanese had launched *Operation Mo* in the South Pacific's Coral Sea, in an attempt to capture Port Moresby, in New Guinea. American intelligence knew the main features of the plan and diverted aircraft carriers to meet the Japanese attack. The battle of the Coral Sea occurred on 7 and 8 May and was the first major naval battle between Japan and America. Compared to later battles, losses were not heavy, but they were significant and were suffered by both sides.

On 8 May, a Special Announcement was made over Radio Tokyo in "German, Italian, French etc. for the World." It stated that

> *. . . The Imperial Navy . . . east of New Guinea, located Anglo-American naval forces on 6th May in the Coral Sea*

south-west of New Guinea. Our ships at once attacked them and sank an American battleship . . . inflicted irreparable damage on a British cruiser . . . and also heavily damaged a British battleship . . . Today . . . our naval forces sank two American aircraft carriers . . . The offensive operations of our ships is still in progress.

This battle shall be named the 'Battle of the Coral Sea.'[53]

Within five days the *USS Lexington* had been added to the list of American aircraft carriers the Japanese claimed to have sunk. In the same period the American Government admitted to having lost the *USS Lexington* only, and claimed to have sunk seventeen Japanese ships. The Japanese admitted losses of one light aircraft carrier and thirty-one aeroplanes. In reality, both sides had lost two aircraft carriers. (Kitayama, 1988b:159-60) Falsification of figures seems to have been a feature of reporting on both sides, as they both wished to make their own destructive power appear greater. However, Japanese exaggeration grew increasingly wild as the war continued, and Japanese propaganda was forced to continually exaggerate further, in order not to undermine previous propaganda.

On 10 May the Japanese transmission to Australia claimed:

The naval battle of the Coral Sea . . . ended on 8th May with a shattering blow for the Americans and the British . . . The United States of America has now been reduced to a third rate naval power, its naval forces will hardly suffice to protect its own shores . . . (Meo, 1968:64)

Over subsequent weeks broadcasts to Australia stressed the vulnerability of Australia, following the huge American defeat, and claims such as this were made:

> *. . . the naval forces in defence of Australia have dispersed; . . . nothing stands now to defend her before the onslaught of the Japanese forces.* [54]

The atmosphere at the Imperial Headquarters Press Section when the news of the actual Japanese defeat in the Coral Sea was received, gives some indication as to why a policy of fabricating such reports was pursued:

> *Who would have thought that the Akagi, Kara, Sōryū and Hiryū would be sunk! Who would have imagined that our first and second air units would be annihilated! . . . "The most important thing is to keep it secret," said the chief of the First Section. "If even a part of the truth should become known it would be difficult to control the nation." No one spoke. These were people who were not trained for defeats . . . (op. cit. Meo, 1968:65)*

Features concerning the glorious results of the Battle of the Coral Sea continued to be broadcast occasionally over the next month, such as a report which claimed to report the truth about the battle, that after the sinking of the USS Yorktown and the USS Saratoga, the aircraft carriers the USS Hornet and the USS Enterprise fled at the sight of the Japanese bombers, without fighting.[55] The main content of news reports, however, concentrated on the war in China and the "mopping-up" operations being carried out around Mandalay in Burma, the fall of which was announced on 3 May 1942.[56] Japanese pressure on Australia was increased when the Head of the Navy Information Section, Captain Hiraide Hideo, announced that three Japanese submarines had entered Sydney harbour undetected on 31 May and had successfully shelled the city, sinking one warship. This was transmitted over the next few hours in all the English language broadcasts to the Pacific and East Asian regions in order to stress the vulnerability of

Australia.[57] In fact the attackers sank one non-military vessel, and failed to hit an American cruiser anchored in the harbour. Calvocoressi et al. 1989:1047)

3.3 The Battle of Midway

The Battle of Midway, 4-6 June 1942, is generally regarded as the turning point of the war in the Pacific. The Japanese attack on Midway Island, a stepping-stone to Hawaii, was intended to lure the depleted American fleet into an inescapable trap. It was preceded by a dummy attack on the Aleutian Islands. American Intelligence, however, had again cracked the Japanese codes and knew that the main target was Midway. The American victory was resounding. Japan lost all four large aircraft carriers and a heavy cruiser in twenty-four hours.

The United States announced complete victory in the naval battle on 7 June. The domestic Japanese audience was told that it was a total Japanese victory. However, in overseas broadcasts there was silence from Radio Tokyo regarding the battle until a military communiqué concerning Japanese landings on the Aleutian islands, issued on 10 June, mentioned that there had been reports of attacks on American ships near Midway on 4 and 5 June.[58]

The following day, reports quoted the United States Government as having admitted that the Japanese navy was now operational in both the Indian and Pacific Oceans. It stated that if the Aleutians fell to Japan, the America-Europe communications and supply lines across the Pacific would be cut, and that if the United States lines of defence were forced to retreat America would be "weakened by dispersal defensive action." It also claimed that Secretary of State Cordell Hull, was clearly cautious about the outcome of the Midway Battle. On 12

June, a news commentary regarding the significance of both the Midway and the Aleutians battles claimed that both battles were proof of the outstanding power, mobility, and superior tactics of the Japanese navy.[59]

The following day, however, the tone was entirely different. In a talk entitled "Australian Anxiety," Radio Tokyo reported that Australians, worried by the Japanese occupation of several strategic points in the Pacific, had warned the Americans not to become "intoxicated with the victory at Midway."[60] This was an admission of the United States' defeat which sought not to draw attention to it. Radio Manila hinted at a similar admission on 15 June when a broadcast to America and the Orient claimed that "Japanese losses at Midway will be more than compensated for by the occupation of the Aleutians."[61] However, on 28 June, a German language talk claimed that the Japanese attacks on Midway and the Aleutians were a planned and simultaneous attack comparable to the combined attack on Pearl Harbor and the Philippines.[62] The implication was that both had been entirely victorious. The battle of Midway was rarely mentioned on overseas broadcasts after this so it is difficult to surmise what, if any, plan existed for reporting it. It may have been that the American victory was treated as common knowledge in broadcasts to Australia and the Orient, but there is little continuation of the theme in the monitoring reports regarding what was said on other occasions so it is impossible to establish any clear trends.

From mid-June 1942 reports regarding the reconstruction of the newly occupied areas in the Pacific and China were the most frequent in all the transmissions, such as a report that the oil wells at Surabaya had been restored and that the Singapore rubber works were scheduled to re-open.[63] Occasional references to Midway and the Coral Sea were made, such as accusations that the Americans had invented results, but these were isolated reports late in a news programmes' running order. Their positioning was intended to emphasise the lack of importance the Japanese wished to attach to them.

CHAPTER 4
INITIAL DEFEATS (JUNE 1942 - JULY 1944)

1. DEVELOPMENTS IN THE WAR SITUATION AND RADIO TOKYO'S RESPONSE

During the two years from June 1942 the Axis powers suffered a series of defeats on all fronts, and the areas under Axis occupation were significantly reduced. In June 1942 Japan's position in the Pacific began to deteriorate. The Battle of Midway was the first United States' victory in the Pacific. At the same time, bitter fighting in the Solomon Islands, to the north-east of Australia, followed a naval and land attack by the American forces. The battle for the Solomon Islands continued into 1943, but in order to make regular claims of victory, Japanese communiqués divided the battle into several smaller battles. Hence the start of the Third Battle of the Solomon Islands was announced in November 1942.

Japan finally began to withdraw her troops from Guadalcanal, a small island in the Solomon Islands chain, on 22 January 1943 and the withdrawal was officially announced on 9 February. Japanese troops had seized the island before the Americans in August 1942, and the American attempt to capture it had originally been expected to take little more than a week.

The American push northwards continued during 1943, and on 17 February 1944 an air raid was carried out on Truk Island, the first American raid within Japan's "Inner Waters." This was followed in June 1944 by attacks on the strategic islands of Guam and Saipan, which were captured a month later.

While American troops were carrying out attacks on Japanese positions in the South Pacific, the situation on the Burma front became increasingly tense. Despite Japanese claims that the British position in North Eastern India was precarious, the expected Japanese victory at Imphal never occurred. Instead, eight weeks of some of the worst hand-to-hand fighting of World War Two took place in the city from March to May 1944.

In China, Japanese forces launched an ambitious and successful offensive in May 1944. The *Ichi-go* Offensive sought to provide a land supply route extending from Manchuria and North China through to Japanese forces in Southeast Asia, as Japanese merchant shipping had been decimated by Allied attacks. One of the principal purposes of the campaign was to prevent the United States from using bomber bases in China for attacks on Japan.

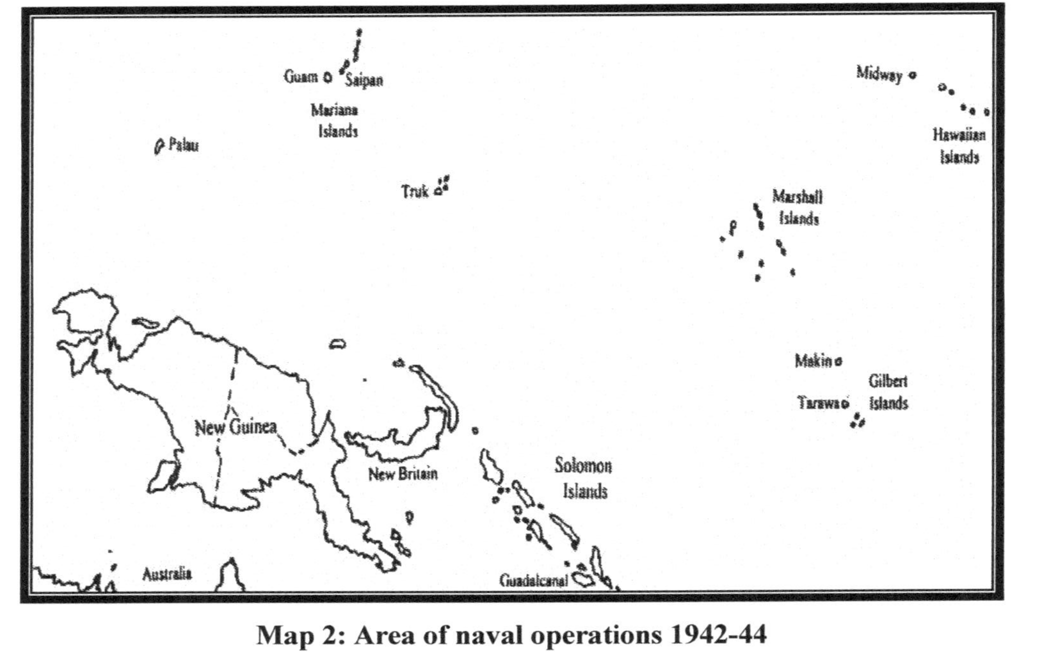

Map 2: Area of naval operations 1942-44

The middle years of the war saw a similar reversal in Axis fortunes in Europe. In January 1943 the Allied capture of Tripoli in Libya was announced and a few days later Allied reports described the first German setbacks on the Russian front at Stalingrad. The battle for Stalingrad had been raging since September 1942, and it concluded in Germany's first major defeat in February 1943. Allied troops attacked Italy across the Mediterranean Sea from positions in North Africa, and on 8 September 1943 the Italian Badoglio Government surrendered to the Allies, after secret negotiations. On 6 June 1944 the Allies opened the awaited second front in Europe with the D-Day landings in Normandy and began the final push towards Berlin.

On the political front, in 1943 the leaders of the Allies met in at conferences at Casablanca in January and Cairo and Tehran in November. At the former meeting, between Roosevelt and Churchill, it was agreed to leave the initiative in military operations in the Pacific to the United States. The Cairo conference, between Churchill, Roosevelt and Chiang Kai-shek, resulted in the signing of the Cairo Declaration, which detailed the division of Japanese territories amongst the Allies following her defeat. The day following the declaration Churchill and Roosevelt met Stalin at Tehran to discuss plans for the conclusion of the European war.

From 5 to 6 November 1943 the Greater East Asia Conference was held in Tokyo and included the leaders of Burma, the Philippines, Thailand, Manchukuo, Occupied China and the Provisional Government of Free India. This meeting was intended to strengthen solidarity and co-operation between these countries and Japan. It also sought to embarrass the Allies and deter them from pressing on with plans for the re-conquest of Asia, by demonstrating that total independence had become the political objective of Asian states. The Joint Declaration issued by the Conference stated that the countries of East Asia would "respect their mutual autonomy and independence." (Iriye, 1981:119) However, its language was not completely anti-Western and it sought to prepare for an eventual end to hostilities. In so doing it partially paralleled thinking in the United States' State Department, which belied the "menacing words" of the Cairo Declaration. (Iriye, 1981:153)

The Japanese short-wave radio response to developments in the middle years of the war was frequently two-fold. Often Japanese reports sought to deflect the listeners' attention from news of Allied successes, and news programmes would frequently devote little time to major battles if the situation did not appear favourable to Japan. Hence after the occupation of the Aleutian Islands of Kiska and Attu, their renaming to *Narukami* and *Atsutu* was announced in programmes on 25 June,[64] being more favourable news than the defeat at Midway. United States' denials of huge losses were described as "useless,"[65] and the strategic importance of Kiska and Attu for attacks on North America was stressed.[66]

The other strategy for broadcasting news about battles in the South Pacific was to pay little regard to the true situation, and celebrate each battle as a glorious Japanese victory. During the battles for the Solomon Islands in the second half of 1942, Radio Tokyo often made "bombastic" claims of losses inflicted on American forces. "War results" were issued frequently, which omitted many of the Japanese losses and exaggerated those of the United States. A Japanese report on 28 November claimed that American losses in the Third Battle for the Solomon Islands had mounted to two battleships and eleven destroyers, rendering the battle a great Japanese victory. In reality, American losses were much lighter than Japanese reports claimed, amounting to three light cruisers and four destroyers. Japanese losses of two battleships, one destroyer, and eleven of their nineteen transport vessels were not reported. (Kitayama, 1988b:238) An American report of January 1943, declared that the Japanese propaganda situation regarding the Solomon Islands could not "be redeemed by anything short of an American defeat as crushing in actual fact as those that Tokyo has claimed in extravagant propaganda."[67]

Radio Tokyo ridiculed the United States' publication of the Pearl Harbor casualty figures late in 1942. It claimed that publication had been delayed for a year in order that it would not seem so devastating to the American public and continued that the Japanese public had learnt the "crippling truth" after ten days, but Americans had to wait twelve months.[68]

The first anniversary of the outbreak of war in the Pacific on 8 December 1942 was marked by "flashback" reports of news reports of a year previously and descriptions of patriotic rallies held in Japan. An outline for the radio commemoration of the anniversary had been drawn up in October and it was to consist of seven days of celebratory programmes. (Kitayama, 1988b:250) A speech to Italy over Radio Tokyo stated, "Like the Italo-German victories, the achievements of Japan during the last twelve months have made the position of the Japanese Empire unshakeable and have strengthened Japan's faith in final victory."[69]

Overseas radio features in 1943 continued to claim high American losses in the Battle for the Solomon Islands. Interestingly, although Radio Tokyo used the word "withdrawal" in regard to Guadalcanal, in some of its English language broadcasts, the Imperial Headquarters statement used the phrase "shift in army positions" [*tenshin*] and this was used in domestic broadcasts and Japanese language broadcasts. (Kitayama, 1988b:288) It is not clear why overseas radio was allowed to use "withdrawal" in its English broadcasts, but it is probably reasonable to assume that it was a mistake, or a misunderstanding by the censor.

On 30 May 1943 the Japanese authorities announced the first "Honourable Defeat" [*Gyokusai*][70] of the war following reports of American landings on Attu Island on 14 May. This was reported on overseas broadcasts on the same day, the communiqué being read out over the air. It said that the garrison had been virtually wiped out as Japanese preferred death to dishonour.[71] Although reticent at first about publishing figures Tokyo soon "fell back on its stock propaganda lines."[72] The withdrawal from Kiska Island was announced on 22 August. The evacuation of the island was described as successful for three reasons: the close collaboration between army and navy, providence which always favoured the Japanese (in this case by sending fog to shield the withdrawal) and the self-sacrificing spirit of the soldiers on Attu.[73]

The battle in the Solomon Islands continued into the winter of 1943 and reports of the "5th Air Battle for Bougainville" announced by the Japanese Army Headquarters on 17 November, claimed that there had been increased United States shipping losses. (Kitayama, 1988b:398) Later that month reports of results for the Gilbert Islands were also included as American troops began landing on Tarawa and Makin on 19 November. (Kitayama, 1988b:412)

On 20 December 1943 the Japanese authorities announced the "Honourable Defeat" of these islands, nearly a month after it had occurred. (Kitayama, 1988b:420) The radio announcement stated that all the 3,000 garrison troops had died the death of heroes against more than 50,000 American troops, but that they had inflicted heavy losses before being wiped out.[74] These reports are remarkable examples of Japanese exaggeration. In fact the invading American force numbered some 17,000 to

18,000 whilst those in the Japanese garrison numbered close to 5,000. The Japanese garrison was almost wiped out, although seventeen prisoners were taken, and it had inflicted heavy losses on the invading force. The losses of 3,301 US Marines killed, wounded or missing were, however, lower than the Japanese garrison losses of 4,690 dead (Hess, 1986:91) and constituted less than twenty percent of the attack force. (Buchanan, 1964:283-6)

With the continued announcement of "Honourable Defeats" Japanese radio turned away from "War Results," and sought to deflect attention to events elsewhere in the Co-Prosperity Sphere. It adopted a theme of "moral superiority." Japan was portrayed as the educator of East Asia, sending textbooks,[75] and opening schools[76] in Macassar in Indonesia. A further commentary claimed perceptively that time could not go backwards in international affairs and that the countries of East Asia could never be passively exploited again by the imperial powers.[77] This proved an accurate prediction as despite efforts by some of the former colonial powers in East Aisa to re-establish colonial rule after the war, most former East Asian colonies gained their independence in the years following the Second World War.[78] However, when American raids on the Marshall Islands began at the end of January 1944 the lists of Japanese "War Results" re-appeared in broadcasts, with a report listing the American air losses in the first two weeks of 1944 over Rabaul, the main city in New Britain.

The American air attack on Truk Island in February 1944 was, unusually, reported immediately on Japanese-controlled overseas radio. Manchurian radio made the announcement on 18 February.[79] In the days, which followed the surrender of the island, however, broadcasts tended to concentrate on the war on the Indian front. An exception was a commentary to Germany on "The Situation in the Pacific Ocean" which claimed that the battle in the Pacific would reach its decisive stage when Japan released for action the hundreds of divisions it had on stand by.[80]

As action on the Burma front became increasingly critical Japanese broadcasts devoted more news time to reports of Indian activity, both in the fighting and in Greater East Asia. On 23 March Radio Tokyo reported that the Indian National Army (INA) had crossed the Burma-India border.[81] The battle for Imphal was closely followed in radio broadcasts and reports were made daily regarding Japanese successes. Radio Shonan declared on 10 April that the "British Empire is heading for collapse" and accused the British of calling on Indians to fight the Japanese invader not for the good of India but that of the Empire.[82] This was not an unreasonable supposition for the Japanese to make about the British regarding Indians in the British army. Naturally, Britain wished to defend her empire from both invasion and uprisings.

On 14 June 1944 the Japanese authorities announced that American planes had attacked Saipan and Guam, and on 20th Japanese General Headquarters announced that the Japanese defenders were inflicting heavy losses on the American troops whilst awaiting reinforcements. (Kitayama, 1988c:63-4) The broadcast did admit, however, that Allied landings had been made. Generally, in stark contrast to domestic broadcasts, overseas broadcasts made infrequent references to the battle for Saipan, simply reporting that violent fighting was continuing,[83] or accusing Allied radio stations of hiding details of the fighting in order to conceal huge Allied losses.[84]

The Japanese authorities admitted the American occupation of Saipan on 18 July 1944. (Kitayama, 1988c:69) Following pressure for reconstruction of the Japanese cabinet, this major defeat drove the Tōjō cabinet to resign at 6.30am on 20 July

1944. This was reported to all overseas transmission regions that day. The achievements of the cabinet in perfecting "the internal system of Japan and in prosecuting the war" and in endeavouring "to liberate all peoples and countries of Greater East Asian from Anglo-American and Dutch oppression" [85] were also broadcast to all regions. Erwin Wickert, a regular commentator on the German transmission, admitted that "Enemy propaganda will undoubtedly try to exploit Tōjō's resignation" but said that the Allies would quickly learn that "the immediate future will show up the enemy's fatal error in believing that Tōjō's resignation means any weakening of Japan's will to prosecute the war."[86] Listeners were reassured that

> *The Japanese people desired the formation of a new cabinet capable of grasping the present excellent opportunity [the fall of Saipan] to force a decision; and the Tōjō cabinet resigned in the expectation that a new and powerful cabinet would be able to fulfil the people's ardent desires.*[87]

Generally Japanese radio had little to say in regard to the war in Europe in these months. Significant events did cause a few comments, but most programmes concentrated on the situation in Asia and the Pacific. Reacting to the surrender of the Badgolio Government in Italy on 8 September 1943, the Government Liaison Committee declared that there should be "strong domestic control concerning this case." On overseas radio hostility towards Italy, which appeared in domestic broadcasts, was largely absent. However, it was decided "as a reflection of present Italian feeling," Japan would "for the time being temporarily suspend for an unspecified period" the Italian weekly exchange broadcasts which were relayed across the Japanese domestic network. (Kitayama, 1988c:376-7)

Both the British capture of Tripoli and German difficulties at Stalingrad were mentioned in Radio Tokyo news broadcasts. These events were, however, played down, appearing late in the running order of news, in short reports, whilst the main headlines concentrated on Asian reconstruction news and reports about the war in China. The first report was an English language broadcast on 26 January which claimed that Allied optimism regarding the capture of Tripoli and German setbacks was unjustified. Typically, this was the eleventh item in the news following reports about the China front and Asian celebrations of "Indian Independence Day."[88]

The D-Day landings on 6 June 1944 were reported by Japanese radio as hastening the decisive turning point of the war. The second European front was, however, said to be developing "according to German expectations"[89] and Radio Tokyo claimed that in finally opening the second front the Allies had walked into a German trap, which would be as devastating as the Japanese strike for victory in India.[90]

Radio Tokyo's response to political and diplomatic events in this period was also muted. It largely ignored the Casablanca Conference, between Roosevelt and Churchill in January 1943, although a news item in a German broadcast did ridicule the Allied leaders for having to hold the Conference in an air raid shelter.[91] Other broadcasts concentrated on the Chungking government's disappointment with the lack of substantial discussions at the conference and a report to Australia and China declared that Chiang Kai-shek had had to order that the volume of criticism be limited.[92]

At the end of January 1943 criticism of the Casablanca Conference was broadcast to all regions and a "Pat to Charlie"[93] broadcast to America inferred that both Stalin and Chiang Kai-shek turned down the American and British invitations to attend the Conference as the talks were "nothing but buffoonery." (Kitayama, 1988b:283-4) In a separate feature Radio Tokyo claimed that the Soviet Union was only of use to Britain and the United States in providing men to die on the European front. (Kitayama, 1988b:284) The perceived split between the Soviet Union and Britain and America was frequently played upon and on 17 February a news item claimed that Britain was "Warning of Soviet Expansion" in the Baltic States. This, it was claimed, was the reason for Stalin's exclusion from the conference. (Kitayama, 1988b:285) Here, Japanese propagandists seized on the enormous ideological differences between Stalin and Churchill and Roosevelt and made logical assumptions in their accusations, for the Allies had little in common besides their joint war against the Axis powers. Churchill's concern over Soviet expansion was real, and although Japan did not have access to confidential British documents Radio Tokyo made a reasonable assessment of the situation.

Following the Cairo and Tehran Conferences, Japanese Prime Minister Tōjō made a radio speech "to the whole world" which was broadcast simultaneously on the domestic and East Asian networks. In it he accused the Allied leaders of making plans which bore no relevance to reality in the light of Japanese successes at Bougainville and in the Gilbert Islands. (Kitayama, 1988b:414) Radio Hsinking claimed that Churchill and Roosevelt delighted in talking about a rosy post-war period in order to take their minds off the real situation.[94] Amid the usual overt denials of the true situation, however, a broadcast from Tokyo revealed to the British audience that Churchill had disliked having to treat Chiang Kai-shek as an equal at the Cairo Conference, but that Roosevelt had insisted on this. He considered Chiang extremely important in the war against Japan owing to the unfavourable position of American troops in the Pacific.[95] This is another case where Radio Tokyo may have reported something closer to the truth than seemed usual. As leader of the British Empire Churchill rarely regarded non-whites as equals, as they were usually in inferior positions beneath British colonial officials. The same was true in British concessions in pre-war China. In fact, Churchill's racism was well known and he frequently referred to the Chinese as "Chinks," "Pigtails" or "Little yellow men." (Thorne, 1978:5-6) Hence, it was reasonable to assume that the imperial leader would dislike being forced to treat someone he considered inferior as an equal. In addition, the military contribution to the overall war effort of Chiang's ground war in China was slight, and this was a further reason that Churchill may have resented his attendence as an equal contributor.

Surprisingly, the evidence that exists implies that Radio Tokyo devoted little broadcast time to the Greater East Asia Conference. The opening of the conference with forty-six delegates in attendance was mentioned in a report to Germany,[96] as was a public meeting attended by many of the senior delegates.[97] In addition, President Laurel of the Philippines, who was in Tokyo for the conference, made a speech from Radio Tokyo extolling the Greater East Asia Co-Prosperity Sphere.[98] However, the conference was a great propaganda event and would have been expected to draw huge coverage. It is possible that there was blanket coverage in broadcasts to Southeast Asia, the target of the propaganda. As neither the BBC nor the National Archive material cover stations which their own monitors could not receive clearly, such broadcasts would not appear in these monitoring reports. However, the conference was called as a propaganda device, so it would be expected to be broadcast worldwide. It must be assumed, therefore, that what evidence exists must be inadequate.

2. CHANGES IN THE STRUCTURE OF SHORT-WAVE BROADCASTING (1942-1943)

On 1 September 1942, as the war situation was increasing the importance of overseas broadcasting in projecting Japan's cause, the status of the International Department was raised to that of the International Bureau [*Kokusai-kyoku*] and a Southern Regions Office [*Nanbyō-shitsu*] was established to reflect the importance of broadcasting to that region. The new International Bureau consisted of two Departments and one Section. Department One was in charge of "editing, broadcast programming and business concerning overseas, international and East Asian broadcasts" and Department Two was responsible for "execution and translation." (Kitayama, 1988b:221) The newly established Administration Section took over responsibility for ensuring that orders regarding censorship limitations were observed and for ensuring that necessary programme announcements were made. It also dealt with issues of copyright and ensured that any other legal or political matters concerning the rest of the Bureau were observed. (Figure 6, page125)

The Southern Regions Office was in charge of broadcasts to the occupied areas, where broadcasts promoting the unification of Greater East Asia were considered to have the highest priority. The office received notification of military and legal decisions regarding broadcasts to the occupied areas and ensured that the NHK broadcasters followed these strictly. The office was also in charge of carrying out requests made by the army or navy that radio stations be established in the occupied areas. In June 1942, an army report regarding operations in South East Asia requested that a means be established to send propaganda directly to Chungking, India and Australia, which were the most important targets to be convinced of Japan's good intentions. This resulted in the rapid rebuilding and establishment of short-wave stations in Singapore (50kw), Manila (10kw) and Rangoon (10kw). Operated by the army and staffed partially by NHK employees, these stations were transmitting programmes by the end of October 1942.

Following a navy request for broadcasts for Japanese living in the occupied areas, the Southern Regions Office supervised the despatch of NHK staff to Burma, the Philippines and Macassar to establish local broadcasts in Japanese for each of these regions. (Kitayama, 1988b:225)

From 20 December two daily broadcasts were made to most of the seven transmission regions over three 50kw and one 20kw transmitters, a total of thirty hours a day. In October 1942 broadcasts in Persian began and during December 1942 and January 1943 Russian, Tamil and Bengali language broadcasts were added to the schedules, as the radio battle for India became increasingly important, bringing the total number of languages being broadcast to twenty-three.[99] (Kitayama, 1988b:246)

The use of an increased number of languages, however, created problems for the censors and in many cases the censor checked only the Japanese version of a script, as the target language was unknown to anyone in the CIB. Hence, particularly with the less widely spoken languages, the translator was often left to alter freely the nuances of a Japanese script whilst still translating what was actually written. Even native English speakers tried to do this in translating English scripts, although English was more widely understood by members of the CIB than many of the other languages. This technique was used in the writing of "Zero Hour," Radio Tokyo's most notorious wartime programme. In the light of this problem, the censors concentrated on ensuring that the Japanese scripts, particularly those for broadcast in Greater East Asia, were entirely accurate, hoping that what was broadcast did not stray too far from the original meaning.

In the Spring of 1943, following American attacks on Truk Island, the schedules of the International Bureau were further revised, as broadcasts to enemy soldiers, now frequently out of range of their own domestic stations, were considered increasingly important. The special news and Chinese language news broadcasts across the Pacific to the United States, Canada, South America and Australia were replaced by further news bulletins in English. The Japanese language news, which was broadcast to Australia was also shortened and the English language news correspondingly expanded. These changes, along with a fifteen-minute extension to Transmission One, virtually doubled the length of time in overseas broadcasts devoted to English language news bulletins. (Kitayama, 1988b:307)

On 1 April 1943 the cabinet's "Epoch-making Reforms of International Propaganda" were put into effect, having a significant effect on overseas broadcasting. A new Inquiry Office was established, which consisted of the president, vice-president and department heads of the CIB, the head of Army Ministry's Information Department, the head of Section Four of the Navy Ministry's Business Bureau and the head of the General Business Section of the Greater East Asia Ministry It was intended to develop CIB prosecution of the ideological war and to tie the CIB more closely to military operations in "a single relationship." (Kitayama, 1988b:320) The effect of this on overseas broadcasting was initially to confuse. However, it was established that under the new system overseas broadcasting was separated from broadcasting to East Asia.

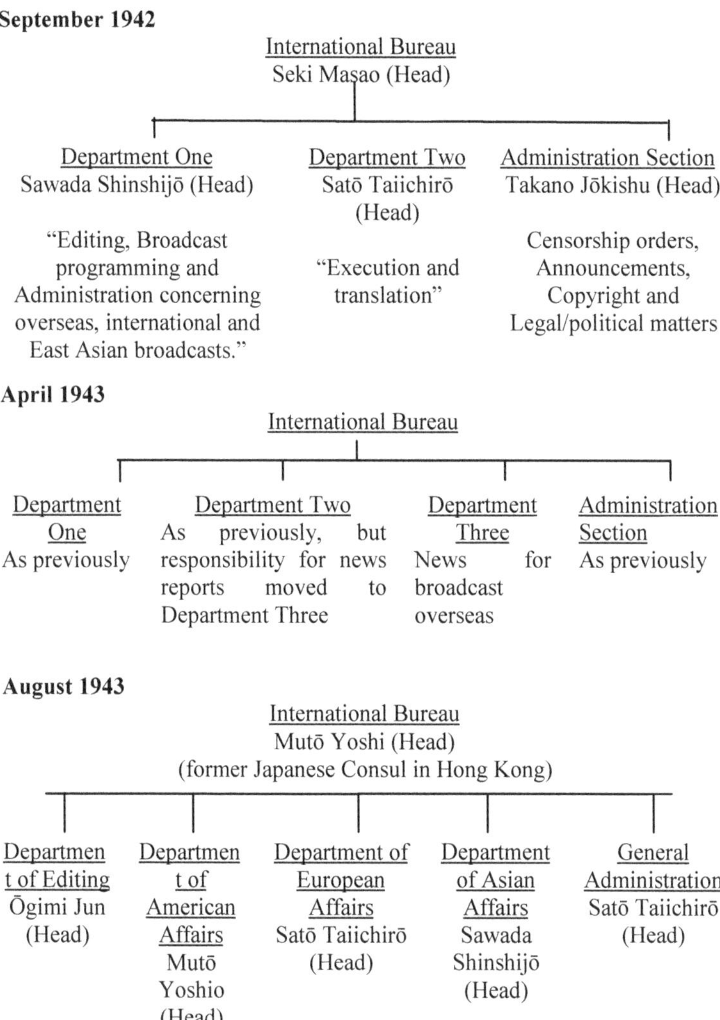

Figure 6: Structure of the International Bureau between 1942 and 1944
(Kitayama, 1988b:221, 244 & 320)

The latter became the responsibility of the Broadcasting Section of the CIB's Department Two, which dealt with domestic broadcasts and relays. This indicated a shift of perception regarding the status of the occupied regions, with them now being seen as "domestic" not "overseas" regions. Naturally, the International Bureau continued to broadcast to those parts of the Southern Regions which could only pick up short-wave transmissions, and to those parts of Asia, which were not occupied, but the task of tying the occupied territories to Japan was removed from the International Bureau.

On 15 May 1943, a new President, Dr. Shimomura Hiroshi, a member of the House of Peers, was installed as the head of NHK. On 17 August the new President announced his "Plan to Strengthen Domestic and Overseas Broadcasting." This included a further expansion of the International Bureau: the previous three departments and one section became five departments. (Figure 6) The effect on broadcasting was for the thirteen transmission regions to be extended to fourteen as broadcasts to the Atlantic Coast of the United States and Canada were separated from those to South America.

3. TOPICS OF JAPANESE PROAGANDA

3.1 The Radio Battle for India (1943-1944)

On 13 June 1943 Indian Independence leader, Subhas Chandra Bose, arrived in Japan from Germany, and on 21st broadcast to India over Radio Tokyo, assuring Indians of his well-being. He reminded Indians of the situation in Europe and Africa but said that,

As far as India is concerned, what is most important of all is the situation near India. No amount of Anglo-American propaganda can either ignore or hide the fact that after achieving brilliant victories in Hongkong, in the Philippines, in the East Indies, in Malaya and Singapore and in Burma, the forces of the Imperial Japanese Army now stand on the frontier of India. (Nippon Times, Evening Edition, 22 June 1943)

In the same broadcast he reminded Indians that the Japanese "Prime Minister has offered active assistance should the Indian revolutionaries need it" and "has repeatedly declared [the Japanese Government's] fullest support to Indian Independence." The following day he made a further overseas broadcasts to Italy comparing the conditions in Italy before 1860 to those in India in the 1940s, and told Italians that this "had enabled your countrymen to understand so well the aims and purposes of another independence movement like ours." (*Nippon Times*, Evening Edition, 23 June 1943)

On 21 October Bose announced the establishment of the Provisional Government of Free India and the Indian National Army (INA), "two vital prerequisites in India's fight for freedom." (*Nippon Times*, Morning Edition, 22 October 1943) On 24th the Provisional Government declared war on Britain and the United States and six days later Rash Behari Bose, head of the Indian Independence League in Japan, broadcast to India from Tokyo, declaring,

Never before were circumstances for India's freedom more favourable or more opportune. You have, today, not only a National Army of your own outside the borders of India ready to come to your aid, but also the powerful co-operation and support of the mighty Japanese Empire and the inexhaustible resources of entire East Asia.

He drew a comparison with Burma which, he said, "after one long century under British tyranny and exploitation did not fail to seize the opportunity for freedom . . ." and urged that "One united, concentrated blow at this hour will seal [Britain's] fate forever." (*Nippon Times*, Morning Edition, 31 October 1943)

Overseas broadcasts to Japan's European allies also continued. On 16 November Subhas Chandra Bose broadcast from Radio Tokyo to Germany, thanking the German Government for its recognition of the Provisional Government. He compared the "pious wishes and false promises for the future" of the Allies' Atlantic Charter with the "principles of justice, national independence, reciprocity and mutual co-operation" on which the Joint Declaration of the Assembly of Greater East Asian Nations was based. (*Nippon Times*, Morning Edition, 17 November 1943)

On 5 December the 50-kilowatt transmitter of the Singapore station was completed, and its operations changed. On the establishment of the Provisional Government of Free India the Japanese authorities handed two hours of the station's daily schedule to Bose's government to make "Azad Hind" [Free India] broadcasts directly to India using NHK equipment. The broadcasts usually consisted of news concerning India, and a commentary denouncing British actions.

As the battle for Imphal intensified in Spring 1944, Subhas Chandra Bose declared it a "decisive fight to the finish" and on 21 March, the Japanese also established Azad Hind broadcasts also from Tokyo, for half-an-hour daily, under the leadership of Rash Behari Bose. "Free India Hour" began at 9.15pm with the Indian National Anthem and proceeded with a commentary in English and recorded commentaries in Hindi, Bengali, Gujarati and Tamil on different days. Despite its name, the broadcast was made over Radio Tokyo and was established to present

"Our developments in the India-Burma War." Hence it was subject to the censorship laws of Radio Tokyo programmes. In reality, then, it was probably subject to closer censorship than those made from Singapore, where the censorship structure was less complex. (Kitayama, 1988c:39)

During a visit to China Subhas Chandra Bose also broadcast over Radio Nanking to unoccupied China. He reminded his listeners that he had once tried to visit Chungking, and had been promised a warm welcome by the Chinese consulate in Calcutta, but had been refused a passport by the British. He described Sun Yat Sen (Sun Wen) as "one of the great personalities of Asia" for Indians, and having attempted to establish his credibility with his Chinese audience, he sought to assuage Chinese fears of Japan. He presented Japan as the defender of the New Order in East Asia rendering "possible the realisations of the dreams of Dr. Sun Yat Sen - for China, for India and for Asia." He sought to persuade Chungking China to unite with Nanking to "bring about peace with Japan . . . economic recovery and national prosperity." (*Nippon Times*, Morning Edition, 6 June 1943) Rash Behari Bose broadcasting to India also warned Chiang Kai-shek, "Asiatics will win final victory . . . It is your duty to join with the people of Asia and not the enemy." (*Nippon Times*, Morning Edition, 16 December 1943)

3.2 Greater East Asia and the War in China

Throughout the Pacific War, many of Radio Tokyo's news reports to all transmission regions concerned the progress of the China War and the reconstruction of Greater East Asia under Japanese rule. On 7 July 1942, the fifth anniversary of the outbreak of the war in China reports to all regions reviewed the

"War Results" for the period. In features regarding the fifth anniversary, Radio Tokyo claimed that the Japanese forces could finish the war against the collapsing Chiang Kai-shek regime at any time, but that Japan, the "elder brother" of Asian countries, had chosen not to pursue this course. Instead she sought to show her "younger brothers" the way. In other words, Japanese patience was the reason Japan had never declared war on China.[100]

A further strand of broadcasting regarding East Asia concerned the reconstruction of Asia following centuries of Anglo-Saxon domination. In November 1942, Radio Tokyo adopted a policy of promoting East Asian culture and East Asian unity. Even before Greater East Asia Broadcasting's shift in emphasis from an "overseas" to a "domestic" operation in April 1943, co-operation between Greater East Asia Broadcasting and the domestic network produced a weekly programme, "Calling East Asia." It was broadcast for forty minutes on a Sunday evening and was designed to promote Japanese culture in the occupied areas. (Kitayama, 1988b:239) It included patriotic songs, a weekly war round-up, and features such as "The Bloody Battle for Reverence of the Emperor and the Expulsion of Barbarians." This was a deliberate variation on the slogan "Restore the Emperor, Expel the Barbarian" used by Restoration activists before the Restoration of the Emperor in 1868. The start of the project coincided with the Greater East Asia Writers' Conference which took place in Tokyo between 3 and 5 November 1942 and which sought to develop a "system of culture for Greater East Asia." (*Japan Times and Advertiser*, Morning Edition, 1 November 1942)

Although as a Christian festival Christmas was not celebrated on domestic radio in Japan, special Christmas programmes were included in overseas broadcasts. For much of December Radio Tokyo appealed to Australians to pressure their government into allowing short-wave broadcasts of messages to Australian prisoners-of-war in Indonesia. The first offer, made on 1 December, was that a message of no more than forty words broadcast from Australia would be delivered to the prisoner by the Japanese authorities[101] and similar offers were repeated most days on the Australian Home News Hour. This programme broadcast prisoners' Christmas messages from 21 December.[102] The monitor of one such message, which the Japanese announcer stated was read by British Group Captain Bish of the Royal Air Force for Britons in Australia, noted that the reader had a "Voice, delivery and manner (which) seemed entirely genuine,"[103] suggesting that the Japanese did allow some of the prisoners to read their own messages.

3.3 Moves Towards East Asian Independence

From the end of January 1943 the topic of Burmese Independence became an important theme in Japanese overseas radio broadcasts. The Burmese leader under the Japanese occupation, Ba Maw, visited Tokyo in March 1943 and broadcasts concerning the visit were transmitted to all regions. It was reported that he received an audience with the Emperor, visited the Diet and was decorated by the Emperor.[104] A Liaison Conference on 10 March 1943 issued a "General Plan for the Independent Burmese Leaders" which fixed the date of independence for 1 August 1943. Despite the continuing war on the Burma - India border and British claims to be penetrating parts of Burma, which were denied in Japanese broadcasts as "British boasts" and "wishful thinking,"[105] Ba Maw declared Burmese Independence and simultaneously declared war on Britain and the United States on that date. News broadcasts to all areas reported the messages of congratulation and official recognition sent by other Axis countries such as Nanking China and Italy[106] and broadcasts to India in particular stressed the importance of Burma's co-operation with Japan in the struggle against Britain.[107]

In March 1942 when Japanese troops had occupied Rangoon, the Rangoon radio station had been burned by the retreating army and become inoperable. It was reconstructed and began operation again on 15 August 1942 with a staff of NHK personnel and an output of 300w. Upgraded to an output of 10kw in September 1942, it broadcast in Burmese, Hindi and Bengali to Burma and India, concentrating on independence issues. After the promise of Burmese independence had been made in March 1943 the scope of the station's overseas broadcasts was increasingly toward India and from April 1943 it broadcast over seven hours daily in thirteen Indian languages. (Kitayama, 1988b:254)

On 14 October 1943 it was announced that the Philippine Islands, too, were to become independent of Japan, under José Laurel. Radio broadcasts claimed that this move to grant independence would weaken the British-American propaganda position significantly, as the former United States' colony, like the former British colony of Burma, could no longer be perceived as passively occupied by Japan. Both countries had entered the war on the Japanese side, against their former colonial rulers. Prime Minister Tōjō sent greetings and congratulations to the Philippines on its independence in a radio message on 15 October. (Kitayama, 1988b:385)

In October Radio Tokyo broadcast a talk entitled "East Asia Rejects Anglo-Saxon Influence." It stated that the declarations of independence of Burma and the Philippines, along with the establishment of the Provisional Government of Free India under Subhas Chandra Bose, which was officially recognised by the Japanese Government on 23 October, demonstrated that

East Asian nations had abandoned their begging attitude towards the Allies.[108] President José Laurel made a speech from Tokyo on 8 November, while attending the Greater East Asia Conference. In it he expressed the gratitude of the Philippine people towards the Japanese Empire and urged East Asian countries "to fight Western imperialism and emancipate themselves." He served "notice to outside powers that they have no reason to differ from us about the maintenance and enforcement in our hemisphere of our ideal and principles." He concluded "we wish to assure them that we shall be guided, not only by the . . . attitude of 'live and let live' . . . but the attitude of 'live and help live', which is the golden rule within our sphere"[109]

The commemoration of the second anniversary of the start of the Pacific war on 8 December 1943 was more low-key than the celebrations a year earlier. There was a talk to Germany by the President of the Patriotic Association of Japan, Professor Kanokogi, on the second anniversary of the German declaration of war on the United States. In it the Professor described Badoglio's surrender of Italy as a breach in the Axis relationship but affirmed that things were back on course. He also expressed Japanese horror at reports of the bombing of German cities and asserted that Japan and Germany would not be defeated.[110]

The New Year of 1944 began with optimistic talks regarding the war situation to most regions. A talk to Germany declared, "Evil cannot triumph over good," and reiterated that Japan opposed Western imperialism and fought to free East Asia and for lasting peace.[111] The Premier of Manchukuo, Chang Ching-hui, (Zhang Zhunghui) gave his "Message to the Nation" address on 2 January and it was summarised for the German audience. In it he declared East Asia was one family with a single destiny.[112]

In May 1944 the Japanese Government announced a major propaganda offensive to coincide with the military *Ichi-go* Offensive in China, and to prevent "the deterioration of public peace and order." Thus at the start of May, stations in Manchuria, Mongolia and China began a broadcasting campaign to counter "the evil of communism." (Kitayama, 1988c:48-9) Japanese concerns were for the rural areas where the number of communists was said to have increased dramatically by 1944, as there was little direct Japanese control in these areas. Twelve North Chinese radio stations were brought into the operation. All were included in plans to broadcast separate programmes for Communists, which outlined Japanese war aims for rebuilding China, and to the people of Chungking, which sought to bring disillusionment with the division between the Nationalist and Communist leadership, and focused on internal squabbles between them. (Kitayama, 1988c:49-51) Previously Radio Tokyo had described differences between Chiang Kai-shek and the communist leadership in broadcasts to other areas of the world and claimed that the Communists were "hampering Chinese operations in Sinkiang[113], Chinghai and Tibet" but this propaganda offensive was directed at China alone and was increasingly emphasised as the seventh anniversary of the start of the "China Incident" approached in July 1944. (Kitayama, 1988c:52) This further illustrates the reasonable assumptions used in Japanese radio propaganda. The ideological differences between Chiang Kai-shek's Kuomintang, and Mao's Communist Party caused severe friction even during the war, finally erupting into civil war after the Japanese surrender.

3.4 Atrocity Broadcasts

On 20 August 1942 the first Japanese repatriation ships from America, the *Asama Maru* and the *Conte Verde* arrived in Yokohama carrying a total of 1,421 people, including the two Japanese Ambassadors to the United States, Nomura Kichisaburō and Kurusu Saburō. Conferences held by the Japanese authorities in late August and early September 1942 to discover details of the domestic situation inside America established that Radio Tokyo was widely listened to in the United States. It can only be assumed that this was the case amongst Japanese communities, and not necessarily the case in the wider community, as the interviewees were all returning Japanese. In addition, the conferences provided the basis for a new propaganda campaign in overseas broadcasting, which emphasised the inhumanity of Americans. Reports regarding American mistreatment of Japanese internees were broadcast to all regions, including a series of thirteen talks on Radio Tokyo immediately following the conferences, entitled "We Reveal American Inhumanity." Radio Tokyo claimed that although many internees were over seventy years old, all were made to work for their food. (Kitayama, 1988b:206-7) This is unlikely. Some internees did work and received between twelve and nineteen dollars a month for a 44-hour week. (Hayashi, 1995:41) However, other former internees remember their internment as follows:

You were not a student.
You were not really employed.
You were
a
something that the government took care of. (Hayashi, 1995:137)

It would appear therefore that not all internees were forced to work to earn their food.

Besides making general statements about the conditions of Japanese in internment camps, Radio Tokyo also took up the cases of other groups in its broadcasts to America. A series in late 1942 presented the cause of Californian Japanese. "Lost Democracy" and "The Moral War" denounced the moving and interning of Californian Japanese as expressions of American hysteria, and claimed that in general the United States was interning elderly, peaceful farmers, thus displaying its fear following a year of Japanese successes. (Kitayama, 1988b:216-7) It is probable that the scriptwriters were able to base their writing on information gleaned from returnees who had been able to read American newspapers and noted the reality of the anti-Japanese hysteria in the United States. It was only the Japanese community which provoked this reaction in the United States. The war with Germany and Italy did not produce the same treatment for German and Italian Americans who were never interned.

The arrival in Yokohama of an exchange ship from Australia on 9 October, however, produced a different reaction. NHK broadcasts described Australian permission for the ship to sail "an act of chivalry." (Meo, 1968:70) Presumably the reason for this lies in Japan's differing propaganda campaign to Australia. The start of the broadcasts of prisoner-of-war messages from Batavia in June 1942 was intended to inspire Australian confidence in Japanese broadcasts, and presumably the use of recently returned Japanese to criticise Australia in the same way as the American campaign would have been considered too damaging. Australia did not intern Japanese so this theme was redundant in broadcasts to Australia. There was also, however, no overt policy of criticising Britain and Australia using the reminiscences of those who had returned on the ship.

Two further incidents added to the "atrocity campaign" in broadcasts to the United States. The first was the American bombing on 1 October 1942 of the *Lisbon Maru*, a Japanese ship carrying Allied prisoners-of-war. The British survivors were said to have denounced the United States[114] and in contrast the Japanese rescuers were described as having had only one thought: that of saving their enemy prisoners.[115]

The second incident cited as evidence of American cruelty and injustice was a report, which appeared in the *Detroit News* on 12 December 1942. It reported that after the war the American government would be under no obligation to restore *nisei* Japanese who were United States citizens to their pre-war status. This, claimed Radio Tokyo, exposed the real intention of the American government - to keep Japanese Americans in a low legal and social position. The response of Radio Tokyo was to issue appeals to "Our Brothers Overseas" on 23 December 1942 and 13 January 1943, although the contents of these broadcasts are unclear. (Kitayama, 1988b:290-1)

A further accusation was made by Radio Tokyo in broadcasts to mark the first anniversary of the implementation of United States' internment policy towards Japanese, on 2 February 1943. A talk, "The Interned Japanese and Agricultural Manpower," claimed that the interned Japanese were soon to be put to work on farms owing to the shortage of American manpower. (Kitayama, 1988b:291) This was another piece of relatively accurate broadcasting by Radio Tokyo for Japanese internees were, indeed employed on American farms.

Programmes at this time also reviewed a riot, which had occurred in the Manzanar Internment Camp near Los Angeles on 6 December 1942, during which one person had died. After the riot the word "atrocity" was used increasingly frequently in references to Americans. A "Pat to Charlie" broadcast on 25 January 1943 entitled "Is this Humanity?" claimed that the majority of Americans agreed with the views of US Naval Commander William Halsey, whom Radio Tokyo accused of stating that "Japanese are monkeys. Therefore one United States soldier is worth four Japanese soldiers." The Radio Tokyo Special News of 9 February, however, accused Americans of being animals. "Look at the Wild Animals" claimed that whilst the Japanese attended to their injured "Enemy planes swoop down very low over the injured soldiers and hurl bombs into the confusion." (Kitayama, 1988b:292-4)

On 17 May Major-General Yahagi Nakao, chief of the Army Press Section, introduced a new charge of American inhumanity when he accused the United States of using poisonous gas on two occasions during the attack on Attu Island. This newest American inhumanity was linked to the continuing atrocity campaign, which accused the United States of attacking Japanese hospital ships in the Pacific.

> *Enemy America has repeatedly revealed its tendencies for inhumanitarianism in the Greater East Asian War. They have bombed or attacked our hospital ships carrying clearly visible Red Cross insignia. On the South Pacific they are using their beast like tactics against our fighting forces and now they have dared to carry out poison gas warfare, defying humanitarianism. . . . It is time to further our determination to crush America, the enemy of humanity.*[116]

Accusations of attacks on hospital ships continued, and on 7 February 1944 Radio Tokyo reported that the Red Cross had formally protested to Britain and America regarding such attacks.[117]

In addition, the confessions of Allied prisoners-of-war were introduced into broadcasts as evidence of the lack of British and American humanity. Information gleaned from interviews with captured pilots in Rabaul was forwarded to NHK for use in broadcasts. Generally the messages revealed how the prisoner now understood that responsibility for Pearl Harbor lay with the United States, but some, such as a message from Ensign J.F. accused Roosevelt of not caring for human life. (Kitayama, 1988c:24)

The intensification of the atrocity campaign coincided with accusations in early 1944 by Britain and America of Japanese atrocities against Allied prisoners-of-war. Radio Tokyo denied such atrocities, and reported that the Allies had begun to make such accusations for several reasons, the most important being that they sought to make barbarism reciprocal, diminishing their own inhumanity. Others included concealing America's inhuman actions towards Japanese civilian internees, diverting the attention of their people from the true situation of the war, and relieving war-weariness amongst their own people.[118] Accusations of atrocities continued to appear regularly in Radio Tokyo broadcasts into the Summer and Autumn of 1944, although the types of atrocities reported remained much the same.

CHAPTER 5
BROADCASTS BY ALLIED NATIONALS AND PRISONERS-OF-WAR

1. ZERO HOUR

On 1 June 1942, the Japanese Ambassador to Iran, Ichikawa Hikotarō, arrived in Japan. During the course of his visit he related to NHK and CIB staff his impressions of Japanese overseas radio. Generally he was critical. He stated that reception of Radio Tokyo programmes was not good as there was frequent interference from British, Russian and French stations. He also indicated that in general, broadcasts by Germany, America and Britain were more appealing to the listener, as there was variety in the schedules, which included plays, different styles of music, and interviews with interesting people. He was particularly impressed with the BBC's techniques of incorporating propaganda into programmes and in broadcasting on both short- and long-wave. In comparison, he declared, Radio Tokyo broadcast too many speeches and not enough entertainment. (Kitayama, 1988b:178-9) This was, in fact, very similar to the format of Japanese domestic programmes.

As a result of this, more music and entertainment programmes were inserted into the schedules of the overseas stations. Plays and dialogues, such as *Who Will be the Next President?* and Æsop's *The Rabbit which Lost its Fur* were transmitted, emphasising American defeats. A monologue, *Twilight*, was broadcast during the Battle for Guadalcanal, in which a dying American youth questioned the validity of the war. It ended with announcer cutting in and pleading with Americans to stop fighting for Roosevelt. (Kitayama, 1988b:179-80) It was also decided that Allied prisoners should be used in overseas broadcasts, as they understood what would appeal to potential listeners.

The Japanese had used allied prisoners in broadcasting from early in the Pacific War. The first "prisoner broadcast" was a letter, read by the announcer, to the mother of an Australian prisoner on 19 December 1941. The number of similar broadcasts made to Australia increased in the early months of 1942, and in June the Japanese-controlled station in Batavia also began to broadcast prisoner-of-war messages to Australia and New Zealand. This feature later became the "Australian Home News Hour," and as the programme developed, recordings of prisoners reading their own letters were also broadcast. The aim of these broadcasts was to attract listeners to the Japanese stations in the hope that they would listen to the propaganda messages while listening for news of relatives and friends.

Probably the best known of Radio Tokyo's overseas programmes was "Zero Hour," which began on 1 March 1943. It was presented and later written by allied prisoners, and became notorious after the war for having been the inspiration for the Tokyo Rose myth. It was christened "Zero Hour" for three reasons. To the American troops, for whom the programme was broadcast, the "Zero Hour" was the moment before an attack began, and so it was felt that they could identify with the name. In addition, the most successful of the Japanese fighter aircraft was the Mitsubishi "Zero," and the sun in the centre of the Japanese flag was considered to represent a "Zero." Hence the title was also thought to be strongly Japanese. (Duus, 1979:76-7)

The central figure in the development of the programme was an Australian prisoner-of-war, Major Charles Cousens, who had been captured by the Japanese at Singapore. Before joining the army he had worked as a broadcaster and producer for the Australian Broadcasting Corporation in Sydney. His background must have been discovered very quickly by his Japanese captors as a broadcast from Singapore in February 1942 mentioned an Australian major, who had previously worked for a radio station in Sydney and who was "anxiously awaiting the end of the war." Presumably the prisoner referred to in the report was Cousens, although no name was given. The same broadcast also stated that as Australia was being treated as a scapegoat, Japan would allow Australian prisoners to broadcast home, although it did not state when such broadcasts would occur. (*Hongkong News*, 28 February 1942)

In June 1942 the CIB decided to use prisoners in broadcasts from Tokyo as part of the drive to add more variety to overseas broadcasts. Cousens was transferred to Tokyo on 31 July from where he broadcast radio essays prepared both by Japanese and himself.

In October 1942, Cousens was joined by American, Wallace Ince and Norman Reyes, a Filipino Eurasian, both of whom had been captured on Corregidor. Prior to their capture they had been involved in an American underground station, the "Voice of Freedom." Ince, who broadcast under the name of Ted

Wallace, and Reyes were initially employed at NHK to check English language scripts. (Duus, 1979:75) Soon after joining Radio Tokyo Ince was interviewed by Domei and during the interview he stressed his good treatment by the Japanese. The newspaper also reported that he did not think his first broadcast would have been popular at home as it contained "nothing but the truth of the Philippines fighting." (*Hongkong News*, 26 October 1942, p5)

When it began in March 1943, "Zero Hour" was a twenty-minute music programme presented by Reyes who loved jazz music. It was a DJ-style programme copied from the format of American broadcasts, which was unfamiliar to NHK staff. The records Reyes frequently played included those of popular American jazz and swing musicians, such as Louis Armstrong, Duke Ellington and Glenn Miller, as well as Japanese jazz and swing bands such as the All Star Jazz Band and the All Star Swing Sisters. The broadcasts also included songs which were intended to make the audience of American troops feel homesick, such as the "St. Louis Blues" and "Home on the Range." (Kitayama, 1988b:317-8) The news scripts in the broadcasts concentrated on bad news items from America, such as a train crash or a flood, as it was assumed that these would lower the morale of the listeners. (Duus, 1979:76)

In August 1943 the programme was extended to forty-five minutes and Cousens and Ince also began presenting sections of it. Japanese wrote the news, but the prisoners tried to "sabotage" it by skipping lightly over bad news and joking about other items in order to turn it into entertainment. (Duus, 1979:77-8)

In November 1943, it was decided that "Zero Hour" should be further extended to an hour-and-a-quarter. The prisoners were concerned that the expansion would mean an increase in the number of Japanese staff. This, they feared would decrease the amount of the programme over which they had control, and would hence increase its propaganda content. Cousens requested time to consider the plan, in order to find a new female presenter, who would be sympathetic to the prisoners' aims in the broadcast. (Duus, 1979:78) Iva Toguri, a *nisei* English language typist who had been stranded in Japan in December 1941, was sympathetic. Cousens asked her to join the team because her voice was not the sweet or gentle type which would be expected of a female DJ, and he hoped to use it to make a comedy of Japanese propaganda. At the suggestion of Cousens, Iva Toguri took on the name of "Orphan Ann" in the broadcasts - "Ann" because in the script the word announcer was abbreviated to "ann." and "Orphan" because the Allied soldiers in the South Pacific were often referred to as "Orphans of the Pacific." (Duus, 1979:80-1) She told investigators in 1946 that Cousens had told her "to pretend that I was among the boys and to speak as if I were talking directly to them." (Howe, 1990:108)

The new "Zero Hour" format from November 1943 began at 6pm with Arthur Fiedler's Boston Pops Orchestra playing "Strike Up the Band," which became the "Zero Hour" theme tune. It was followed by five minutes of prisoner messages read by Cousens and the fifteen to twenty minute "Orphan Ann" spot, a light music spot for which Iva was the DJ, and read a script prepared for her by Cousens. The "American Home Front News" which followed, was written by Japanese and read by Ince. It was given a five- to ten-minute slot, but frequently there was not enough material to fill the slot and it ended with more light music records. At the end of the slot, Iva, who introduced each slot, repeated, "Thank-you, thank-you" five or more times at the instruction of Cousens. This was repeated after each of the sections not written by the prisoners themselves, in order that the material written by the Japanese would be "wiped" from the listeners' memory. The "American Home Front News" was followed by Reyes' "Juke Box," a fifteen to twenty minute jazz slot, in the format of the original "Zero Hour" programme, and "Ted's Highlights tonight." This was a five to ten minute slot written by Japanese using news monitored from foreign short-wave broadcasts. It was edited and read by Ince, but again was "wiped" at the end of the slot by Iva repeating "Thank-you" several times. Occasionally this was followed by a commentary by Charles Yoshii, described as a "renegade *nisei*" and the "Japanese Lord Haw Haw," who had worked at NHK since 1935. [119] "Zero Hour" ended with a military song and a sign off by Ince.

Cousens and Iva usually chose British bands for the light music "Orphan Ann" spot. They thought that British music would be less popular with the American audience and in their attempts to make a mockery of the Japanese broadcast, they often included pre-World War One accordion pieces, such as Ketelby's "In a Persian Market," in the slot. (Howe, 1990:50) In addition, Iva spoke quickly and used many slang expression and puns in her chatter between the records in order to make it difficult for the Japanese censors to follow what she said. Hence she could slip in things, which were not flattering to the Japanese without the censor halting the programme. (Duus, 1979:83) As part of the mocking tone of the programme, Iva's scripts included pseudo-Japanese translations such as "you onable boneheads" and "you are liking, please?" (Howe, 1990:113) and her scripts described her own chatter as propaganda. For example, on 27 March 1944 Iva began:

> *Ann.*: *Greetings every body! This is your little playmate, I mean your bitter enemy, Ann, with a program of dangerous and wicked*

propaganda for my victims in the South Pacific.

On 21 April, she read:

> *Ann.: Dangerous enemy propaganda, so beware! Our next propagandist is Arthur Fiedler with the Boston Pops Orchestra playing Ketelby's "In a Persian Garden."*[120] *. . .Please to listening.* (Howe, 1990:113)

Ince tended to state the German or Japanese sources and datelines in his news segment in order to make it less believable to the listeners. In addition, he read very quickly to that listeners would not bother to listen properly to his section. The plan of the "Zero Hour" team to minimise the Japanese propaganda value of the programme was made easier as the censors did not check the scripts every day, or make the participants pre-record any of the broadcast. (Howe, 1990:98, 110-1) Hence censorship often relied solely on the ability of the censor listening to the broadcasts to understand English. The tactics of using slang expressions and speaking quickly made it much simpler for the team to convey meanings other than the Japanese intended without the censor questioning them. Similarly, the Japanese censor had little idea of what kind of Western music appealed to American troops so the choice of out-dated tunes was not queried.

Ince became ill in December 1943, owing to mistreatment in the prisoners' camp. (Howe, 1990:171) He continued to work on "Zero Hour" until the end of April 1944, when a severe beating following a fight with a camp officer left him too ill to present the programme. He later appeared in other radio broadcasts as an actor in dramas, but he did not return to "Zero Hour" and the other prisoners assumed that he had been executed. He was replaced by Kenichi Ishii, a Eurasian Japanese with a voice very similar to that of Cousens. (Howe, 1990:57)

The name "Tokyo Rose" was first heard by Cousens in the spring of 1944. A report from Sweden mentioned it was the nickname given by American troops to the presenter of a Sunday programme. The report described the sweet voice of the presenter. Cousens and George Mitsushio, the Japanese in charge of "Zero Hour," concluded it would be Myrtle Lipman, a former Miss Manila, who had just begun broadcasting to American troops from there, or Ruth Hayakawa, who took Iva's place on the Sunday programme. (Howe, 1990:56-7) Indeed, a United States Office of War Information (OWI) report issued shortly before the Japanese surrender in 1945 concluded:

> *There is no Tokyo Rose; the name is strictly a GI invention. The name has been applied to at least two lilting Japanese voices on the Japanese radio . . . Government monitors listening in 24 hours a day have never heard the words Tokyo Rose over a Japanese controlled station. (Howe, 1990:65)*

Cousens left "Zero Hour" following a heart attack on 15 June 1944. Reyes, a "friendly alien" following the establishment of the "independent" Philippines under Laurel in October 1943, was given more responsibility, and increasingly new *nisei* were given parts in the programme. The Japanese put increasing pressure on Iva to allow the politicisation of the "Orphan Ann" spot. She resisted, re-working Cousens' old scripts, using traditional English tunes, and visiting him in hospital for advice. Although an American herself, she even tended to continue using Cousens' British English grammar in her scripts. In one such script, dated 14 August 1944, her introduction began:

> *Ann.:* *Hello, you fighting orphans of the Pacific. How's tricks? This is the after-the-weekend Annie back on the air, strictly on the Zero Hour. Reception OK? Well, it had better be, because this is an all-request night and I've got a pretty nice program for my favorite little family – the wandering boneheads of the Pacific islands.* (Howe, 1990:199-200)

In it Iva used the grammatically correct "it had better be" rather that the American "it better be," and "I've got" rather than "I've," both of which are more common in British English. To the censor this would have been an imperceptible difference, but it is possible that an American speaking British English would have seemed odd to the listeners. At times Iva surpassed Cousens in her mocking tone. A script dated 3 May (but with no year) reads:

> *Ann.:* *You are liking, please? Well, keep listening in because in a few moments you'll be hearing your News from the American Home Front. But first we'll hear from George Scott-Wood and his accordeon. (sic) A lousy little tune, "In a Gypsy Tea Room," but nicely played.*

Howe concludes that, "Cousens . . . would probably have ruled that the phrase 'lousy little tune' was going too far in self-mockery." (Howe, 1990:200-2)

As the format of "Zero Hour" altered from entertainment to propaganda, Iva Toguri, whose "Orphan Ann" slot remained, tried to leave the programme on several occasions, but was not given permission. Increasingly in late 1944 and 1945 she did not arrive at work to present the slot, and regularly failed to turn up if there was an air raid. This was partly as she feared that those loyal to Japan would seek revenge on a pro-American announcer as the war situation worsened for Japan.

During her periods of absence, Iva's place on "Zero Hour" was taken by several of the other female presenters, who did not write scripts to undermine the propaganda role of the programme. One of the more frequent replacements was Miyeko Furuya and an occasional replacement was Ruth Hayakawa, presenter of the Sunday programme, whom the prisoners suspected of being a *kempei* (Military Police) agent. (Howe, 1990:97) In May 1945 Miyeko married Kenichi Oki, the producer of the programme, and under her and the other replacements the "Orphan Ann" spot changed, and like the rest of the programme, increasingly contained more propaganda than entertainment. Hence in the latter months of the war, the programme reverted to the kind of heavy propaganda broadcasting, which the Ambassador to Iran had criticised, and which "Zero Hour" had sought to counter.

2. HI NO MARU HOUR

In May 1943, at the suggestion of the Joint Chief of Staffs' office, NHK began work on creating a programme for the West Coast of the United States, to have a similar content to "Zero Hour" which was broadcast to American front-line troops. From September 1943 forty prisoners in Japanese camps throughout the Empire were moved to Tokyo Camp, as it was considered that their background and personality made them suitable for work on this programme. Once they had arrived in Tokyo Camp, NHK representatives visited them ten times in three weeks to interview them in more detail. Through this, the "mysterious men," as the interviewers became known in the camp, selected thirteen prisoners, whom they considered particularly suitable, and these were transferred to a separate camp. (Ikeda, 1979:23-4)

The thirteen prisoners arrived at the former Suragadai Cultural Institute (*Bunka Gaku-in*), in Kanda, Tokyo, on 1 December 1943. On 18th they were joined by Cousens and Ince, but as a "friendly alien" from October 1943, Reyes was forbidden to enter the camp. On 7 January 1944, four further Americans joined the camp, which became nicknamed "*Bunka* Camp." (Ikeda, 1979:28-30)

The first "*Hi no Maru* Hour" broadcast, named after the Japanese flag, was scheduled for 2 December 1943, so work was to begin immediately on the prisoners' arrival at the camp. First, however, the thirteen prisoners were taken into the camp garden, where the camp rules were read out. Essentially these were that the prisoners were to co-operate with the Japanese until the end of the war, and that if they did not the Japanese could not guarantee to safeguard their lives. On 9th, at a repeat of this, the prisoners were asked if they agreed to co-operate and a British officer, Charles Williams, replied, "No, Sir." He was removed from the camp by the *kempei*. He was not executed but it was decided not to send him back to an ordinary prisoner-of-war camp as it was felt that he would reveal sensitive material regarding the propaganda war on America to other prisoners. At the suggestion of Ikeda Norizone, who was in charge of "*Hi no Maru* Hour" he was sent somewhere where he could not be expected to live very long. He survived the war in a mine worked by prisoners-of-war and was later decorated by the British government for this act of defiance. (Ikeda, 1979:55-6)

However, the other prisoners in *Bunka* Camp presumed that he had been executed, and this had a profound effect upon their willingness to co-operate. (Ikeda, 1979:42-3, 53-6)

After the rules had been read on 2nd, three American prisoners, Edwin Kalbfleisch, George Henshaw and David Provoo, were taken to the studio to rehearse for the first broadcast, which had been written three weeks previously by the Japanese involved in the programme. The following day the same three prisoners arrived at Studio Five of the Uchisaiwaichō broadcasting complex at 11am, and had a second rehearsal before the broadcast. They were joined on the programme by a Japanese, who played the records, while the prisoners performed the spoken slots, Provoo acting as radio host. As the programme was, like "Zero Hour," broadcast live, the director and censor sat in a room next to the studio, with the "cut button" near them.

"*Hi no Maru* Hour" was a daily half-hour show broadcast at 1pm, and the lives of the prisoners at *Bunka* Camp were structured around it. Five hours of the day were spent writing scripts and making copies, whilst a further one-and-a-half hours were spent at the studio.

Initially, the prisoners read scripts and news commentaries previously written by a Japanese, like Ikeda Norizone, but from the start it was envisaged that, as with "Zero Hour," the prisoners would write the material themselves. However, the Japanese produced a list of appropriate propaganda themes and ideas. Roosevelt was portrayed as a ruthless imperialist, who ignored the wishes of his people, and who had established a secret police to spy on them in the form of the FBI. The Japanese queried the American alliance with Stalin, emphasising their own strong stance against Communism, in signing the Anti-Comintern Pact, and asking, "Who is the real enemy of America?" (Ikeda, 1979:88-91) Asia was compared to eighteenth century America, fighting for its freedom from the European powers, and black soldiers were warned that although they fought for their country, the Ku Klux Klan would be waiting for them on their return. In addition, all soldiers were reminded of the Government's mistreatment of the "Bonus Army," an "army" of more than 15,000 war veterans which had marched on Washington in 1932 to demand immediate payment of a veterans' cash bonus that Congress had voted in 1924. (Ikeda, 1979:92-9) When Congress dismissed the bill before going into summer recess, the President became nervous at the number of veterans still in the capital and ordered General Douglas MacArthur to clear their shantytown. His troops burnt the shantytown to the ground, directly violating a presidential order. It is plausible that this topic was chosen because MacArthur was now Commander-in-Chief of the American Army's Pacific operations.

Ikeda drafted a British officer, John McNaughton, who had been an actor before the war, into assisting him to write a series of thirty-minute dramas to be performed weekly in "*Hi no Maru* Hour" broadcasts. The first, broadcast on 3 December 1943, was entitled "The Issue of the Monroe Doctrine" and claimed that just as President Monroe had declared in 1823 with regard to European affairs, America should refuse to interfere in Asia. (Ikeda, 1979:102) "I Met Napoleon," broadcast in early January 1944, was based on George Bernard Shaw's *The Man of Destiny*. Ikeda writes that the play was not very good, (although he does not specify whether he means the content or the production) but was considered good propaganda, as it was based around a quote of Napoleon, "Blood is cheap but wine costs money." It was followed by two plays, which dramatised the capture of two Allied prisoners. The first, "The Story of the Shooting Down of Major Cox" detailed the capture of one of the group of four prisoners at Suragadai, who arrived in January 1944. The second was about the capture of a prisoner who was held in Ōmori Camp in Tokyo, Lieutenant-Colonel Pike, who had been shot down over China. Tsuneishi, Commander of *Bunka* Camp, asked that this story be used as it contained several good propaganda points. Pike had been shot down following a raid on Japan, and had received horrific burns to his face. The Chinese farmers who had found him were terrified at his burnt face, and had handed him over to Chiang's Army, but it had lost him to the Japanese in ground fighting. The story contained many elements considered good propaganda – the failure of a raid on Japan, the Japanese power to inflict horrific injuries, the unwillingness of ordinary Chinese to help an injured American and the inability of Chiang's Army to keep hold of him. The Japanese, therefore, acquiesced to a request by McNaughton that the drama be extended over two days. (Ikeda, 1979:103-5)

For the second set of broadcasts it was decided to adapt English language anti-war novels and plays for broadcast. The first, John Steinbeck's *Of Mice and Men* was criticised by some in the Bureau of International Broadcasting for being short on propaganda, and because it was felt the prisoners enjoyed producing it too much. However, Ikeda and other Japanese associated with "*Hi no Maru* Hour" justified their use of the drama by quoting research done by the British in World War One. This stated that the propagandist needed to create a "favourable atmosphere" in the target country prior to broadcasting strong propaganda, in order to make the audience receptive to the second wave of propaganda. (Ikeda, 1979:106-7)

The second adaptation was of R.C. Sherriff's *Journey's End*, the story of the final three days in the lives of three British soldiers in the World War One trenches, who die when they go "over the top" in March 1918. The anti-war message was obvious. Ikeda claims that all those in the studio during the broadcast were touched by the story, including McNaughton, Provoo and Henshaw, who acted the parts of the soldiers, "even though it was not their propaganda." (Ikeda, 1979:109-12)

The final radio play in the series was Irwin Shaw's *Bury the Dead*, originally a 1936 Broadway production, set "in the second year of the world war beginning the eve of the day after tomorrow." It was the story of the ghosts of American soldiers, who remained unburied as the ceremonies were always reserved for senior officers. As producer, Ikeda did not like the story as much as *Journey's End*, but as it was an American anti-war play it was thought it would have wider appeal in America. (Ikeda, 1979:112-14)

Despite Radio Tokyo's portrayal of Japan as the true enemy of Communism, it was decided that the next series of plays would be based on socialist writers, beginning with Upton Sinclair's *The Jungle*, as much socialist writing was out of print in the United States. Anti-war novels also considered for future adaptation included Hemingway's *Farewell to Arms* and Remarque's *All Quiet on the Western Front*. (Ikeda, 1979:116) The use of such material to produce subtle propaganda, which appealed to the audience, is a clear indication of the sophisticated approach to propaganda that developed at NHK over the course of the war.

Despite criticism in February 1944 that "*Hi no Maru* Hour" broadcasts in January had included the word "peace" fifteen times, (Ikeda, 1979:117) the broadcasts continued and on 1 April they were renamed. It was felt that the reference to the Japanese flag in the title of the programme was too strong a propaganda reference, so the broadcasts became "Humanity Calls," although the format remained the same. In addition, a new programme, "Postman Calls," was begun on 18 September, (Kitayama, 1988c:120)[121] in the half-hour slot immediately following "Humanity Calls" (1.30 – 2.00pm) doubling the length of the prisoners' programmes. This was a programme devoted to prisoner messages. "Humanity Calls" included one or two prisoner messages, but these were generally very short extracts indicating that a given prisoner was in Japanese hands, such as one on October 13 1944 from Edward L. Kirkpatrick, interned in Fukuoka, which read:

Dearest Mom, hope you are well. I am in good health, don't worry. When you write send some pictures.

Best wishes to everyone, Love Ed.[122]

"Postman Calls" was a programme devoted exclusively to prisoner messages, and it included much longer messages, similar to the prisoner letters broadcast by the Batavia station to Australasia, such as one from Private Angelo Pluchino on 13 November:

Dad and Sister, I am happy to have the opportunity once more of getting word to you. I have recently received a radiogram from you which made me very happy. I am enjoying good health here in our camp. I seriously hope you are also in excellent health. I am looking forward to the day I shall again be with you. I hope Emily is fine and enjoying herself. I am doing my regular duties as a Medical Orderly in our Prisoner of War Hospital Camp. We have American and British doctors and orderlies. We have patients of all nationalities and are able to treat them very well. In our spare time we can read, listen to music and play cards. Therefore please do not worry about me. I am getting along fine. Please take care of Dearest Mother yourself mother and tell dad (sic) and Emily to do the same. I am longing to eat your excellent cooking and smoke Dad's cigars. God bless you,

Your loving son, Angelo.[123]

In anticipation of this new programme Ikeda and Yamaguchi, another of the Japanese involved in the broadcasts, spent a week in March 1944 visiting prisoner camps in Kyushu to obtain material. Although the Japanese at the camps knew the nature of their visits, they went under the guise of Red Cross workers when they spoke to the prisoners. As a genuine member of the Red Cross Ikeda says he was uncomfortable with this, but that he completed the tour in any case. (Ikeda, 1979:127-132) The usefulness of the material they gathered regarding the lives of the prisoners, particularly their lives in the camps, varied between camps, and depended on how closely supervised the visit was. When the prisoners were allowed to meet the "Red Cross" representatives without close supervision, they were, naturally, more inclined to talk than when there were camp officials close by.

In December 1944 messages read by the prisoners themselves were broadcast increasingly frequently as Christmas approached. One on Christmas Eve is typical:

> *This is Walter Adam Shapcunic, Warrant Carpenter, U.S. Navy formerly 16th Naval District, Cavite P.I. I am broadcasting to my brother, Mr. John P. Shapcunic, Cementon, Penn. U.S.A.*
>
> *Hello folks. My treatment as prisoner of war is as good as can be expected under the present conditions. My health is good. Weight now 165 pounds. Hope that every one at home is in good spirits and sound health. I pray daily that we may be reunited very soon. My thoughts often wander to*

> *days of past, recalling the various party celebrations and good times we had together. It has been a very long time since I have been on a good fling. So keep your keg (?) [sic] filled to the brim. We will be in all probabilities remain here [sic] until the hostilities cease. Convey my best wishes and regards to all our friends and relatives. A very Merry Christmas and a Joyous New Year to every body. Your loving brother, Walter.*[124]

"Humanity Calls" and "Postman Calls" continued to be broadcast until the Japanese surrendered in August 1945. However, as with "Zero Hour," problems in broadcasting increased as the war situation became grave for Japan. As food became increasingly scarce for all, rations were reduced for both the prisoners and Japanese at the camp. However, the prisoners in *Bunka* Camp received better rations than those at other prisoner-of-war camps. Rice was replaced by kaoliang, a variety of millet, and when the prisoners complained that it was unhealthy to eat the cereal alone, they received a ration of bread to accompany it. In addition, camp commander, Tsuneishi provided money for the wives of Japanese soldiers in the camp to buy meat and vegetables for the prisoners on the black market, and tacit approval was given for them also to obtain tobacco, the supply of which remained constant throughout the war. (Ikeda, 1979:75-7) In fact, this practice was approved at the highest levels, and when one person was discovered buying for the camp on the black market and reported to the General Staff Headquarters, the only action taken against the camp was to limit the smoking of cigarettes to work time although the person caught buying from the black market lost his job. The powerful camp commander, Tsuneishi, was simultaneously head of Section Eight of the General Staff. Hence, when one of the prisoners, Quille, lost the use of his arm, Tsuneishi ordered a military hospital, unwilling to treat a mere prisoner, to operate immediately, overriding the local *kempei*. (Ikeda, 1979:82-4)

As many of the Japanese at *Bunka* Camp returned to their home regions to prepare for the "Decisive Battle for the Japanese Fatherland" in the Spring of 1945, however, replacements became involved in the broadcasts. One was a German, who had previously been involved in anti-enemy broadcasting. Often these people, sent by the Foreign Ministry, prepared broadcasts before the group from *Bunka* Camp arrived at the studio, so the nature of the broadcasts changed. Increasingly the prisoners had less involvement in the preparation and writing of programmes. As with "Zero Hour," the programme gradually reverted to the strong propaganda, which it had been established to replace.

3. JOHN HOLLAND

Japanese overseas broadcasting did not only rely on prisoners for native English speakers. John Holland was an Australian, who voluntarily broadcast regular strongly anti-British commentaries over Radio Tokyo in 1942-3.

Holland had lived in Shanghai since 1937 and from April 1941 broadcast as David Lester for XGRS, the German-run station in Shanghai. (Boelke, 1977:433) He took over the Walla Walla broadcasts, which were transmitted in "English for Occupied China," broadcasting local news and some entertainment features.

In the winter of 1942, monitors detected the same voice broadcasting from Tokyo under the name of John, or Jack, Holland.[125] The first such broadcast monitored in Britain was a commentary in the transmission to Australia and New Zealand entitled "Americans' Warmongering," on 6 December.[126] The following day, Holland repeated the Japanese claim that the United States was trying to blame the outbreak of war in the Pacific on Japan, by labelling the Pearl Harbor attack the cause. He continued that the 26 November note clearly showed that the blame lay with America.[127]

Generally, Holland's commentaries reflected the world situation more than other regular commentators on Japanese radio stations, who tended to concentrate on Asian affairs. Radio Batavia's Abdul Wahid, for example, broadcast to India, urging unity against Britain, and Erwin Wickert broadcast from Radio Tokyo to Germany, offering insights into aspects of life in Japan and other Greater East Asian countries for German listeners. On 17 December Holland returned to German affairs in a commentary, which described the 1940 Franco-German Armistice as an example of German generosity, in stark contrast to the harsh war terms inflicted on Germany in 1918.[128] At the end of December he analysed Allied problems caused by the situation in North Africa,[129] and a commentary in February 1943 described the affront caused to Stalin, in particular, and Chiang Kai-shek in being excluded from the meeting between Churchill and Roosevelt at Casablanca.[130]

The other recurring theme of Holland's broadcasts was Roosevelt's incapacity to lead, and the growing resentment against him. Holland described Roosevelt's inability to recognise his own limitations as "a tragedy for America,"[131] and stated that the American public doubted his ability to uphold the naval and military strength of the American forces.[132] He also criticised Roosevelt's lack of judgement in appointing Flynn, a man with "no international diplomatic experience," Ambassador to Australia.[133]

American monitors in San Francisco suspected that Holland was never in Tokyo, and that his daily commentaries in the

Winter and Spring of 1942-3 "were recorded in Shanghai and shipped to Tokyo."[134] Commentaries indicating the situation in Shanghai, such as one in March 1943 which detailed new restrictions on the businesses and residences of Jews in Shanghai,[135] seem to bear out this supposition. However, after March 1943, neither John Holland nor David Lester was heard in broadcasts from Tokyo or Shanghai. There was "no excuse or reason given for his sudden precipitation to oblivion,"[136] so it is impossible to ascertain precisely where he was when his broadcasts were made, or why they stopped suddenly.

4. THE USE OF PRISONERS IN PROPAGANDA BROADCASTS

The use of prisoners for propaganda purposes was undoubtedly a violation of the 1929 Geneva Convention. Whilst the employment of prisoners-of-war was permitted, Article 31 of the Convention stated:

> *Labor furnished by prisoners of war shall have no direct relation with war operations. It is especially prohibited to use prisoners for manufacturing and transporting of arms or munitions of any kind, or for transporting material intended for combat units. (op cit. Van Waterford, 1994:347).*

Propaganda, although not mentioned specifically, must be considered as having a direct relation with war operations, as its purpose is to weaken the enemy's prosecution of the war. Indeed, early in the war the Japanese authorities declared short-wave radio broadcasting "munitions." As such, then, it must have been subject to the Geneva Convention. In addition, Japanese officials posing as Red Cross members in order to obtain information from prisoners for use in propaganda broadcasts must be considered a violation of the spirit of the

Convention, as well as a violation of that organisation's regulations. The Tōjō cabinet justified these violations, stating that Japan had never signed the Convention, and was not, therefore, bound by it.

Nazi Germany also violated the 1929 Geneva Convention and as a result of the treatment of prisoners by Japan and Germany during World War Two, the Convention was revised in 1949, being expanded and more forcefully worded. From late 1941 the number of prisoners working in agriculture, construction and mining was steadily reduced, while those working in such "other employment" as the armaments industry, became the government's top priority. However, there is no evidence to show that prisoners were used in propaganda in the same way as in Japan. There were foreign nationals working for German overseas radio, such as William Joyce, (the notorious Lord Haw Haw) who broadcast to Britain, and the German-American, Fred Kaltenbach, who broadcast to America's Mid-West under the name of Lord Hee-Haw. (Rolo, 1944:77) Like John Holland, these were individuals who had volunteered to work for the enemy, and were employed for their expert knowledge of their own countries' tastes in programmes. In the same way, Japanese-Americans volunteered to be involved in American broadcasts to Japan, and many Europeans, who had escaped Nazi occupation, broadcast from the BBC to their home countries on behalf of the Allies. As volunteers, none of this group was subject to the conditions of the prisoner broadcasters in Japan. For the prisoners, however much they influenced the programme, there were inevitably sections of the broadcasts, which directly opposed their own beliefs, and although conditions at Suragadai Camp were better than elsewhere, the broadcasts were made under duress.

For Iva Toguri D'Aquino, the situation is less simple. As a Japanese brought up in the United States she could have easily volunteered to broadcast for Japan, as many did in her situation. The unfortunate circumstances surrounding her entrapment in Japan indicate that Howe and Duus are correct in their claims that she was not a totally willing participant in anti-American propaganda. However, both books were written seeking to redress Iva's treatment by a hysterical government. A discussion of whether or not she was a traitor is, however, not the subject of this study. As Iva was neither a prisoner nor an internee, and volunteered to work for NHK, whatever her motives, she was not subject to the Geneva Convention, and must be classed with the other volunteer broadcasters.

The use of Allied prisoners-of-war in overseas broadcasts was very important to the Japanese radio propaganda campaign. There had been several attempts to increase the entertainment value of Japanese broadcasts before the war, and jazz music, banned on domestic broadcasts, was permitted in short-wave broadcasts because of this. However, after the outbreak of war, it was felt that it was essential to increase the number of listeners, and broadcasts to Australasia began to include letters from prisoners-of-war.

The use of prisoners in producing and presenting programmes under Japanese supervision was the next step for Japanese programme makers, who recognised that their own knowledge of western entertainment was minimal. The use of prisoners with a background in broadcasting and entertainment was intended to ensure that the programmes appealed to western listeners. Hence for much of the time, the prisoners working on "Zero Hour" and "*Hi no Maru Awâ*" were allowed considerable freedom in producing entertainment slots for the programmes.

The Japanese invested considerable time and money in the prisoner broadcasts, an indication of the importance of these programmes. First, all the camps in the Japanese Empire were scoured for prospective broadcasters and then the most promising were transported to Tokyo. Initially, Cousens, Ince and Reyes were installed in the Dai-Ichi Hotel, one of the most prestigious hotels in Tokyo before the war, which had, in fact, been built for the 1940 Tokyo Olympics that were never held. It was reported that there they were "treated as any other guest" and had "living conditions and food . . . better than even those of the average Nipponese." (*Hongkong News* 26 October 1942)

Once Japanese officials had selected the remaining prisoners, following numerous visits, Suragadai Cultural Institute was converted into *Bunka* Camp, and the prisoners moved there. Whilst conditions at *Bunka* Camp were harsh by peacetime standards, they were better than in other Japanese prisoner-of-war camps, as it was considered imperative that these prisoners remained healthy and contented. Thus, on Christmas Eve 1943, the prisoners were allowed a Christmas meal, consisting of three courses, and were permitted to decorate the camp with their national flags, the Japanese flag remaining in the centre of the camp. They were also all presented with an extra Christmas ration of tobacco. (Ikeda, 1979:64-5) The more lenient policy continued throughout the war. As the war situation deteriorated in 1944-5, many Japanese suffered from malnutrition and disease owing to shortages of food and clean water. The protected position of these prisoners was, therefore, frequently very good by comparison. It is clear that the installation of a powerful official as commander of *Bunka* Camp, and the money and time invested in seeking out the prisoners and then ensuring that they remained healthy and co-operative, are clear indications of the importance attached to the prisoner broadcasts by the Japanese authorities. They are also perhaps indications of the depth of Japanese uncertainty regarding the effectiveness of their overseas broadcasting, following criticism from their own Ambassador to Iran.

CHAPTER 6
THE FINAL STAGE OF THE WAR (JULY 1944-SEPTEMBER 1945)

1. DEVELOPMENTS IN THE WAR SITUATION

The military situation in the South Pacific continued to deteriorate in the final year of the war. In June and August, Saipan and Pulao were captured by American forces and at the end of September the Japanese authorities announced the "Honourable Defeats" of Guam and Tinian. The capture of Saipan and Tinian were particularly significant, as they enabled the United States to mount air attacks on Tokyo using land-based bombers.

On 17 March 1945 Japan announced that the island of Iwojima had been lost. This was a great psychological blow for it was formally under the administration of Tokyo City and was hence the first part of the "Japanese mainland" to be surrendered. This preceded the intensification of Allied air raids over Japanese cities in March and April 1945.

American troops pressed north. Progress was slow and casualties high during the bloody battle for Okinawa, which lasted almost three months and ended with both the Japanese commander and his deputy committing ritual suicide. Over a hundred thousand Japanese were killed in the battle, and the number who survived as prisoners were very few. (Calvocoressi et al., 1989:1163)

In Europe, the advance on Germany begun by the Normandy landings in June 1944 culminated in the surrender of Germany on 8 May 1945.

The political and diplomatic situation developed rapidly in the last year of the war, in line with the rapidly changing military situation. In Japan, the formation of the Koiso-Yonai cabinet was announced on 21 July 1944, replacing the Tōjō cabinet. The new cabinet represented a compromise between the Army and Navy factions, removing some of the power of the Army Ministry. It was headed by General Koiso Kuniaki, with Admiral Yonai Mitsumasa as unofficial Assistant-Premier. The appointment of the moderate Yonai, who had opposed the Tripartite Pact, was an encouragement to those in Japan who hoped now to find a way for peace.

In February 1945 the Yalta Conference between Roosevelt, Churchill and Stalin completed Allied plans for the defeat and the post-war administration of Germany. An agreement was also reached that the Soviet Union would declare war on Japan some three months after the defeat of Germany. This agreement was not included in the Yalta Communiqué, and was denied by Russian Foreign Minister Molotov when the Japanese Ambassador to Moscow visited him. However, in its meeting on 19 February the Japanese Supreme War Guidance

Committee concluded that it was very likely that the Yalta Conference had discussed Japan. (Kitayama, 1988c:178)

In March, a crisis in the cabinet, which had been developing for months, finally erupted. It concerned the developing war situation in the Pacific, and the cabinet's failure to agree to make peace with the Chinese government in Chungking. The Prime Minister resigned on 4 April and a new cabinet was formed under Admiral Suzuki Kantarō.

On 13 April 1945 (12th in the United States) President Roosevelt died and was replaced by Harry Truman, but the policies of the United States and the Allies remained basically unchanged. Hence it was Truman who met with Churchill and Stalin at Potsdam in July to discuss the political and economic principles which would govern the treatment of Germany. During the conference, a general election in the United Kingdom removed the Conservative Party from power, and Churchill left the conference to be replaced by the new Labour Prime Minister, Clement Attlee. Before Churchill's departure from the conference, however, he, Truman and Chiang Kai-shek issued the Potsdam Declaration, calling for the unconditional surrender of Japan. It was broadcast to Japan in Morse code, and on both short-wave and medium-wave radio.

2. RADIO TOKYO'S RESPONSE TO THESE DEVELOPMENTS

News of the capture of Pulao in August 1944 was not broadcast by Radio Tokyo until 18 September, when the Japanese authorities announced enemy landings on the island. However, the broadcasting station on Pulao, which broadcast on short-wave to Australia and the Southern Regions, suddenly stopped transmitting on 1 August, indicating that conditions on the island were no longer favourable to the Japanese.

The capture of Saipan, Guam and Tinian were commemorated on domestic radio. (Kitayama, 1988c:97) However, in overseas broadcasts news reports concentrated on rumours of Allied plans to attack Burma. The Japanese Commander-in-Chief in Burma, General Kimura, vowed that Japan would not confine herself to defence, but would fight on into India to free her from Western imperialism.[137]

Broadcasts concerning the battles in the Pacific continued to ignore the true situation, making optimistic claims of great Japanese "war results." Broadcasts from Tokyo continued to emphasise that the American troops, despite dropping leaflets asking the Japanese to stop fighting,[138] were being "exposed to death defying Japanese assaults."[139]

American landings on Iwojima were admitted in Japanese overseas broadcasts, although they reported that Japanese troops on the island were "in high spirits"[140] and broadcasts sending tributes to the "brave heroes on Iwojima" were transmitted on domestic and Greater East Asian services. (Kitayama, 1988c:183) Radio Tokyo continued to report on the battle on Iwojima, describing it as a "whirlpool of American blood" where no Japanese soldier had died without killing at least ten of the enemy.[141] As with other defeats, Iwojima's capture was not openly admitted on overseas radio, but reports concerning Iwojima soon disappeared and were replaced by news of fighting elsewhere. Reports on Greater East Asia broadcasting described Iwojima's capture as within the Japanese plan. A commentary on 13 March declared that the Japanese had allowed enemy landings on the Philippines and Iwojima, and that the enemy had "pigheadedly approached within our reach" and "the supreme time to crush him [had] arrived."[142]

American air raids over Tokyo prompted accusations of "indiscriminate bombing from above the clouds" but they were mentioned infrequently in overseas broadcasts. However, occasional reference was made to the number of American planes shot down over Japan, such as a broadcast on 3 April which claimed that forty-five to fifty planes had been destroyed or damaged over Tokyo the previous day.[143] Despite reports that raids caused only slight damage, other news items gave some indication of the damage that was being inflicted on Japan by the continual bombing. The reported suspension of Japanese express train services was presumably prompted by damage to the track and shortage of fuel and rolling stock; it can be assumed that a reported "adjustment" in rice and wheat prices was upwards owing to a shortage of supplies as good news of any food surplus would have been reported extensively as an example of Japanese efficiency;[144] reports that a supplementary budget was to be drawn up for repairs to air raid damage[145] were an indication of the extensive damage being caused by the Allied raids.

The American bombing of Okinawa was regularly reported in overseas programmes. Radio Tokyo reported that Okinawan civilians were fighting alongside Japanese troops and that the mounting American losses being inflicted by the combined force showed that "an enemy landing on Japan would have as little success as his bombing attacks."[146] The news that Okinawa had finally fallen was not broadcast directly in overseas transmissions. There was only an "emergency announcement" on 23 June that United States planes were only an hour from Kyushu. (Kitayama, 1988c:254) However, over the next few days, the focus of broadcasts shifted to developments elsewhere, as was usual when a battle had been lost. A commentary declared that this blow had renewed the confidence of the "hundred million" citizens in Japan who were determined to fight any invader hand-to-hand until the last person, as the Japanese troops on many of the Pacific islands had done. It reminded the United States that it could not ignore its own losses in the Okinawan campaign.[147]

Rumours of Hitler's suicide prompted a defiant response from Radio Tokyo. A report on 1 May declared that Japan would be unaffected by it, as she had long been preparing for the worst in Europe.[148] A day later it claimed that the unconfirmed German surrender was because Hitler had failed to bring about the solidarity of all the peoples of Europe for a New Order. This was compared unfavourably to the Asian solidarity achieved by Japan.[149] The predominant theme in Japanese broadcasts about the end of the war in Europe was that although it left Japan with no ally in Europe, Japan would succeed in creating a New Order in Asia: "Evil may temporarily prevail but it cannot completely destroy us."[150]

The political events of 1944-5 also prompted reponses by Radio Tokyo. Kitayama claims that its response to the Yalta Conference is unclear, but that from headlines in the Japanese press it would seem that broadcasts would have accused Britain and America of flirting with Communism in order to end the war. (Kitayama, 1988c:177-8) Although the conference did not conclude in any precise arrangements for post-war Europe, it is true that Stalin succeeded in side-stepping Churchill's proposal for early and free elections in Poland. He also used Roosevelt to assist him in forcing Chiang to agree to the continued "independence" of Communist Outer Mongolia (rendering it virtually dependant on the USSR) Port Arthur, a Russian naval base in South Manchuria, and a Russian share in the Manchurian railways. (Calvocoressi et al, 1989:70)

The BBC's *Summary of World Broadcasts* records several overseas broadcasts by the Japanese which dealt with the Yalta Conference. Broadcasts based on press reports certainly accused Britain and America of trying to cover over their own withdrawal from the European political scene in deference to the Soviets[151] and described the outcome of the conference as proof of British and American humiliation by the USSR.[152] However, commentaries broadcast to Germany also described the plan to complete the European war by the end of September 1945 as optimistic and arrogant.[153]

The resignation of the Koiso-Yonai cabinet on 4 April and the formation of a new cabinet under Admiral Suzuki Kantarō were discussed little on Japanese overseas radio. Tokyo reported that the new cabinet would meet any day, at any time of the day or night (unlike the previous cabinet, which had met on Tuesdays and Fridays).[154] In addition, a commentary to Italy stated the change of cabinet was due to the need for a more vigorous cabinet, just as the Koiso-Yonai cabinet had been more energetic than the Tōjō cabinet.[155]

The death of Roosevelt prompted an unusually sympathetic response from Radio Tokyo. Prime Minister Suzuki sent his condolences to the American nation and this was reported in international broadcasts. It was, however, omitted from domestic broadcasts, as it was considered that it would be seen as a move towards peace. (Kitayama, 1988c:214) A commentary to Germany stated that Roosevelt was responsible for the war, but described him as a great politician and a huge loss to the United States.[156]

Broadcasts from the Provisional Government of Free India in Singapore were less generous. In November 1944, Subhas Chandra Bose, on a visit to Tokyo, had been told by Rash Bihari Bose, leader of the IIL in Japan, that he "should not increase our number of enemies." This was a reference to the strongly anti-American propaganda, which was frequently broadcast from the IIL's Rangoon station. Despite this "last advice," (Nair, 1985:258) however, the station continued in its propaganda campaign against the United States. On 13 April 1945, a commentary entitled "Roosevelt, the Arch-Enemy of the Asiatic Peoples" claimed that it was impossible to feel sympathy over his death as he had entered the war because of his own greed and ideas of world domination. His death was, the commentator concluded, a relief.[157] This was a strange propaganda line for Bose to take, as Roosevelt was, in fact, well known for presenting anti-colonial views.

Radio Tokyo's response to the Potsdam Conference was to ridicule the conditions in which the conference took place. It compared the conference to the earlier San Francisco conference, which had established the conditions for creating the United Nations to replace the League of Nations. It claimed that there were more press representatives than diplomatic delegates at San Francisco, which is possible since the conference had included large numbers of countries and security had been low key. Conversely, reported Radio Tokyo, the Potsdam Conference dealt with real business and Stalin "held all the cards" so security was tighter and the media were absent. However, it concluded no security curtain was "thick enough to disguise American and British anxiety."[158] This was a reasonable assumption for Japanese propagandists to make, for having seen the Soviets take control of much of East and Central Europe following the defeat of Germany, Britain and

America were naturally anxious about the consequences of such action.

Japanese-controlled stations capitalised on Churchill's election loss, describing it as an indication of war weariness in Britain. They claimed that the wartime election was an indication of the major domestic problems Churchill had been facing.[159] In response to the issue of the Potsdam Declaration itself, the CIB immediately placed a complete ban on reports about the ultimatum within Japan. For overseas listeners the first response of the Japanese was transmitted in Morse code by Domei and declared that:

> *It is authoritatively learned that Japan will ignore the joint proclamation . . . calling upon the Japanese to announce their unconditional surrender. Japanese will prosecute the war of GEA to the better end, in accordance with her fixed policy . . . (Kitayama, 1988c:268)*

An early evening broadcast on the Greater East Asia broadcasting network dismissed the declaration as a British and American attempt to save face having failed to draw the Soviet Union into the Pacific War during the conference. It preceded a report of the terms of the declaration with the following comment:

> *The American diplomacy that attempted to draw Stalin into the Japanese issue at Potsdam has failed . . . The Chungking Regime, which has no actual power, was allowed to participate, a joint declaration was issued . . . in order to patch up the situation.*[160]

Although the situation for Japan became increasingly desperate in 1944-5 and finding "Good News" to report increasingly difficult, Radio Tokyo succeeded in presenting the listener with broadcasts from festivals and celebrations. 1 August 1944 marked the first anniversary of Burmese independence under Ba Maw and it was celebrated over five days. (Kitayama, 1988c:79) The first anniversary of Philippine independence on 14 October 1944 was similarly celebrated and included an exchange of radio messages between Prime Minister Koiso, Philippine President Laurel, Prime Minister Chang of Manchuria, Cheng Kung-Po, vice-president of Occupied China, and Prime Minister Kovit Abhai Wongse of Thailand.[161] Similar radio exchanges were broadcast to Germany and Italy to celebrate the anniversary of the Tripartite Pact on 27 September, (Kitayama, 1988c:96) and to countries of Greater East Asia such as one to celebrate the third anniversary of the Thai Defence Treaty on 21 December 1944. (Kitayama, 1988c:141-2) However, as 1945 progressed this type of programme virtually disappeared from the schedules, and the reporting of "good news" was restricted to reporting of internal Japanese celebrations, such as Navy Day,[162] or news of a good harvest.[163]

3. CHANGES IN THE STRUCTURE OF NHK BROADCASTING

The establishment of the Koiso-Yonai cabinet on 22 July 1944 coincided with a change in the structure of NHK. This was initiated to ensure that NHK worked more closely with the War Ministry, and to minimise the risk of radio transmissions being used for navigation purposes by American aircraft. (It was common for all the belligerent nations to close down radio transmissions during air raids, so that the raiding aeroplanes could not use the signal emitted by the transmitters for navigation.) A new Director-General's Office was established which included a new Department of Defence, and a Wartime Radio Research Institute. In addition, the International Bureau became the Overseas Bureau and the Southern Regions Office, which had been established to handle broadcasting to the occupied islands of the South Pacific, was abolished as the situation in the region became increasingly difficult for Japan. Its remaining business was incorporated into the Private Secretary's Section of the Director-General's Office. (Kitayama, 1988c:74-5) In addition it was decided to run-down certain transmitters in anticipation of Allied air raids to prevent bombers using the signals as aids to navigation. Hence from 1 August 1944 the output of the smaller relay stations was reduced.

On 5 November the International Bureau was once more enlarged, to its largest wartime operating size. Broadcasts for the Southern Regions were removed from Transmission Thirteen, which broadcast to Thailand, Vietnam and Burma only, and a new Transmission Fourteen was established broadcasting to the Philippines and Indonesia. (Kitayama, 1988c:120-1) At its largest, then, Radio Tokyo broadcast fifteen transmissions, for thirty-three hours and five minutes a day, in twenty languages. This was fewer languages than previously, as Urdu became treated as a dialect of Hindi, and items in Gujarati, Turkish and Dutch were dropped from the schedules completely. The complete Radio Tokyo schedule was as follows: (Kitayama, 1988c:117-8)

Transmission 1	Western United States	00.00-03.40	(3 hours 40)
Transmission 2	India	00.00-01.45	(1 hour 45)
Transmission 3	Middle East	02.00-03.40	(1 hour 40)
Transmission 4	Europe	04.00-07.00	(3 hours)
Transmission 5	Eastern United States	07.15-09.15	(2 hours)
Transmission 6	South America	09.30-10.30	(1 hour)
Transmission 7	India and Middle East	10.45-11.45	(1 hour)
Transmission 8	Western United States	12.00-17.00	(5 hours)
Transmission 9	Europe	17.15-20.00	(2 hours 45)
Transmission 10	Australia and the Central & Western Pacific		17.15-19.15 (2 hours)

Transmission 11	China	19.30-21.15	(1 hour 45)
Transmission 12	South America	20.15-21.15	(1 hour 30)
Transmission 13	Thailand, Vietnam, Burma	21.30-23.40	(2 hours 10)
Transmission 14	Philippines and Indonesia	21.30-23.40	(2 hours 10)
Transmission 15	Eastern United States	22.00-23.40	(1 hour 40)

At the same time as the expansion of overseas radio, the East Asia Relay Broadcasts were also re-organised, following the destruction of several transmitters in an air raid. The short-wave network broadcast from 5.30am to 10.20pm and relays were made via Shanghai, Hsinking, Peking, and Taipei. On 5 October the network was separated from overseas broadcasting and renamed East Asia Broadcasting. It established transmissions to twelve regions, Taiwan, Korea, Manchuria, Central China, Northern China, Singapore, Malaysia, Java, Burma, Celebes, Vietnam and Thailand broadcasting for sixteen-and-a-half hours daily. The re-organisation included a plan to strengthen Japanese news broadcasting to Asia, and the daily number of Japanese news broadcasts was increased to nine. The network included some Japanese domestic broadcasts, but the re-organisation sought to create a new "Asian section" of overseas broadcasting. Hence it attempted to create local programmes for East Asia, and used programmes from domestic and international broadcasts. (Kitayama, 1988c:121)

The expansion of broadcasting activity in both overseas and East Asia broadcasting, and the collapse of the Pulao station in August 1944 meant that the larger stations in the Greater East Asia Co-Prosperity Sphere became increasingly important in maintaining the level of overseas broadcasting. The Korean Broadcasting Corporation's Chongjin station broadcast regularly on medium-wave for Russia and the Taiwanese Broadcasting Corporation's Taipei station broadcast to much of South-east Asia, Australia and North America. It also relayed Radio Tokyo broadcasts for Burma, India and overseas Chinese. Radio Amoy broadcast to Nationalist and overseas Chinese and the Hainan station broadcast for China and the Pacific. Radio Hsinking's "Voice of Manchuria" transmitted to America, China, Europe and Russia. The Kalgan station of the (Inner) Mongolian Broadcasting Corporation broadcast to China, Mongolia and Chungking. It also co-operated with Radio Hsinking to produce anti-Communist broadcasts (Kitayama, 1988c:122-3)

Within China there were two broadcasting corporations, one based in Peking and one in Shanghai. The former broadcast on short-wave for Chungking and on medium-wave for the Chinese Communist stronghold of Yenan and the Shanghai station broadcast for Chungking, "Chinese in a third country" and Australia. In addition a station in Canton operated by staff from Taiwan also broadcast to Chungking. (Kitayama, 1988c:123)

Radio Shonan (Singapore) was the most important of the Greater East Asian stations, and Japan's most important short-wave station after Tokyo. In addition to the Provisional Government of Free India broadcasts, it broadcast Japanese short-wave programmes to India, Australia and enemy troops in the South Pacific. In 1944 it expanded its operation and began broadcasts to Chungking, Europe and the Middle East. It also relayed Radio Tokyo's European transmission in order to boost the signal. (Kitayama, 1988c:123-4)

The Saigon station broadcast to Australia and India and Radio Bangkok also broadcast to India, although its transmitter output was low. A further station in the radio war on India was Rangoon, which broadcast programmes for India, along with those for Chungking. Like Radio Shonan, Indians operated part of Radio Rangoon's schedule. In this case the operator was the IIL not the Provisional Government, but in reality this station, too, came under the control of Bose. In addition, Kitayama claims that there was a "Free Ceylon" station operated over Radio Rangoon, although details regarding it are unclear. (Kitayama, 1988c:124)

Radio Manila broadcast over two transmitters to North America, and from 8 March 1944 to enemy troops in the Western Pacific. (Kitayama, 1988c:123) In Indonesia, the Jakarta station[164] broadcast on short-wave to India, North America and Australia and the station in Makassar broadcast to Australia after December 1943. (Kitayama, 1988c:124)

Even as late as November 1944 the scale of the Japanese short-wave broadcasting operation throughout the occupied territories was enormous. However, as some records have not survived, it is impossible to establish the total number of hours broadcast by Japanese-controlled stations each day. (Figure 7 and Appendix 2)

Less than three months after the final expansion of short-wave broadcasting, however, the first contraction in overseas broadcasting was made as the deteriorating situation in both Japan and the Co-Prosperity Sphere made the over-stretched schedule impossible to maintain. On 1 February 1945, thirty minutes of Japanese language broadcasting was cut from Tokyo's East Asian broadcast. The reason was stated frankly:

> *. . . We will have to cease (the transmission) . . . on account of the difficulties in relays we are now experiencing due to local circumstances caused by developments in the war situation. (Kitayama, 1988c:168)*

At the same time as this reduction the Japanese broadcasting authorities began to plan for emergency broadcasting should NHK's Uchisaiwaichō site be damaged or destroyed during an air raid. It was considered essential that the overseas schedule be maintained with as little disruption as possible. A studio was constructed under the Dai-Ichi Life Insurance building in Tokyo, and plans were drawn up immediately to dispatch two members of staff from the American Department and one from the Performance Department to the underground studio should the station be bombed out. They were to continue the transmissions with news and records until others could arrive. In such an emergency, it was agreed, Transmission Fourteen for the Philippenes and Indonesia could be omitted from the schedules. It was specified that broadcasts to the Western United States would consist of the "German Hour," "Humanity Calls" and "Postman Calls," while the "Zero Hour" programme, broadcast to Australia, and the Pacific would continue. (Kitayama, 1988c:169)

Station	Languages	Target audience
Radio Chongjin (Korean Broadcasting Corp.)	Russian	Oriental USSR
Radio Taipei (Taiwan Broadcasting Corp.) 10kw	English, Cantonese, Vietnamese, Fukien & Beijing dialects of Chinese	South-west China, French Indo-China, Vietnam, Eastern India, Northern Australia, East Pacific. Relays of Radio Tokyo broadcasts for Burma, India, overseas Chinese
Radio Amoy 100kw	Mandarin	Chungking, overseas Chinese
Voice of Manchuria Radio Hsinking (Manchuria Telephone & Telegraph Co.) 20kw	English, Chinese, German, English, Russian	Western United States & Canada, China, Europe, USSR Co-operation with Radio Kalgan in anti-Communist broadcasting.
Radio Kalgan (Mongolian Broadcasting Corp.) 10kw	Chinese, Mongolian	Western & Northern China, Outer Mongolia, Chungking Co-operate with Radio Hsinking in anti-Communist broadcasting

Radio Peking (North China Broadcasting Corp.) 10kw	Chinese	Chungking, Yenan
Radio Shanghai (China Broadcasting Corp.) 10kw, 1kw	Chinese, English	Chungking, "Chinese in a third country," Australia
Radio Canton (Taiwan Broadcasting Corp.)	Chinese	Chungking
Radio Shonan 50kw	Hindi, Tamil, English, Mandarin, French, Arabic, Persian, Turkish	India, Australia, Enemy troops, Chungking, Europe, Middle East, Provisional Government of Free India broadcasts Relays of Radio Tokyo European transmission
Radio Saigon 12kw	English, Hindi, Punjabi, Tamil	Australia, India
Radio Bangkok 5kw, 2kw	Various Indian languages	India
Radio Rangoon 10kw	Hindi, Bengali, Chinese	India, Chungking I.L.L. broadcasts "Radio Free Ceylon"
Radio Manila 25kw, 10kw	English	North America, Enemy troops in Western Pacific
Radio Batavia (Jakarta) 10kw	English	India, North America, Australia
Radio Makasar 10kw	English	Australia

Figure 7: Short-wave broadcasting operations of the Japanese-controlled stations in Greater East Asia. (Kitayama, 1988c:122-4)

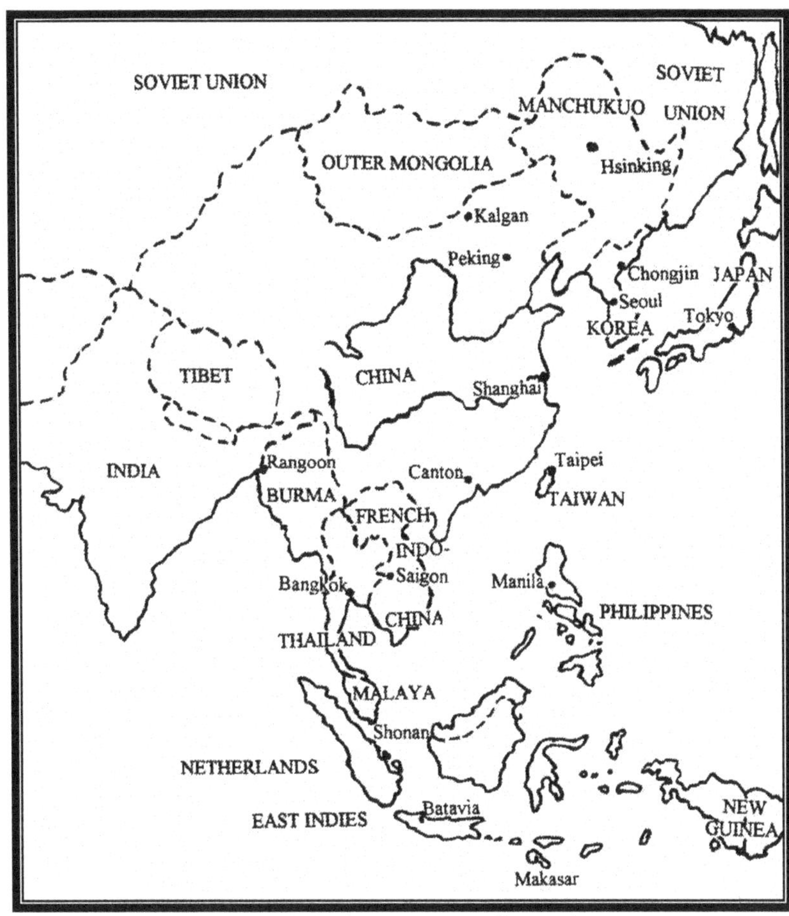

Map 3: Japanese-controlled Short-wave radio stations

On 4 May 1945, the day on which the Koiso-Yonai cabinet resigned, there was the first drastic reduction in the output of overseas broadcasts from Tokyo, which reduced the total daily usage time of the transmitters by eleven hours. (Kitayama, 1988c:211) Under the plan, broadcasts to the United States and Greater East Asia were considered the most important. Hence, even before the defeat of Germany was announced, the early morning transmission for Europe from 4 to 7am was dropped from the schedules and an additional transmission for China was created, increasing the total broadcasting time to Chungking by forty-five minutes. The former transmission to India and the Middle East, Transmission Seven, was also dropped. In addition, the separate transmissions for the Eastern and Western United States, Transmissions One, Five, Eight and Fifteen, were amalgamated forming two transmissions to North America, Transmission One from midnight to 2am and Transmission Six from 11am to 5pm. The new transmissions included the "Humanity Calls" and "Postman Calls" programmes, and were an hour longer than the previous transmission in order to include a new "huge propaganda projectile" in English and Japanese. Hence, the new transmission schedule was as follows: (Kitayama, 1988c:211)

Transmission 1	North America	00.00-02.00	(2 hours)
Transmission 2	Middle East	02.15-04.15	(2 hours)
Transmission 3	South America	05.00-09.00	(4 hours)
Transmission 4	Chungking	09.30-10.30	(1 hour)
Transmission 5	Philippines	09.30-10.30	(1 hour)
Transmission 6	North America	11.00-17.00	(6 hours)
Transmission 7	Europe	15.15-19.30	(4 hours 15)
Transmission 8	Philippines and Australia	17.30-19.30	(2 hours)
Transmission 9	South America	19.45-21.15	(1 hour 30)
Transmission 10	Chungking	19.45-21.15	(1 hour 30)
Transmission 11	India	21.30-23.45	(2 hours 15)
Transmission 12	Southern Regions	21.30-00.00	(2 hours 30)

An air raid on 21 May 1945 destroyed the factory which supplied vacuum tubes for NHK's short-wave transmitters. The number of stockpiled tubes was sufficient to continue the overseas schedule begun at the beginning of May for two months but it was agreed that a further reduction in transmission time would extend this to three months. The reduction was dramatic, reducing the daily programming time by eleven hours forty-five minutes. The number of transmissions was reduced to nine as the former Transmissions Three (South America), Four (Chungking) and Five (The Philippenes) were dropped. In addition, most of the remaining transmissions, were reduced significantly, although the "Zero Hour," "Humanity Calls," "Postman Calls" and "Free India" broadcasts continued as before in their respective transmissions. Although this reduction in transmission time was to prolong the life of the supply of vacuum tubes there does not seem to be any indication as to what, if any, plans existed for short-wave broadcasting after the three month period had elapsed. It is possible that the Japanese authorities hoped that a new factory to produce tubes could be established in that interval. However, it could also have been that by the end of May 1945 the unofficial view of Japan's decision-makers was that Japan could not prolong the war effort for significantly more than three months. Whatever the reasoning, this remained NHK's overseas broadcasting schedule in the latter months of the war: (Kitayama, 1988c:235-6)

Transmission 1	North America	00.00-01.30	(- 30 minutes)
Transmission 2	Middle East	11.30-12.30	(- 1 hour)
Transmission 3	North America	12.45-17.00	(- 1 hour 45)
Transmission 4	Europe	17.15-19.45	(- 1 hour 45)
Transmission 5	Philippines and Australia	18.00-19.30	(- 30 minutes)
Transmission 6	Chungking	19.45-21.15	(unchanged)
Transmission 7	South America	20.00-21.15	(- 15 minutes)
Transmission 8	India	21.30-23.45	(unchanged)
Transmission 9	Southern Regions	21.30-00.00	(unchanged)

4. RE-EVALUATION OF PROPAGANDA STRATEGIES FOR OVERSEAS RADIO

Throughout the final year of the war, the propaganda strategies of the Japanese government were re-evaluated and altered as the war situation developed. On becoming Prime Minister in July 1944, General Koiso decided to create a new body to guide policy and public opinion in order to increase Prime Ministerial control, which was not sufficiently strong in the Cabinet Liaison Committee. The resulting Supreme War Guidance Committee consisted of the Prime Minister, the Ministers of Foreign Affairs, the Army and the Navy, and the Army and Navy Chiefs of Staff. It met with the Emperor for the first time on 15 August 1944. The policy decisions agreed at the meeting were wide-ranging and included policies for the guidance of public opinion within Japan and policies for propaganda to be used in the occupied territories and overseas. As part of the latter, it was agreed that future plans for the independence of Indonesia should be promoted, along with propaganda to encourage the Soviet Union to remain neutral in the Pacific War. A principle clause of the agreement was the "Strategy for Propaganda Towards the Enemy" which stated that it was important to create divisions between the United States, Britain, the Soviet Union and China whilst providing "clarification of the war aims." (Kitayama, 1988c:81-2)

In August 1944, the "Atrocity Campaign" re-surfaced in both Japanese domestic and overseas propaganda. It began with a report in the *Asahi Shimbun* that American soldiers on the front line in the South Pacific had paraded the head of a decapitated Japanese general in front of Japanese as part of a victory celebration. (Kitayama, 1988c:83) The campaign, entitled "American Barbarity," spread to broadcasting and on 6th Radio

Tokyo reported that Japanese were indignant over a report from Zurich that Roosevelt had accepted a gift of a paper knife made from the bone of a Japanese soldier.[165] A further broadcast to Germany included a commentary, "American Cannibalism" which accused Americans of keeping Japanese skulls and bones as souvenirs, and reported that American children played with the skulls as toys.[166] A later White House report that Roosevelt had returned the paper knife to Congressman Francis Walter, who had given it to him, was cited as proof that the Japanese accusations were true.[167]

A new twist to the atrocity propaganda was its denunciation of American behaviour as anti-Christian. After reports about soldiers keeping bones as trophies appeared in the United States, the Catholic Church there denounced it and this was taken up by propagandists in Japan. Japanese Catholic Archbishop Doi was reported as calling for barbarism to be punished.[168] Radio Tokyo told Americans that the culprits would not escape God's judgement, warning that the decay of Europe began when European civilisation denied reverence to Christianity. As this broadcast was to Germany, it can probably be assumed that Nazi Germany was not included in the "decayed Europe" described by the commentator, but that it was a warning as to the moral standards of the Allied troops now in mainland Europe. It continued, "You Americans have sold your soul for materialism", but there was no explanation as to how the mutilation of Japanese bodies constituted "materialism."[169] The "Atrocity Campaign" continued and in October the "Real Values of Americanism" were discussed. A broadcast entitled "The Civilised Savages" claimed that the educated civilisation of Americans was only a veneer covering savage instincts. The savage character of Americans was attributed to their impure blood, and this became a further slogan of the campaign. In fact a broadcast on the effect on Japan of an American victory cited the dilution and eventual obliteration of Japanese blood as one of the worst occurrences. (Kitayama, 1988c:87-8)

A meeting of the Supreme War Guidance Committee on 5 October 1944 produced an agreement for a "Policy on Crushing the Enemy's Ideological Strategy" which included a three point plan to discredit the Allies' strategic medium-wave Japanese broadcasts from Hawaii and Saipan, which had begun in February 1944. The committee was particularly concerned about these medium-wave broadcasts. Previous short-wave American broadcasts were less threatening, as short-wave receivers were banned in Japan and the occupied areas.

The Japanese government had, however, encouraged medium-wave listening to facilitate its own control of the population. Hence, American medium-wave broadcasts were potentially threatening. The new policy sought to explain the war aims of Japan, whilst discrediting those of Britain and America, and warnings about the American broadcasts were published in Japanese newspapers. However, following the boosting of the Saipan transmitter to 1,000kc on 31 December 1944, the Supreme War Guidance Committee decided, instead, to jam the American transmitter's signal. (Kitayama, 1988c:146-8) This policy was extended to American medium-wave broadcasts from Iwojima, which began on 23 February 1945. Initially the short transmission was ignored as it clashed with a popular programme on the Greater East Asia network but it was jammed when length of the transmission was increased. (Kitayama, 1988c:190)

The "Policy Outline of Propaganda towards the Enemy," produced at the same time, specified the topics to be promoted in broadcasts to different enemies. Generally they dealt with the probable post-war situation in each country. Broadcasts to the United States claimed that the reign of Roosevelt indicated clearly the "emptiness of any post-war management," and those to Europe reported British unease over American policy towards her after the war. (Kitayama, 1988c:104) Radio Tokyo claimed that America's policy was to take over the governing of British colonial territories after the war, and sought to scare the British government into opposing the United States. A broadcast about the American "invasion" of India stated that American soldiers were paid three times as much as those from Britain, and claimed that they "overstepped the conventions observed by the British for many years . . .(taking) . . . half-caste girls into the best restaurants."[170] Broadcasts to neutral countries had a similar theme, and their inhabitants were warned that they would be caught between a power struggle between Britain and America and would be sacrificed by both. (Kitayama, 1988c:104)

In February 1945, Radio Tokyo claimed in the "Humanity Calls" and "Postman Calls" programmes that what prisoners-of-war feared most was bloodshed. The aim was to heighten American fears of a protracted and bloody struggle. However, prisoner letters, which also continued to be broadcast, tended to undermine this. The prisoner letters were in the same kind of cheerful language as in earlier years. However, the principal difference in 1945 was that as American troops pushed northwards in the Pacific, prisoner-of-war camps in the Philippines and Indonesia were closed and the prisoners were moved to camps on the Japanese mainland. This meant that the gathering and recording of prisoner letters for transmission over Radio Tokyo was much simpler than previously, and there was now an opportunity to broadcast larger numbers of letters. Increasing numbers of letters using cheerful language undermined the claim that American prisoners were in fear of a long and bloody war. A letter from Staff Sergeant Virgil Maye is typical of the kind of letter which continued to be broadcast:[171]

Dear Mother and Dad. I'm sending just a few words to say that I am well. The weather here is very much the same as at home and I feel much better than when I was in the Philippines. Please send my regards to all my family, have them write short messages, send pictures, and if possible another wonderful package like last year. Give my my (sic) best regards to all my friends. Do not worry, say 'hello' to Vivian, Frank Patterman, and all the Letterman gang. My prayers and hearts (sic) love to you always, from your son.

5. THE "ZACHARIAS" BROADCASTS

On 9 May monitors at Atagoyama picked up a broadcast by Captain Ellis Zacharias of the United States' Navy, which included a statement by President Truman. It reminded Japan of the surrender of Germany, which spelt "Japan's inevitable defeat" but reassured listeners that this referred "only (to) Japan's military defeat." (Zacharias, 1946:399) The broadcast by Zacharias was the first of a significant series of fourteen recorded in Japanese and English and transmitted to Japan. In this first broadcast, Zacharias stated clearly why he had been chosen as America's official spokesman. He had spent considerable time in Japan, and had developed relationships with many high-ranking Japanese officials, including former assistant Prime Minister, Admiral Yonai, and Nomura and Kurusu, the Japanese Ambassadors to Washington at the outbreak of war. He had been active in many diplomatic exchanges with Japan and mentioned many of his Japanese contacts in this first broadcast, in order to establish his credibility with the Japanese authorities, expressing confidence that "those . . . who have known me personally will trust me."

(Zacharias, 1946:400) He followed his own introduction with a statement by President Truman stressing "Unconditional surrender does not mean the extermination or enslavement of the Japanese people." He concluded the broadcast by offering his listeners a choice:

> *Your future lies in your own hands. You can choose between a wasteful, unclean death for many of your forces, or a peace with honor. (Zacharias, 1946:401)*

The second broadcast followed four days later. It repeated President Truman's statement, and followed it with a commentary which pointed to criticism of the war's prosecution even within the Japanese High Command:

> *It is . . . clear to thinking Japanese that those who made the estimates three years ago and promised you quick victory over the United States are now trying to conceal the facts . . . .The shadows of . . . defeat are . . . evident in the communiques of your own High Command. (Zacharias, 1946:402)*

The following broadcast followed a similar format and stressed that the United States' good treatment of prisoners-of-war contradicted the notion of extermination upon surrender, which was presented by the Japanese authorities. (Zacharias, 1946:403-5)

The fourth broadcast by Zacharias, on 27 May,[172] did not repeat Truman's statement. It claimed that the Japanese people wanted peace, especially since their German ally had capitulated, but that Japanese leaders did not. It called on Japan to replace its leadership with leaders "who have the best interest of Japan at heart [and will] repudiate these failures and embark on the only course which can save Japan." (Zacharias, 1946:406)

The following day, the FBIS monitored a response to the broadcasts from Japan, noting that it believed the Japanese government had officially selected the person making the broadcast. This was the case. The three people chosen to make broadcasts were Ōya Kusurō, Inagaki Kazuyoshi who had been involved in pre-war negotiations with the United States; and Inoue Isamu, the former editor of a Los Angeles newspaper. (Kitayama, 1995:8-9) The initial broadcast made no mention of the term "unconditional surrender," and was inserted into the schedule of Transmission Three for North America, probably in the 4.40pm commentary slot. (Kitayama, 1988c:244) The contents of this broadcast have not been established. However, Inoue's broadcast of 2 June demanded clarification of the term "unconditional surrender," and ended with the accusation that the call for Japanese surrender was because American soldiers in the Pacific wanted to go home. This lack of commitment was compared to Japan and her allies in Greater East Asia which "wanted to join hands to build an international world structure which pressed on for world peace and human benefit." (Kitayama, 1995a:9) It is probable that the theme of replies to Zacharias' broadcasts had not changed much in the period between the two, and that the earlier transmission had been similar in tone. The latter point of the Japanese reply was very similar to a point made in the 1943 East Asia Declaration. Much of the declaration dealt with Asian solidarity, but it too ended with talk of world peace. This was a reflection of the growing influence of moderate leaders in Japan.

The fifth broadcast by Captain Zacharias was on 3 June. It repeated the call for the Japanese people not to "follow leaders whose unbroken record of failure has . . . brought their nation to the brink of disaster." (Zacharias, 1946:407) It was followed by a further broadcast a week later, which sought to reassure people, that the unconditional surrender called for by Truman would mean only:

> *The end of war . . . the termination of the influence of the military leaders . . . provision for the return of soldiers and sailors . . . [and] not the extermination or enslavement of the Japanese people. (Zacharias, 1946:410)*

The series of broadcasts continued on 17th when Zacharias reminded listeners of the good relations enjoyed by Japan and the United States in the pre-war period. He also sought to increase Japanese trust in him by mentioning his relationships with prominent Japanese, such as Rear Admiral Yokoyama Ichirō, whom he had known in Washington. (Zacharias, 1946:410-2)

On 24 June Zacharias described the American victory in Okinawa, which he described as "a milestone in the Pacific War." (Zacharias, 1946:412) On 1 July he stated that the equipment of the advancing American Army was superior to that of the Japanese Army, as Lieutenant General Kosuda Katsuzo, Head of Japan's Ordnance Administration, had admitted in 1944, and concluded, "Time is running out for Japan." (Zacharias, 1946:415) The broadcasts continued throughout July, appealing to Prime Minister Suzuki to make a wise decision for peace, (Zacharias, 1946:416-7) and repeating the meaning behind "unconditional surrender." (Zacharias, 1946:418-9) However, Japanese scheduled short-wave broadcasts continued to re-iterate that "The unconditional surrender slogan has no effect on Japan" whose citizens would "fight until we finally achieve victory." (Kitayama, 1995a:10)

Zacharias made his twelfth broadcast on 22 July. In it he stated that there were two choices for the leaders of Japan: "the virtual destruction of Japan followed by a dictated peace . . . [or] unconditional surrender with its attendant benefits as laid down by the Atlantic Charter," which would bring renewed "peace and prosperity for Japan." (Zacharias, 1946:412) Scheduled broadcasts continued to deny that any plans for peace were being considered, such as one from Hong Kong on 22nd:

> *Lately she (Chungking) has again been circulating peace rumors . . . about . . . peace proposals made by Japan . . . to alienate people from the military & destroy their will to carry on the war. . . . Such propaganda is far too transparent ever to be effective. (op cit. Kitayama, 1995a:11)*[173]

However, the secret reply, broadcast by Inoue on 25th, responded differently. It began with the declaration that Japan had "no problem" with a "liberal America" and seems to have attempted to sound out American officials as to what was meant by the term "unconditional surrender." At the end of the broadcast Inoue respond to Zacharias' mention of the Atlantic Charter with the news that Japan was now willing to talk about an end to the fighting:

> *. . . Should America show any sincerity of putting into practice what she preaches, as for instance in Atlantic Charter . . . Jap. (sic) . . . would automatically . . . follow in stopping of conflict . . . & then only sabers cease to rattle both in East & in West. (Kitayama, 1995a:11)*[174]

It was noted in America that Japan had stated that peace was now possible.

The penultimate broadcast Zacharias made was on 29 July, following the issue of the Potsdam Declaration. He appealed to "both the leaders and the people of Japan" to "allow tranquillity again to return to the city and the countryside." (Zacharias, 1946:421-2)

The final broadcast by Zacharias was on 4 August 1945, two days after the United States had decided that should peace not be forthcoming, the 20th Air Force in Guam would arm a bomber with an atomic bomb and attack Hiroshima's factory and military areas. (Kitayama, 1988c:272) The broadcast described the continued struggle of Japan as a problem of leadership and repeated that all hope for a Japanese victory was lost. In a final appeal, Zacharias stated:

> *The [Japanese leaders] must recognize their present situation, and take suitable steps to correct the tragic mistakes of the recent past. They must plan for their inevitable defeat and for Japan's future with whatever loyalty, intelligence, and courage they can still command. (Zacharias, 1946:424)*

There was no immediate response broadcast by NHK.

6. THE END OF THE WAR

On 6 August 1945 an American B29 bomber exploded the world's first atomic bomb over Hiroshima. At 1.30am the following day a monitor at Domei picked up an announcement by Truman that he had ordered the attack: "This bomb was . . . the most powerful bomb in history. It was an atomic bomb." This was reported immediately to Foreign Minister Togo. (Kitayama, 1988c:273)

The CIB devised a propaganda counter offensive the same day, deciding that whilst the domestic population should be encouraged to prepare themselves for the final battle for the mainland, in overseas propaganda, the atomic bomb was to be denounced as an inhuman weapon. There was some dispute between the CIB and the Army Ministry, which wanted to omit use of words "atomic bomb," but eventually the term was used in both overseas and domestic propaganda. (Kitayama, 1988c:274-5)

The transmission to North America (Transmission Three) carried a statement that a small number of B29 bombers had carried out a raid on Hiroshima the previous day, and that use of a new kind of bomb, possibly atomic, was being investigated. (Kitayama, 1988c:273-4) The transmission to Europe reported Truman's statement in its French language section[175] but the first full reports of the situation in Hiroshima were not made until the following day. The French language report called the attack "indescribable" and declared that the "cruel result of the attack is such that one cannot distinguish between the men and women killed by fire." It accused the United States of disregarding the Hague Convention by attacking "open towns and defenceless civilians" and reminded its listeners of American accusations of Japanese inhumanity regarding much smaller scale attacks in China.[176] The German language section continued the attack on American inhumanity with an eyewitness report by a Domei correspondent. He declared that,

> *The enemy . . . has revealed . . . this lust for the slaughter of innocent Japanese civilians. The Americans have . . . torn off the mask of humanity.*[177]

The following day the Japanese-controlled stations took up the denunciation of the attack. Radio Batavia reminded listeners of

British and American protests about indiscriminate bombing over the use of V1 and V2 rockets by Germany on London. These it claimed were "carefully aimed and . . . controlled by radio" and were much less indiscriminate than the "atomic bomb which the Anglo-Americans now produce with apparent irresponsibility of guilt."[178] In a show of defiance, Radio Shonan derided the West for finding atomic energy so new. It claimed that atomic power had long been understood in Japan, and threatened that Japan would retaliate in kind, employing "weapons like the atomic bomb", attached to suicide bombers.[179]

On 9 August 1945 the Soviet Union declared war on Japan and her troops entered Manchuria. The same day a second atomic bomb was exploded over Nagasaki.

The second bomb was largely ignored by short-wave radio stations, which on 10th continued to describe children in Hiroshima in contradictory reports. An eyewitness account described the children probably accurately as a "pitiful sight" with "legs and bodies scattered."[180] However, another report defiantly made light of the situation, claiming that children had received only minor burns, not even suffering any bleeding, and were now playing in the streets as before.[181] A further Radio Tokyo report of 12 August, anticipating some later historical writing, accused the American government of using the bomb in order to intimidate the Soviet Union, rather than to force Japan into surrender.[182]

At 14.20 (22.20 in Japan) on 10 August 1945 British monitors received the following transmission from Domei:

The Japanese Government is ready to accept the terms enumerated in the Joint Declaration issued at Potsdam on 26 July, 1945, by the heads of the Governments of the USA,

> *Great Britain and China, and later subscribed by the Soviet Government, with the understanding that the said Declaration does not comprise any demand which prejudices the prerogatives of His Majesty as a sovereign ruler.*[183]

This information was repeated on short-wave radio to each transmission region over the next 24 hours. The Allied reply stated that "From the moment of surrender, the authority of the Emperor and the Japanese Government to rule the state shall be subject to the Supreme Commander for the Allied Powers." (Kitayama, 1988c:292-3) On 13 August whilst the Japanese Government considered its response, Soviet troops attacked Chongjin in Northern Korea, and twelve of the radio station staff committed suicide, blowing up the station in an "honourable suicide explosion."

At 10.50am on 14 August the Cabinet and the Supreme War Guidance Committee met with the Emperor and heard that he had decided to comply with the terms of the Potsdam Declaration. It was decided that the Emperor should broadcast the decision himself at noon the following day. During the course of the day the Chiefs of Staff broadcast secret transmissions to the armies in the field instructing them to listen to the broadcast, and at 11pm the Foreign Minister contacted the Ambassador to Switzerland telling him to indicate to the Swiss authorities that the Japanese Government would accept the terms of the Potsdam Declaration. Between 11.20 and 11.50pm the Emperor made two recordings of the speech to be broadcast.

Zealous elements of the military were opposed to surrender, and sought to continue the war for the Japanese mainland. Some of these sought to destroy these recordings to prevent the broadcast being made. On the night of 14 August they tried to take over the Imperial Palace, but when they failed to find the recordings, they took hostages and moved on to the NHK studios. Their occupation of the studios lasted three hours, delaying the start of the domestic schedule. However, it had no effect on the short-wave schedule, which did not start until 11.30am. (NHK, 1977c:124)

The Emperor's broadcast was to have been relayed simultaneously by all the stations in the Empire. However, broadcasters in Radio Batavia refused to carry the relay, as they feared that the surrender of Japan would jeopardise the promised independence of Indonesia, which had been strongly promoted in the spring and summer of 1945. Monitors in Australia instead picked up news items regarding food shortages, and one-and-a-half hours after the surrender, heard a commentary from Radio Batavia proclaiming, "Asia Marches On." (Kitayama, 1988c:314-5) Free India stations and the Bangkok station also refused to relay the message so the response of Radio Batavia could also have been part of a co-ordinated refusal. Four days later, however, it was announced that the cease-fire order had been received in Jakarta and that the military administration disassociated itself from the Indonesian Independence Movement, which had refused to surrender.[184]

Overseas broadcasts in the days which followed the Emperor's broadcast, were largely concerned with the text of the Emperor's speech and the formation of a new cabinet under Prince Higashikuni, following the resignation of the Suzuki cabinet on 15th. On 18th the transmission hours of Radio Tokyo were reduced by 2.5 hours. (Kitayama, 1988c:325) Singapore's Free India broadcasts continued, and messages from Bose were read out calling for Indians "hold your heads erect and face the future with unending hope and confidence."[185]

Towards the end of August there were also broadcasts to the Allied occupation forces about to take over areas of Asia. On 25th Singapore instructed the Japanese troops that the cease-fire included a ban on looting, and urged the Allies in Malaysia and Singapore to co-operate in keeping the peace.[186] The same day Radio Saigon appealed to Allied troops to give advance notice of medical supply drops for prisoners-of-war on Borneo.[187]

On 1 September 1945 the American Supreme Commander for the Allied Powers (SCAP), General Douglas MacArthur, arrived in Japan and a day later the formal surrender ceremony took place on the deck of the American battleship, *Missouri*. It was described in overseas radio broadcasts throughout the day. The following day the second order given by SCAP announced the cessation of all radio transmissions in foreign languages after midnight, 3 September 1945. The programme schedule was further altered on 6 September, to nine daily transmissions. (Figure 8) Kitayama claims that as a result of this SCAP order all these transmissions were only broadcast in Japanese.

Transmission One	North America	00.00-00.40
Transmission Two	China	10.30-11.10
Transmission Three	North America	13.00-13.40 and 15.00-15.40
Transmission Four	Europe	17.00-17.40
Transmission Five	Philippines and Australia	18.00-18.40
Transmission Six	China	19.30-20.10
Transmission Seven	South America	20.00-20.40
Transmission Eight	India	22.00-22.40
Transmission Nine	Southern Regions	22.00-22.40

Figure 8: NHK International Department schedule from 6 September 1944
(Kitayama, 1988c:326)

This was generally the case, although monitors at the BBC recorded having listened to English language broadcasts from Radio Tokyo to North America on 20 and 25 September.[188] These seem to have been regular scheduled broadcasts, not transmissions of official messages by the American authorities in Japan, so it must be assumed that English language broadcasts were also permitted. In addition, broadcasts from the stations in Singapore, Saigon, Bangkok and Batavia were not covered by MacArthur's directive and these continued to broadcast in English.

Kitayama also claims that a Civil Censorship Division (CCD) directive of 10 September superseded the SCAP order and forced the cessation of all overseas broadcasting. He writes, too, that there was concern for Japanese working overseas, who needed the radio link to their homeland, but that the American authorities declared it impossible to maintain this. (Kitayama, 1988c:326) However, the monitoring reports of the BBC show that overseas broadcasts continued throughout September 1945. It is probable that they also continued into October although this study includes material from the BBC's *Summary of World Broadcasts* only up to number 2267, 1 October 1945. The reports are much shorter than previous ones and are noted as having been monitored by the New Delhi station, but as the target regions continued to be noted as previously it must be assumed that the shortened transmission schedule of September 6 continued to be broadcast. The content of the broadcasts primarily concerned the reconstruction of Japan, such as reports on the Ministry of Education's proposed "science drive,"[189] and the resumption of treasury bill and government securities transactions.[190]

The role of short-wave broadcasting in the period after the surrender of Japan seems, therefore, to be somewhat unclear.

Much of Japan was in turmoil in the period between the Emperor's speech and the arrival of the American occupation forces, so there can be little surprise that this turmoil extended to NHK. However, this is less understandable following the implementation of SCAP rule in Japan. The SCAP directives should have clarified the situation completely. Both Kitayama and the official history of NHK state that short-wave broadcasting was banned early in September 1945. (NHK, 1977c:137) [191] The BBC's *Summary of World Broadcasts*, however, shows that short-wave broadcasts continued to be made in Japanese and English throughout September 1945. There seems to be no explanation for this, for according to NHK there was no short-wave broadcasting until experimental broadcasts were permitted in 1949. (NHK, 1977c:197)

By the end of September 1945 references to Japanese short-wave broadcasts in the *Summary of World Broadcasts* were increasingly infrequent and it may be assumed that this trend continued into October. It is possible, therefore, that early SCAP directives did not take effect immediately but gradually, in the confused situation in immediate post-war Japan. If this were the case, it would appear that although overseas broadcasting was the subject of the second SCAP order to be issued to the Japanese authorities, this order was less important and effective than it appeared. Perhaps the occupation government perceived some liberalism in the later Japanese broadcasts, and the responses to the "Zacharias Broadcasts," and felt that broadcasting would adjust itself gradually, hence exerting less direct control than over other aspects of Japanese administration. (Kitayama, 1995a:8-9)

CHAPTER 7
PROPAGANDA THEMES

1. THE WAR IN ASIA

During the China Incident and the Pacific War there were several themes regularly employed in Japanese overseas broadcasting. Some were not employed throughout the period, but were used intensively for a short time or to a specific target region, whilst others appeared in broadcasts to most regions throughout the war, albeit with varying intensity.

The most important subject in Radio Tokyo news reports was the war situation, and war reports constituted the majority of news items in transmissions to all regions. Immediately after the Marco Polo Bridge incident in July 1937, the Information Committee issued a directive stating that the propaganda line for overseas radio was that the Japanese were making the sacrifice in order to keep the peace, and oppose Communism in Asia. (Kitayama, 1988a:200) Over the next four years there were frequent references to the fighting in China in reports to all the transmission regions. A commentary from May 1941 is typical in its assessment of the situation in China:

> *Recent Japanese war operations . . . aimed . . . to break the resistance of the Chiang Kai-Shek regime. The Chungking army is no longer a Regular Army, and one can hardly call it*

fit for battle. It has lost all hold over the Chinese people and its main function today is that of a smuggling gang, trying to secretly import merchandise through gaps in the Japanese blockade . . . Chungking today suffers from an eighty-fold increase in the cost of living. . . . Chungking, which is no longer fit for fighting, is today faced with the alternative either to collapse or to amalgamate with the National Chinese Government in Nanking.[192]

There were of course elements of truth in this assessment, as the Chinese army did try to smuggle goods through the Japanese blockade, and Chungking China did suffer from high inflation.

After the outbreak of war in the Pacific in December 1941, war reports concerning China and the Pacific often constituted most of a newscast.[193] Often the reports took the form of 'war results,' lists of the numbers of dead and injured on each side, and the amount of enemy 'booty' (weaponry) captured by the Japanese. The reporting of 'war results' was not confined to the Japanese media. During the Battle of Britain in the late summer and autumn of 1940, posters at newstands in Britain advertised results of air battles as "Their's 78, Ours 17," as though it was the scoreline from a football match. (Fussell, 1989:58) Japan's war results had been given out occasionally in reference to the fighting in China before 1941. After Pearl Harbor, however, lists of 'war results' became increasingly frequent in broadcasts to all transmission regions. Most 'results' gave figures from a single battle or attack. However, occasionally there were huge lists of 'results' covering whole campaigns, which were perhaps intended to impress the listener when the on-going situation had reached a stalemate. In April 1942 Radio Tokyo reported the total Chinese 'war results' to the end of March 1942, from the start of the Greater East Asian War in July 1937. The following list was read out on air:

In 30 operations there were:

58,313 enemy troops killed
18,453 prisoners captured
5 planes captured
17 tanks captured
1,470 automobiles captured
309 railway cars captured
3 torpedo boats captured
201 (- ? -) or cannon captured
1,363 machine guns captured
12,443 rifles captured
30 planes shot down
4 gunboats sunk
32 ships sunk

This was contrasted with the reported Japanese losses of 536 killed and 6,382 wounded.[194]

However, generally the reports concerned short time periods and small areas of battle, and Radio Tokyo continued to read out ‘war results’ until the end of the war. Even in August 1945 ‘results’ continued to appear in news bulletins, although by this time they consisted of reporting the number of planes Japanese troops claimed to have shot down during recent American air raids. Radio Singapore reported on 30 July, that 190 planes had been shot down or crippled on 28th, and more than 537 between 10th and 28th.[195]

The reporting of 'war results' was the most frequent way that broadcasts from the Japanese-controlled station sought to impress upon listeners the power and strength of the Japanese Army. The enormous lists were impressive and tended to appear when there was little else of worth to report, particularly concerning the situation in China. However, the China Incident itself became the focus of Japanese reports when the situation in the Pacific worsened. In the latter half of the war, reports regarding the China War dominated the war report broadcasts. In contrast to the huge naval battles in the Pacific, which appeared in the news reports of all the Allies, only Radio Chungking was in a position to present an opposite view. This meant it was easier to present the skirmishes in China as major victories with little contradiction.

Japanese radio stations did report great Japanese naval victories in the Pacific battles in a similar way. However, when their propaganda position became untenable, a defeat was rarely admitted. Usually reports concerning that field of operation merely disappeared from the newscasts, often to be replaced with more optimistic news from China.

2. THE WAR IN EUROPE

References to the European War in broadcasts by Japanese radio were not frequent. Soon after the outbreak of war in Europe Radio Tokyo expressed the astonishment of Japanese over the lack of hostilities during the period of the phoney war, and the desire of Japan to benefit from the war, particularly in the supply of canned goods.[196] A later report in April 1940 expressed Japan's worries over the German invasions of Denmark and Norway and its apparent disregard for their neutrality.[197] This was a strange propaganda line for Tokyo to take, as Japan had still not declared war on China, and the fighting there continued to be termed the "China Incident."

In 1942 there was occasional reference to the dilemma over a second European front. The fighting between the Allies and Germany was concentrated in the USSR where Russians were resisting a German invasion. The plan was to establish a Second Front in France in the West to draw German troops away from the East and attack Germany from two directions. A commando landing at Dieppe in August 1942 produced heavy casualties from heavy German fire, due to inadequate beach reconnaissance, and a lack of integration between air and sea bombardments of the French coast. (Macksey, 1987:179) Japanese broadcasts tended to highlight differences between Britain and the Soviet Union and to conclude that the establishment of a Second Front was unlikely as Britain was content to allow Russians to fight the war for her, without endangering any of her own troops. A statement by a CIB spokesman in October 1942 claimed that whilst, "For Russia, the Second Front question is a matter of life and death," Britain had "several million fully trained soldiers" garrisoned to defend the British Isles, and "thousands of American soldiers . . . having nothing better to do [than] . . . (?flirting) with women and meddling in purely British affairs." It concluded:

> *To a practical people like the British, the creation of a Second Front (?with) the possibility of another Dunkirk is inconceivable. Such a disaster (?took place) at Dieppe, where the British sacrificed more than 3,000 (?Canadian) youth for a futile, . . . experience.*[198]

When Italy's Badoglio Government surrendered to the Allies in September 1943, there was little reaction on Japanese overseas radio, and the only significant change to Italian broadcasts was the suspension of the weekly radio exchanges which were broadcast across the domestic network. (Kitayama, 1988b:376-7) News programmes carried reports of the situation regarding Italian embassies and communities in Greater East Asia. Radio Tokyo reported that the Italian Embassy in Manchuria was being guarded, and that the Italian settlement in Tientsin was under the administration of the Nanking Government.[199] Reports in English concerned the return of Mussolini, who, Radio Tokyo reported, was "at Hitler's headquarters in Germany and [was] expected to form a new fascist government."[200] It is interesting that whilst broadcasts for the German audience sought to reassure them that Italian people and property were being protected by Italy's former ally, reports in English made boastful claims about the re-emergence of Mussolini, presumably to undermine Allied morale.

The eventual establishment of the Second Front, by the D-Day landings in Normandy in early June 1944, received little more than a cursory mention in Japanese overseas broadcasts. According to Radio Tokyo, the "second front [was] opening according to German expectations" and the Allied landings were "exactly at the most fortified zone . . . [and would] end in a second Dunkirk."[201] A further line taken by Japanese-controlled radio was that the Allies would "provide Germany with the spring-board she needs for a victorious general offensive [and had] walked into an elaborate death trap."[202] Interestingly, the regular German commentator, Erwin Wickert, whilst not expressing it directly, implied that the fighting in the Pacific was a sort of Axis "Second Front," declaring, "Japan must inflict blows on the Allies in the East in order to relieve pressure on Germany."[203] However, a week later he made a plea for Germans not to forget that the Pacific and European conflicts were one war, and occasionally to remember their allies in the East.[204] Presumably, the Japanese authorities were concerned that their monitors had heard only news about the European War in German radio broadcasts.

The response of Japanese radio to the surrender of Germany in May 1945 was to declare that it would have no effect on the prosecution of the war in the Pacific. A commentary on 5 May declared,

> *Japan now has no allies in Europe, everyone is an enemy . . . Evil may temporarily prevail but it cannot completely destroy us . . . Japan will build a New Order*[205]

Other broadcasts claimed that Hitler's failure had been to achieve solidarity and collaboration amongst all the peoples of Europe. East Asians were, in contrast, described as united in their struggle.[206]

In a final comment on the war in Europe, Radio Shonan informed British troops in Asia in June 1945 that it had been the Soviet Union, not the British and Americans which had won the war in Europe.[207] At that time, the Japanese government was unaware that the Soviet Union had agreed to declare war on Japan after the defeat of Germany, and the Russo-Japanese Neutrality Agreement remained intact. Presumably the intention was, therefore, to imply that even if the troops who were listening sacrificed themselves in an invasion of Greater East Asia, it would be in vain as Britain and America could not hope for victory without the assistance of the Soviets.

3. THE PROMOTION OF JAPANESE CULTURE

The promotion of Japanese culture by short-wave radio was important to the Japanese government from the early 1930s. In 1932, the Head of NHK, Iwahara Kenzō, had stressed the importance of clear short-wave broadcasts to the *gaichi* in order to encourage a policy of assimilation. In 1933, the departure of Japan from the League of Nations over the League's refusal to recognise the state of Manchukuo left her in an isolated position. The role of overseas broadcasting in expressing the Japanese viewpoint to the rest of the world hence became increasingly important.

The first scheduled overseas broadcast proper from Tokyo on 1 June 1935 was made in both English and Japanese, an indication that the broadcasts were not merely intended for overseas Japanese. Unlike the BBC Empire Service which at that time only broadcast in English for British abroad, the Japanese overseas service sought to foster an audience of foreign listeners and develop their understanding of the Japanese position through an appreciation of Japanese culture. Soon after the start of scheduled broadcasting, in July and August 1935, a series explaining the "Japanese Spirit" and "National Structure," "to Our Countrymen Overseas" was transmitted to America in order to increase the awareness of American-born Japanese of their roots. (Kitayama, 1988a:119)

Following the attempted military coup in Japan in 1936 known as the 26 February Incident, radio again became the primary tool the government used to restore the image of Japan abroad. Programmes broadcast included "Japan Presentation Hour," which dealt with a different aspect of Japan each week. Whilst most of these programmes were aimed at North America, the promotion of the joint Japanese-German film production, "*Atarashiki Tsuchi*," by radio in February 1937, was aimed at German listeners. The film itself, and the radio promotion it received, sought to familiarise Germans with the culture of their ally, Japan.

In August 1941, a further lecture series was broadcast to acquaint Germans with the national character and traditions of the Japanese. The first lecture was entitled "The Spirit of Chivalry" and outlined the principles of the Samurai code of *bushidō* for the German audience.[208] *Bushidō* was re-discovered and promoted by the Japanese Government to encourage and justify the actions of Japan.

At the start of 1939 a new drive was begun in the form of the "Japan Culture Series" which emphasised both the unique nature of the Japanese spirit, and the Japanese vision of a New Order in East Asia. This drive was reinforced in 1939 with the introduction of weekly programmes in August and September. "*Nisei* Radio Hour" and "Let's Tune In" in the Western United States schedule presented traditional Japanese stories and talks by *nisei* in Japan, for the American audience.

After the outbreak of war in the Pacific in December 1941 the superiority of the Japanese character was frequently cited in overseas broadcasts to most regions, although it was often with the aim of intimidating the enemy rather than promoting the Japanese way. The following description of the Japanese and American navies is typical:

> *A strong navy must have two essential qualities - durability and spirit . . . The main success of the Japanese Navy is its solid strength against paper force . . . Although the US has enormous natural resources and great wealth and can build a great navy, the present naval engagement has definitely shown how fragil [sic] it is. Due to haste of navy building, US warships are mostly ill constructed . . . Furthermore, US economic strength is not very great. Therefore, although the US Navy is superior numerically, its actual strength is very weak.*[209]

In April 1942, the superiority of the Japanese *bushidō* was repeated in broadcasts to Britain. In describing the rescue of

British sailors from *HMS Exeter* off Surabaya, in Java, Radio Tokyo reported,

> *The British Commander wept . . . [and] some of the rescued British sailors had brought their pets with them . . . Many of the rescued sailors insisted on singing popular jazz songs to give vent to their feelings. The Japanese sailors looked (?agape) at them . . . . No wonder the British Navy always lost its battles with the Japanese.*[210]

Japanese language courses were a further tool Japanese overseas broadcasting used to inspire interest in Japan. A Japanese language course for English speakers was conducted fortnightly over short-wave radio in 1940. It was broadcast first to the United States and then repeated in the European transmission. A Spanish version of the course was also broadcast to South America, (Kitayama, 1988a:312) and the full courses were re-broadcast again before the start of the Pacific War. After the outbreak of war the Japanese language became important to the Japanese in the 'assimilation' of East Asia and Japanese became an important subject in the schools of Greater East Asia. News items gave occasional glimpses as to the success of the programme. In 1942 a report declared,

> *Answering the ardent desire of the Burmese people for learning the Japanese language, a three month's course will be given at a newly-opened Japanese school from 1st June. Over 800 Burmese have already applied for the course.*[211]

Abdul Wahid, Radio Batavia's regular Indian commentator, made an unusual observation regarding the promotion of Japanese culture within Greater East Asia. He asked, "Must the government and the governed be of the same religion? . . . Japan does not try to impose Shintoism on Malays."[212] As the broadcast was to India the implication, presumably, was that Britain had tried to impose her own religion on those she governed. This is an unusual argument for a Japanese station to use, and from the records that are available, it seems as though this was the only occasion on which it was. Although the promotion of a religion may be included in campaigns to promote the culture of a country, this was not a theme used by Japanese radio. It seems that by 1943 some at least, including Wahid, had noticed this omission and thought it something that in turn could be used to further promote the benign nature of Japanese rule.

After the battles of Midway and the Coral Sea in the summer and autumn of 1942 the references to Japanese culture in overseas broadcasts dwindled. The superior spirit of the Japanese continued to be exalted, but largely in reference to the fighting ability of Japanese soldiers. Campaigns to increase listener numbers and familiarise them with the culture of Japan such as had taken place before the outbreak of war did not continue. This is not surprising as the station was now perceived by Allied listeners as 'the enemy' and the sympathy a campaign of exposing the audience to Japanese culture was intended to generate would be extremely hard to create. In addition, the tactics of Radio Tokyo changed and the reporting of huge Allied losses became common. This could be expected to intimidate and perhaps impress an Allied audience more effectively than a programme of broadcasts describing the moral superiority of the Japanese.

4. THE GREATER EAST ASIA CO-PROSPERITY SPHERE

Throughout the war period, broadcasts concerning the Greater East Asia Co-Prosperity Sphere contained two principal themes, those of Asian liberation from colonial oppressors, and the advances made in the development of each country's economy. Following the outbreak of war, Japanese-controlled stations throughout Asia encouraged anti-British feeling, in particular. Britain was described as the "greatest influence and power in the Far East" after Japan, supported by "Chiang Kai-shek's 'running-dog' regime and the 'softened up' Netherlands East Indies."[213] America on the other hand was told that the Pacific was large enough that, "if both sides [Japan and America] keep to their own business . . . peace in the Pacific is not difficult to maintain."[214]

The Japanese capture of Singapore, long described as Britain's impenetrable fortress, in February 1942 was celebrated widely by Japanese overseas radio. Victory broadcasts were made to all regions, such as one to Europe, which declared "the people of Asia today rise in a chorus of thanksgiving on this, the attaining of a freedom so long denied them."[215]

The prospect of achieving independence with help from Japan was an important propaganda theme used towards the countries of Asia. As early as January 1942, Prime Minister Tōjō was reported as having said that Japan would encourage Philippine and Burmese independence in return for their co-operation within the Greater East Asia Co-Prosperity Sphere.[216] This contrasted with the poor prospects for Philippine independence under the United States portrayed by Radio Tokyo. "The hope of Philippine independence," it declared in December 1941, "is far away," as "the US, despite its promise of independence, is 'utterly ignoring the sincere desire of the Philippines.'"[217]

When the Japanese entered Burma, in May 1942, Radio Tokyo reported "Burmans joyfully welcome Japanese in Mandalay."[218] On 1 August 1943 Burma was declared 'independent' under Ba Maw and Japanese radio broadcasts to all regions included celebrations and congratulations for the new state. On 14 October the same year the Philippines, too, became an 'independent' state, led by José Laurel. For both countries the nominal independence from Japan was accompanied by formal assurances that they would retain complete political, economic and military involvement in the Greater East Asia Co-Prosperity Sphere. In radio broadcasts the moves to independence were portrayed as gallant actions by the Japanese. In a radio speech in November 1943, Laurel expressed his country's gratitude to the Japanese, and urged other Asian countries "to fight Western imperialism and emancipate themselves."[219]

In 1945 it was Indonesia which was promised independence. A broadcast in July reported that the Sumatran Council had drafted a Declaration of Independence and made provision for the establishment of a League of Freedom and the raising of a native army.[220] Broadcasters in Radio Batavia even refused to relay the Emperor's speech which explained the surrender of Japan on 15 August, as they feared that the surrender would jeopardise the promised independence of Indonesia.

An important target for broadcasts which urged national independence was India. Broadcasts from Tokyo to India began in March 1942 at the time of the Cripps Mission and the heightening of the Civil Disobedience campaign led by Gandhi. The arrival of Subhas Chandra Bose in Japan in June 1943 precipitated a huge increase in the number of broadcasts to the subcontinent. Bose was an eloquent speaker who used radio to deliver his message to Indians, both within India and in the rest of Asia, and to the rest of the world. Under his leadership the Provisional Government of Free India, which was established on 21 October 1943, was given daily airtime in the schedules of the Singapore station to broadcast directly to India. In addition, the IIL, also led by Bose, broadcast daily from the Rangoon station, and in March 1944, Rash Bihari Bose leader of the IIL in Japan, began 'Free India' broadcasts from Tokyo. These were in addition to the regular broadcasts made by Radio Tokyo and other East Asian stations, particularly Batavia, which broadcast to India.

The themes of the broadcasts did not vary much throughout the war. Abdul Wahid in Batavia frequently urged Indian Moslems to accept the leadership of Gandhi, and urged the Moslem League to unite with the Congress Party in order to achieve independence. In his first broadcast his appeal was that settlement of the Pakistan issue should be left until after independence was achieved: "Why do they [Indian Moslems] want to divide India? . . . Join hands with Hindus now and you can settle your differences later."[221] This remained the main theme of broadcasts from Batavia to India.

Speeches made by Bose from both Singapore and Tokyo continually promoted independence. Even towards the end of the war he remained confident of Japan's ultimate victory and when a Japanese victory seemed too remote a possibility, he continued his broadcasts from Singapore, declaring,

> *If India has not emerged as an independent State by the end of the war, our next plan should be a post-war revolution inside India. If we fail in that too, World War No. 3 [sic] will give us another opportunity to strike for our freedom.*[222]

Even after Japan's surrender Bose's tone remained defiant. His final message read over the Singapore station was, "The roads to Delhi are many, and Delhi still remains our goal."[223]

The second principal strand of propaganda relating to Greater East Asia concerned the reconstruction and development of the economies of the Co-Prosperity Sphere countries under Japanese administration. In part, this was in order to impress upon both Japan's allies and enemies that there had been minimal disruption to normal life as a result of the Japanese occupation. A report in April 1942 that horse-racing meetings had been recommenced in Hong Kong[224] was typical of this type of broadcast. Broadcasts also sought to show that the former Western colonies had become increasingly productive once the inhabitants began to work for themselves (the Co-Prosperity Sphere) rather than their imperial master. As the war continued, however, and shortages became widespread, the broadcasts were also to convey the image that the Co-Prosperity Sphere was not suffering through shortages. In so doing Japan sought to intimidate her enemies by implying that her capacity to wage war had not diminished.

A regular theme of the broadcasts seeking to reassure listeners that all was well in the Co-Prosperity Sphere was that of food production. In June 1942 it was reported that normal rice production had been resumed in Java[225] and the following year, a 300% increase in the Manchurian grain harvest was reported.[226] Even at the end of the war reports regarding food production continued to be monitored. At the end of July 1945, Radio Tokyo reported "Yams and potatoes are to be grown in bombed areas of Tokyo. Osaka and Nagoya will follow."[227] The early broadcasts sought to indicate that life had largely returned to normal in the occupied territories, or to imply that Japanese production methods were superior to the enemy's. However, the later reports were broadcast to convince the enemy that Japan was not suffering from food shortages, and could continue the war for the foreseeable future. Perhaps the reporting of vegetable plots in bombed out areas was also intended to show Japanese resourcefulness in the face of adversity.

A similar pattern existed in the reporting of Japanese development of the natural resources of Greater East Asia. A typical commentary in November 1942 informed Australians of the wealth of natural resources, including silver, copper, lead, zinc, tin, cobalt, oil and virtually fat free beef now available in Burma. This was said to ensure that "the natural resources of East Asia [would] revert to East Asians for fostering this war effort."[228]

Besides reporting the restoration of normal economic life and the development of the known natural resources of East Asia, Japanese broadcasts were also keen to present the listener with the impression that Japanese technology was more advanced than that of the Allies. Hence there were numerous reports which described both scientific advances and the resourcefulness of the Japanese. These included claims of a new Japanese synthetic fibre which was more durable than cotton and more moisture resistant than wool,[229] and the development of pineapple leaf fibres for making fishing nets, ropes and bicycle tyres.[230]

As the war progressed and the number of shortages increased, frequent claims of new Japanese inventions were made in order to suggest that Japan's capacity for war had not diminished. In a single week in January 1944, there were reports of new techniques which allowed for the construction of wooden aeroplane parts,[231] a new anti-freeze to protect soldiers hands when they were working in sub-zero temperatures,[232] the development of non-flammable rubber,[233] and a new method of extracting salt from sea water.[234]

Besides technical developments, there were also claims of medical advances in the latter part of the war. Radio Tokyo reported in August 1943 that Japanese scientists had developed "a 100% cure for tuberculosis . . . [and] . . . a 100% cure for morphine poisoning."[235] The following month a commentary by Radio Tokyo detailed the success with which the Japanese had dealt with outbreaks of cholera in China. "Japan Beating the Cholera Scourge" claimed "Shanghai is free from cholera for the first time . . . [and following] . . . anti-cholera inoculations in Peiping . . . there have been less than 1,000 deaths."[236]

A further theme in broadcasts during the early part of the war, was that of the acceptance of Japanese ideas by the countries of Greater East Asia. Reports about the enthusiastic co-operation of citizens in reconstruction were made regularly, although it is impossible to ascertain from the broadcasts whether such co-operation was through desire to assist the Japanese, or a simple wish to return life to normal. Occasionally, however, there were intimations by Japanese radio stations that the native populations openly welcomed the new administration. In 1942, Radio Tokyo reported "the Philippines are grateful to the Japanese . . . [and] . . . people are adopting Japanese surnames."[237] The following year, it was reported that the people of Burma "usually celebrate New Year on 3 April but have decided to celebrate on 1 January with Japan as of this year."[238] It was not stated that this had been something the Burmese had wished to do under British occupation. However, presumably it was hoped that the listener would reach the conclusion that native co-operation in Burma was much freer than it had been under the British, a sign that life was better in the Greater East Asian Co-Prosperity Sphere.

5. PORTRAYING THE ENEMY

5.1 Britain and America

Even before the outbreak of war in the Pacific the Japanese authorities developed plans for Radio Tokyo's portrayal of the 'enemy.' The anti-British campaign began within Japan over the death of a Japanese Maritime Customs Inspector in the British concession in Tientsin in April 1941. In December 1941 this campaign spread to broadcasts to South East Asia in order to persuade the local populations of the benefits of their countries' incorporation into the Greater East Asia Co-Prosperity Sphere.

Immediately before the outbreak of war, and in later commentaries, it was the Allies, particularly the United States, which were blamed for the conflict. The American and British governments were accused of unprovoked aggression against Japan, excluding her from her rights and denying her

> *. . . the right to support a regime whose sole objective is to bring the joys of a civilized life, a Christian life, as it is called in the West, to a people long persecuted by brilliant and profiteering racketeers.*[239]

Radio Tokyo broadcasts were eager to denounce American actions. In August 1943, Radio Tokyo aired a commentary regarding the United States entitled, "A Nation Without Scruple." It reported, "Mrs. Roosevelt has revealed Stalin told Hull that all American casualties amounted to what Russia suffered before breakfast." Like the Japanese accusations against the British, this report continued, "This shows

Americans let others fight for them . . . [it has] a lot of praise for Russia but nothing else." It concluded on the note, "if it can't use foreigners to fight it will use the downtrodden American minorities."[240]

The lower social status of blacks in America was a further theme in Japanese radio propaganda. In January 1942, Radio Tokyo reported that America had decided to form a "negro corps officered by whites" which would "be rapidly drafted into the Service to be used as shields to save the lives of white Americans."[241] American calls for an end to racism were said to be of no significance. They were, according to Radio Tokyo, only to ensure that blacks could be used in the war effort.[242] A later commentary from Radio Batavia noted that although blacks were now doing the same work as whites, white disdain towards them remained. Discrimination against blacks in the United States meant that there was segregation in public buildings, and legislation to prevent inter-racial marriage. This, it continued with sarcasm, rendered blacks an 'untouchable' class in the very country that claimed to be fighting for democracy.[243] Of course, many of these accusations were true.

5.2 Australia

An important aim of Japanese propaganda early in the Pacific War was to split Australia from the Allied cause. Australian listeners were reminded that geographically Australia was closest to Asia, and her "logical place [was] within the Co-Prosperity Sphere." (Meo, 1968:103) Britain was reported to be interested in Australia solely as a source of front-line troops. In December 1941 Radio Tokyo cited evidence from captured Australian soldiers that Britain used Australian troops in the Malayan campaign, while "British home forces were 'engaged in the rear.'"[244] In a broadcast to Australian troops Radio Tokyo appealed, "Go back to your peaceful homes in Australia and forget war!"[245] This theme was repeated in broadcasts regarding Malaya, Singapore and India. Over the battle for Singapore Radio Tokyo declared,

> *The British Government confirms the English habit of fighting with the blood of others. Perhaps it is even proud of its intelligence in exploiting its own colonial peoples. Our compliments!*[246]

Australia was considered such an important propaganda target that the Japanese took unusual steps to try to ensure that Australians were exposed to Japanese propaganda. In June 1942, Radio Batavia began broadcasting letters from Australian and New Zealand prisoners, in the "Australian Home News Hour," to attract Australians to listen in to the station. Generally the letters described camp life and reassured the addressee (usually a close relative) that the prisoner was healthy and grateful to the Japanese for their good treatment. Often the letters also included the names of other prisoners in the camp, and asked the addressee of the letter to contact their relatives to reassure them that the prisoners were well. Such was the concern of the Australian government, that in January 1943 it formed a body responsible for making a written copy of the letters and sending them to relatives addresses, thus negating the need of the Australian public to listen to the broadcasts.

5.3 Allied Atrocities

Accusations of atrocities committed by Britain and America were a regular theme in Japanese overseas radio propaganda after the outbreak of war in the Pacific. In December 1941 it was decided that it was important for Radio Tokyo to expose the British and American atrocities against Chinese in Hong Kong and Mindanao respectively. A series of talks was broadcast, beginning with "The Slaughter of Chinese At Mindanao - The Responsibility of the United States-Philippine Army," which accused American troops of carrying out a slaughter of Chinese women and children on Mindanao. (Kitayama, 1988b:57)

The inhumanity of Allied bombing raids was a frequent theme in Japanese atrocity broadcasts, and the bombing of hospital ships was a regular accusation throughout the war. In January 1942 a commentary stated,

> *Japanese submarines sank a Lexington-type aircraft carrier, but American submarines sank a hospital ship. . . . America does not know the words 'justice' and 'humanity.'*[247]

This theme continued to appear throughout the war. A commentary in 1944 explained "The American Way and the Japanese Way:"

> *When Japan sunk the Prince of Wales and the Repulse it allowed a rescue ship to reach the sailors, when it could have sunk it. . . . This was not an isolated incident. . . . America attacks hospital ships.*[248]

Cruelty, Radio Tokyo concluded, was hereditary in the West, and although "the Anglo-Saxons always favour propaganda alleging inhuman acts, . . . American crime statistics show that they are hardly ever committed by Japanese."[249]

The Doolittle raid over Tokyo, Osaka, Nagoya and Kobe of April 1942 was similarly denounced as an inhuman raid, which targeted hospitals, schools and temples.

Broadcasts stated:

> *School children were machine-gunned by the American raid and thirty innocent little children were wounded. . . . There was no damage to military installations and the only effect of the raid was to increase the patriotism of the people.*[250]

This patriotism was described a few days latter when Radio Tokyo reported, "School boy dies in the American raid on Tokyo. His school-fellows have sworn to avenge themselves for his death."[251] In October 1942, when the pilots, captured after the raid, were tried, Radio Tokyo assured listeners that the pilots, who had ignored the "principles of humanity" would be severely punished.[252]

In addition, Radio Tokyo was critical of the Allies' "indiscriminate bombing" of the European Axis powers. Professor Simoi, who was described as having lived in Italy and still having relatives in Rome, stated that there was a "Japanese sense of affliction" regarding the raids on Rome in July 1943 and declared, "Unprecedented hate must rise from Rome's ruins."[253] The Vatican and the Italian government were deemed to be closely connected, as the fascist leaders of Italy were Roman Catholics, so the raids were also described as attacks on Roman Catholicism. Thus, the Catholic Bishop of Malacca was reported to have been indignant and sorrowful over the raids,[254] and the Pope was said to have condemned them and other "terror raids" in Europe.[255]

Japanese-controlled stations also accused the Allies of mistreatment of Japanese prisoners and civilians. Accusations of British mistreatment of Japanese civilians appeared in March 1942 when the Japanese army took control of a British hospital in Ipoh:

The British gathered all the Japanese there together during Japanese air-raids and when the planes swooped down they put them directly in the line of machine-gun fire. When Japanese troops arrived the British staff tried to pretend that it had been a mistake, and offered the patients fresh bandages, but the Japanese refused, thinking they were poisoned.[256]

Following the arrival of the first repatriation ships in late 1942, information about the domestic situation in Allied countries was gleaned from the repatriated Japanese and used in propaganda. The initial response was to denounce the internment of Japanese on the West Coast of America. It began in the Autumn of 1942 with a series of talks entitled, "We Reveal American Inhumanity." In addition, a riot in the Manzanar Internment Camp near Los Angeles on 6 December 1942, which caused one death, fuelled the accusations that Japanese were being mistreated in the internment camps. (Kitayama, 1988b:292-3)

A peculiar allegation of Allied cruelty was made in May of 1943, when Major-General Nakao Yahagi, chief of the Army Press Section, accused American troops of using poison gas during their attack on Attu island in the Aleutians. The Chinese had accused the Japanese of making gas attacks in March 1943, but this had been denied by Radio Tokyo: "Washington will not be tricked any more with Chungking's lies of poison gas in Hupeh."[257] It is possible that Yahagi's accusation which was reported on Radio Tokyo, was triggered by this and previous similar Chinese accusations. However, accusations of poison-gas use seem not to appear elsewhere in Allied monitoring reports. It would seem, therefore, that it was not a theme that NHK or the CIB, which controlled the output of NHK, wished to embrace, and it remained the comment of Yahagi only, not the Japanese propaganda machine.

In the latter part of the war, the images of American barbarity portrayed by Radio Tokyo became increasingly repellent. It made accusations of American children playing with the skulls of Japanese soldiers[258] and Roosevelt accepting a bone paper knife.[259]

Accusations of American inhumanity concluded in August 1945 with criticism of the dropping of the Atomic bombs. Radio Batavia cried,

> *Remember the angry British and US protests against their (V1 & V2) . . . indiscriminate bombing. . . How much more indiscriminate is the atomic bomb.*

In the stunned numbness and the chaotic situation following the attacks, however, Radio Tokyo did not use descriptions of the devastation as vividly as it had descriptions of American barbarity a year previously. It is true that news regarding the situation in Hiroshima and Nagasaki was slow to reach the rest of Japan as all communication systems were destroyed in the blasts, and that the worst effects of radiation did not become apparent for months and years afterwards. However, the only definite picture the listener was given of the effects was that, "one cannot distinguish between the men and women killed by fire."[260]

In contrast to its denunciation of Allied atrocities, Japanese overseas radio refuted British and American accusations of Japanese atrocities. In February 1942 Radio Shanghai reported, "the American Red Cross says American prisoners-of-war in the Far East live in excellent conditions."[261] The following month Japanese radio strongly denied British Foreign Secretary

Anthony Eden's accusations of atrocities committed by Japanese in Hong Kong following its surrender. According to Radio Tokyo:

> *In a feeble but desperate effort to conceal the myriad defeats, which the British Forces have suffered in the Pacific, Eden made an effort to make the Japanese look atrociously cruel and degenerate in the conduct of war.*[262]

In order to confirm that Allied prisoners were well-treated by the Japanese, there were regular references made to their condition. In April 1942, Radio Tokyo reported that American troops in the Philippines were "starving and trailing to prisoner-of-war camps" for better conditions.[263] As confirmation of this, the prisoner letters broadcast from Batavia always described life in the Indonesian camps favourably. Many described a prisoner vegetable garden, medical facilities or classes established by the prisoners themselves and encouraged by the Japanese. One by Lieutenant Rohan Rivet was typical in nature:

> *The food is boring but my health is good. . . . We have . . . classes in the camp and I teach French. . . . I have suffered no violence [from the Japanese.]*[264]

In June 1942, it was also reported that all IIL and wounded Filipino prisoners were to be released by the Japanese army to return to their families,[265] as a further demonstration of Japanese good treatment of prisoners.

Assurances of Japanese good treatment of prisoners continued throughout the war, and early in 1944, Japanese radio sought to explain why Allied stations made claims of atrocities against Japan. Amongst the reasons it included, "to make barbarism reciprocal, by establishing the Japanese as an accomplice," "to cover up their government's 'inhuman acts' against Japanese civilian internees," and "to cover up their tracks in preparing some future 'real atrocities' which they have already plotted against Japan."[266]

5.4 Anti-Semitism: A Borrowed Theme?

Throughout the war Radio Tokyo used a propaganda theme which seems to have been borrowed from Japan's Axis ally, Germany, that of anti-Semitism. Despite its importance in Nazi ideology, anti-Semitism was not an important element in Japanese thought and propaganda. The Jewish community in Asia was small and the presence of the imperial powers was a much more significant concern. Hence, within Japan and the Greater East Asia Co-Prosperity Sphere, anti-Semitic slogans did not appear and the national hatred of Jews, which was central to German policy, was absent. Indeed, in his book, *Die Macht Des Radios*, the most significant work in German regarding wartime broadcasting, Willi Boelke notes that even after the Japanese occupation of Shanghai in 1937, emigrant Jews with German passports were welcomed to the city. (Boelke, 1977:432) It was nationality, not race, which was the important factor, and even if these Jews had fled persecution in Germany, their German nationality made them welcome to the Japanese.

Despite this, however, a thread of anti-Semitic propaganda ran through the overseas broadcasts of Japanese-controlled stations throughout the war. As it did not stem from a Japanese policy it must be concluded that it was one of the "stereotypes, clichés and watchwords [borrowed] from the arsenal of National Socialist Propaganda." (Boelke, 1977:439) In January 1942, a commentary declared "When the American people realise they have been duped by the policy of the Jewish element it will be too late." The rest of the commentary derided the American army for having to offer a cash incentive of $500 per Japanese aeroplane destroyed, in order to induce troops to fight,[267] and the Jewish theme was not continued. It would seem therefore that anti-Semitism was no more than a political gesture, something without emotional substance for most Japanese, and so there was no explanation or elaboration.

A particularly peculiar commentary broadcast to India in March 1943 was entitled "What One Jew Did For England." In it Radio Batavia briefly described the life of Trebitch Lincoln, an ethnic Jew who, it claimed, had posed as a Christian priest in Canada, served as a Member of Parliament in Britain, and been tried as a German spy in World War One. It continued that he later posed as an anti-Semite in Germany, a Soviet Bolshevik in China and a Buddhist monk in Burma in his quest for power and influence, as a pseudo-messiah. This, declared Radio Batavia, "is the kind of Jew for whom the English, Australians and Americans are asked to despoil their homes" and continued that the three countries would "do better to take action to improve the lives of their own slum dwellers."[268] As the broadcast was to India, perhaps the aim of this story was to imply that Indians were among the "slum dwellers" who should be considered.

It is interesting that many of the references to Jews were made in broadcasts for India from Batavia. It is possible that this was on account of the situation in Palestine in the early 1940s. Under the British mandate administration, Jews had been migrating to Palestine in the 1920s and 30s, and this had led to the Arab revolt (1936-9). A report issued by the Peel Commission in 1937 had advocated the partition of Palestine into separate Jewish and Arab states, although this had not been carried out before the outbreak of war in 1939. At the end of 1942, a Radio Batavia commentary stated that Britain was likely to agree to sending more refugee European Jews to Palestine, which would "oust the Arabs."[269] In one commentary Abdul Wahid declared that Britain always favoured Jews, who were the cause of the present Arab problems.[270] It is possible, therefore, that Japanese propaganda regarding Jews was used not to cause fear and hatred of Jews in the same way that German propaganda intended, but because it was felt that Indians could relate to the experiences of Arabs. Both were ruled by Britain, and Japanese-controlled stations suggested that Arabs already resident in Palestine were being out-numbered by immigrant Jews with the encouragement of Britain. Perhaps the implication was not that "Jews are Evil," but that rather, if Britain could dictate changes to countries under its administration, against the wishes of the local populace, "What Will Britain Inflict on India in the Future?" In addition, there was a significant Moslem community in India, which naturally opposed Britain's policy in the Middle East. The Radio Battle for India was intense, so it is plausible that propaganda about Jews would be used, along with other more common themes, to persuade Indians that India would do better to join Japan in order to evict the British.

In Japanese anti-Semitic propaganda, Jews were equated with capitalism. A broadcast from Singapore to Australia urged, "'Australia for Australians!' should be your cry, not 'Australia for the Shylocks of New York and the City of London.'" (Meo, 1968:102-3) Anti-Semitism was a concept borrowed from Nazi Germany without genuine belief. Its equation with capitalism in the mind of the Japanese propagandists rendered useful an otherwise less than useful theme, which could be inserted into broadcasts from time to time, to make them more memorable. This kind of borrowing gave the impression of close Axis collaboration over propaganda. Boelke's conclusion, however, that, "In reality, . . . each partner made its own propaganda [and] borrowed the propaganda expressions of the other when they crossed their path" (Boelke, 1977:439-40) seems to be borne out. Hence, anti-Semitism was a theme which could be added to existing anti-capitalist propaganda for emphasis, but it had very little meaning.

The propaganda themes traceable in Japanese overseas radio propaganda are many and varied. In her book, *Japan's Radio War on Australia*, L.D. Meo identifies seven general themes[271] used in broadcasts to Australia, which she discusses in some detail. In a wider survey of this nature, it is not possible to investigate all the propaganda of all the Japanese overseas radio stations in great detail. However, there were general themes, which were common to most transmission regions and time periods. These themes seem readily distinguishable in a survey of available material, and provide a clear insight into the aims of Japanese radio broadcasts and the mode of thought of Japanese propagandists throughout the war.

CHAPTER 8
HOW EFFECTIVE WAS JAPANESE WARTIME SHORT-WAVE PROPAGANDA?

1. PROPAGANDA ANALYSIS

Definitions of propaganda vary. However, certain essential elements remain: that propaganda is an attempt by one party to influence or manipulate another party into thinking and behaving as the first party wishes.

In order for a propaganda campaign to be deemed successful there are several considerations which need to be taken into account. Firstly, the target audience must be in a position to receive the message, so the appropriate means of communication must be selected. Secondly, successful propaganda is related to the prevailing mood of the time and to the beliefs, values and personalities of the audience as "messages have greater impact when they are in line with existing opinions, beliefs, and dispositions." (Jowett & O'Donnell, 1986:163) Different people react in different ways to propaganda messages depending on how the messages are perceived to link with what readers or listeners already know.

Hence a recognised and prestigious expert is considered more credible than an unknown voice, because the audience already has a perception of the person from previous experience. (Hoyland & Weiss, 1954:337-47) In addition, the use of symbols, both visual (such as flags) and verbal (such as the as the use of language associated with authority figures like parents, teachers, heroes or gods) can create a sense of authority with which to impress the target audience. (Jowett & O'Donnell, 1986:166-7)

The success of a propaganda campaign must finally, however, be measured by whether the changes desired by the propagandist can be perceived in changes in behaviour in the target audience over the time period allocated by the campaign organiser. In an advertising campaign, which is the form of propaganda cited most frequently by modern studies, the rate of success is assessed by market research questionnaires, opinion surveys, and in the sales figures of the product. However, such data is rarely available to the historian, particularly the historian assessing wartime propaganda campaigns.

In war, few of the pre-requisites for a successful campaign exist. An enemy source, if it is disclosed, immediately creates suspicion in the minds of a target enemy audience, and it is unlikely to be wholly appeased by the voice of a famous or prestigious person. In addition, the situation of war often increases the general patriotism of the belligerent peoples, rendering enemy propaganda less likely to relate to the beliefs and values held by the general target audience. As a consequence, changes in behaviour may occur in a significantly smaller percentage of the audience than under normal circumstances, rendering it harder to detect. This difficulty in detection is increased as material is often destroyed or concealed by participants in a war. Many fear their change in thinking may be discovered and punished by their own side. At the end of the war, the defeated side may try to prevent war crimes trials occurring by destroying evidence.

Naturally, there are exceptions to this. Many of these difficulties do not occur when the target is an audience in a neutral country, which is not necessarily hostile and so may perceive the propaganda message more openly. Colonial subjects, too, may perceive a propaganda campaign differently, as a message which does not relate to the beliefs of the belligerent, may still appeal to the colonial subjects of that country. Acceptance of the message, though, may still have to remain concealed from the colonial ruler. In these cases the task of the propagandist may be generally easier because the conditions may make the message more acceptable.

Despite these difficulties, analysis of wartime propaganda is not impossible. The range of analysis may have to be limited in nature, depending on the material available, but certainly general conclusions may be drawn, and for certain well-documented campaigns a more detailed analysis may be made. This chapter deals with specific campaigns made by Japanese short-wave radio, for which material regarding the audience response exists, such as the "Tokyo Rose" broadcasts and those made by prisoners. It also draws, in a more general way, on the responses to Japanese campaigns made by Allied propagandists, in order to infer the effects Japanese overseas radio was perceived as having at the time.

2. BROADCASTS TO AUSTRALIA

Letters written by prisoners were read out over Japanese-controlled radio stations from early in the Pacific War, in order to attract listeners to these stations, particularly in Australia. By February 1942 1,100 prisoner letters had been written for random broadcast from Tokyo, (Kitayama, 1988b:126) in order to ensure that once attracted, the listeners remained tuned in to Radio Tokyo, so as not to miss a letter. In June 1942 the station in Batavia also began broadcasting prisoner letters, along with lists of the names of prisoners in camps in Indonesia. The letters were censored, and were usually similar, largely describing scenes of life in the camp. However, there was enough personal information included in the letters for the listeners at home to assume that they were genuinely written by the named prisoner.

This presented problems for the Australian government, which became increasingly concerned that Australians were, in fact, tuning into Japanese stations in increasing numbers, to hear news of friends and relatives. In November 1942, W. Macmahon Ball, the chairman of the Government's sub-committee on enemy propaganda expressed this growing fear, which was recorded in an appendix to the minutes of the 3 November meeting:

> *It is not possible to estimate with any precision the number of regular listeners . . . but it seems safe to assume that they have won a very wide and interested audience . . . We have had a number of insistent requests . . . for information about the content of these broadcasts, and about times and frequencies . . . We have evidence that in some parts of Australia the relatives of prisoners are listening to a large number of Japanese-controlled sessions in the hope that they may pick up some information about prisoners.*
>
> *Bearing in mind the large number of Australian prisoners in Japanese hands, it seems reasonable to assume that some tens of thousands of Australian listeners are deeply interested in these broadcasts. (op cit. Meo, 1968:166-7)*

In response to this concern, the sub-committee sent a questionnaire to the AIF Women's Association in November 1942, asking for information about the listening habits of the Association's members. Three of the Association's officials attended a sub-committee meeting to present their findings. Their answers indicated there was indeed significant interest in the Japanese broadcasts among their members. The AIF officials admitted that listening was restricted to those who had both short-wave receivers, and the leisure time to listen to the radio for prolonged periods. However, they indicated that as far as they were aware, "everybody that has a short-wave set and leisure does listen in, and communicates with those who cannot listen," and that available figures showed a definite increase in interest. (Meo, 1968:167)

The sub-committee was also interested to know if "unofficial listening bureaux" existed, which listened and passed on messages to the addressees of letters. The Association's findings indicated that the Prisoner-of-War Relatives Association did carry out that service, and that many of the relatives of prisoners relied on others listening in for them, even if there was no specific roster organised. The officials at the meeting cited examples of members who had been contacted by several people following the broadcast of a relative's letter. One, described as Mrs. B., had received a radio letter from her husband from Tokyo. In response "she was telephoned by over sixty people, received letters from twenty-five, including letters from South Australia, New South Wales and Queensland, [and] six people whom she did not know called on her." (Meo, 1968:167-8)

It thus appeared that the Australian government was correct in its suspicions regarding the audience for broadcasts of prisoner letters from Japanese-controlled stations. This heightened its concern over the reactions of listeners to Japanese news and information. Most authorities assumed that listeners would subscribe to the view that "the Japanese wouldn't say all these things if there weren't some truth in them." (Meo, 1968:168)

The idea that the Australian government sought to refute most clearly, was that there would not be any damage to Australia resulting from a Japanese victory. Australian official sources emphasised, both on the radio and in the press, the ill treatment of prisoners by Japanese, and atrocities committed by the Japanese in their exploitation of occupied territories. (Meo, 1968:169) In addition, in January 1943, the jamming of enemy short-wave broadcasts was considered, but the idea was dropped under technical advice that it would be impracticable.

The problem of growing listener numbers to the Japanese broadcasts remained, however. In January 1943, the sub-committee on enemy propaganda received a service recommendation that the text of the letters should not be disclosed to the addressee, but that they should be merely informed that Radio Batavia claimed their relative was a prisoner. The sub-committee wholly rejected this recommendation, concluding that this would foster short-wave listening rather than curb it. In his rejection of the proposal, W. Macmahon Ball added, "It is idle to suppose that a wife or mother to whom a prisoner's letter is broadcast will be satisfied with anything but the full text of the letter." Instead, he proposed "if the relative knows that the full text is recorded under the best technical conditions, and that it will be sent on without delay, this will remove the biggest incentive to direct listening." (Meo, 1968:170)

This formed the basis of the sub-committee's counter proposal - that after verification of the prisoner's name and any others mentioned in the letter, the full text of the letter be sent to the addressee without delay. This change in policy was accompanied by official announcements in the press, so that people would realise there was no longer any need to listen in.

Meo claims that there is "little or no evidence upon which to base an opinion as to long-term effects of Japanese propaganda, or even short-term effects." (Meo, 1968:171) The lack of evidence of further fears over Australians listening to Japanese broadcasts after 1943 seems to imply that, as far as the Australian government was concerned, the danger had subsided. It is probable that most people returned to their usual favourite stations, and as the war situation for Japan worsened, and Japanese claims conflicted so clearly with Allied claims, even those who remained listeners believed less and less in the Japanese version of events. Indeed, as the situation in the South Pacific continued to deteriorate, Radio Batavia stopped broadcasting prisoner messages, as the prisoners in Indonesia were moved to camps further north.

However, the reaction of the Australian government to the prisoner broadcasts of the Japanese is an indication of their effectiveness. The Japanese were not alone in broadcasting prisoner names and letters, clearly identifying the addressee and the sender, in order to personalise their message. German stations listed names of war prisoners in order to draw enemy listeners to German radio programmes (Doob, 1954:513) and in 1945, during the Allied advance on Berlin, the Allied station, Radio Luxembourg, broadcast a programme for Germans entitled, "Letters Which You Do Not Receive." In it a female presenter read out love letters found on the bodies of dead German soldiers, again clearly identifying the writer and the addressee, in order to lower the morale of the German home front. In the end it was stopped, not because it was considered ineffective, but rather because it was considered to be in bad taste. (Doob, 1948:326) The personalisation of messages in broadcasts was, then, a recognised method of rendering the broadcast acceptable to the enemy audience. The findings of the AIF Women's Association, that those who had both a short-wave receiver and time to listen tuned in regularly to Japanese-controlled stations, confirmed that this was indeed the case in Australia. Hence the concern of the Australian government to ensure that this increasing trend was reversed is understandable. It seems evident, then, that the use of prisoner letters and lists of names was an effective tool in drawing Australian listeners to Japanese stations. Not only does the statistical work carried out at the time confirm that the number of listeners was high, but the concern of the government to find a means of preventing listening indicates clearly that the method was an effective propaganda tool.

3. THE RADIO BATTLE FOR INDIA

One of the major propaganda battles of the Pacific War was the one between Japan and Britain over India. The Japanese radio attack began from Tokyo in December 1941.

From the outbreak of war in the Pacific in December 1941 and throughout 1942, when the political situation in India seemed particularly critical for the British, the propaganda offensive towards India was waged intensely by both sides. Following the heightening of tension in India after the arrest of Gandhi and Nehru by the British authorities in August 1942, Radio Tokyo began a "Propaganda Offensive" on India and Britain. Broadcasting time to India was increased and broadcasts were modified so that the messages could permeate all classes of Indian society. There were two main points in the plan - to recruit more Indians to broadcast on Japanese radio, as NHK did not have available people able to speak all the Indian languages in which it wished to broadcast, and to ensure prompt reporting of disturbances in India, as the British-controlled New

Delhi station had a forty-eight hour delay before reporting such incidents. (Kitayama, 1988b:202) The offensive was spearheaded by a series of talks to India, which warned against both Britain and the United States. There were also speeches which portrayed India as part of Asia and rightfully in alliance with Japan, and those which praised the Indian Spirit, much as the Japanese and Asian Spirits were extolled in other overseas broadcasts.

During 1942, there was a real feeling on both the British and Japanese sides that the anti-British disturbances in India would erupt into violence. Indeed, the Japanese saw this as an opportunity to extend the Greater East Asia Co-Prosperity Sphere across the subcontinent. The increase in radio propaganda to India, not only from Tokyo but also from stations in the surrounding Japanese occupied territories, was a natural response to this. If the population of India was, as it seemed, already openly hostile to British rule, the objective of harnessing that hostility and creating a Japanese-backed revolution, did not appear too difficult to achieve.

This revolution did not occur. In a broadcast on 8 July 1942, Gandhi accused Japan of an "unprovoked attack on China" which lay waste "mercilessly to a great and ancient country," (Kitayama, 1988b:200) and declared it unwise for India to be reliant on Japan. Although Radio Tokyo ignored the comments, they made an impact on Indians in India and therefore reduced the perceived credibility of Japanese broadcasts there. The arrival of Subhas Chandra Bose in Singapore and the establishment of the INA and Azad Hind broadcasts may have raised the expectations of some Indians. By this time, however, broadcasts to India appeared only occasionally in the monitoring reports of the BBC, an indication that British concern over the situation in India had diminished. The feeling of impending internal crisis had subsided, and the changing war situation showed the Japanese army not to be the all-powerful force it had in 1941-2. Hence whilst Japanese-backed broadcasts to India continued until the end of the war, the reality of the war situation undermined the credibility of their claims.

Early in the war, however, the British had certainly been extremely concerned about the effect of Axis broadcasting on India. Japan was not the sole source of radio propaganda that Britain perceived as threatening. BBC reports concerning German broadcasting to India were scathing and concluded that the broadcasts only offend most Indian opinion." (*op cit.* West, 1987:290) However, they admitted that,

> *By reason of the excellent reception from German transmitters, the entertainment value of the colourful content of their broadcasts and the pleasure afforded by the comparison of German and British versions of news items, they undoubtedly attract may listeners [in the uneducated classes].*

And they recognised that,

> *German 'Hindustani' announcers are excellent broadcasters. Their delivery is well-timed, and the language employed easily understood . . . They are undoubtedly potentially dangerous. (op. cit. West, 1987:291)*

In 1942, concern over this danger was considerable in the light of Japanese victories in Malaya, Singapore and Burma, which resulted in Japanese troops reaching the Indian border. The growth of the protest movement inside India itself similarly caused concern, for India was extremely important to Britain in terms of prestige, war manpower and raw materials. Both Japan and Germany, then, played significant roles in determining the structure of British broadcasting to India.

In late 1944 and 1945 despite the setbacks of the Indian National and Japanese armies in Burma and the South Pacific, and the surrender of Germany, Subhas Chandra Bose remained confident that Japan would ultimately win the war. Bose believed that the only way India could achieve independence was through armed struggle and "would broadcast from Radio Singapore putting forward his ideas of another armed attack and blaming the Indian National Congress for its 'defeatist attitude.'" (Nair, 1985:261) During June and July 1945, he broadcast almost daily at length on the subject of the Simla Conference, which had been called by the Viceroy, Wavell, for members of Congress and the Moslem League. On the 18th Bose commented that he had "no doubt that acceptance of the offer would seriously jeopardise all chances of securing even self-government"[272] and on 25th he asserted in a broadcast from Singapore,

> *If India has not emerged as an independent State by the end of the war, our next plan should be a post-war revolution inside India. If we fail in that too, then World War no. 3 (sic.) will give us another opportunity to strike for our freedom.*[273]

It would appear that the establishment of BBC broadcasts to counter Axis broadcasts is a measure of the success which Japanese broadcasts to India did achieve. Although early in 1942 it appeared that few of the Indians to whom the broadcasts were aimed owned radio sets, the BBC employed George Orwell to produce cultural programmes for intellectuals in India. It granted him permission to use "impressive processions of literary men and professors such as T.S. Eliot and E. M. Forster", (*op cit.* Crick, 1980:284) in his broadcasts. This is an indication of the importance attached to these BBC broadcasts.

The India Section of the BBC's Eastern Service was established at this time, in order to assuage India Office worries that "the BBC was not doing enough to counteract the propaganda offensive from the Germans." (Sheldon, 1991:371-2)

Orwell was disappointed that the British Government was not doing more to reassure the Indian Congress that independence would be achieved after the war. This is perhaps an indication that very little BBC broadcasting time was spent explaining the British view of the future to India, whilst much of the time was spent countering the claims of the Axis stations. It would appear, therefore, that the BBC's India broadcasts were largely reactions to the broadcasts made by Japan and the other Axis powers.

In the short-term, the Japanese propaganda broadcasts to India did not result in the changes in behaviour the propagandists hoped for within the time-scale the Japanese intended. Thus, according to the definitions of propaganda given above, the campaign must be viewed as a failure.

That is not, however, an entirely accurate view of the situation. The influence of Bose was not hampered noticeably by his association with the Japanese, and his broadcasts reached a large section of the population. After the war British plans for India's dominion status ultimately proved untenable and she became a Republic in 1950.

Whatever the reaction within India to Japanese and Indian nationalist broadcasts, it would appear that their effect on the British government was considerable. Broadcasts by Japan and the other Axis powers caused considerable concern in Britain, and resulted in the British establishing BBC broadcasting to India which seemed constantly to react to these broadcasts, and not to lead in a "radio offensive." This was, naturally, not the primary aim of the Japanese propagandists, but it is an indication that the broadcasts were not entirely ineffective, and that the British clearly recognised their potential influence.

4. BROADCASTS TO ENEMY TROOPS

Early in the war, the propaganda team of Section Eight of the General Staff under Major Tsuneishi Shigetsugu, became responsible for producing propaganda to demoralise enemy troops. Apparently convinced that American men thought of little other than women and sex, leaflets were produced for dropping over Allied zones, which showed "bosomy hometown girls languishing in diaphanous nightgowns, pining away for their absent boyfriends - and often succumbing to fleshy temptations with other men." (Duus, 1979:66) As far as the recipients of these leaflets were concerned, they were amusing, but ridiculous.

However, the same team was also responsible for "psychological warfare" by radio and eventually for "Zero Hour." In the early stages of the war, the simple broadcasting of the truth regarding the Japanese victories was enough to make a clear impression on the minds of listeners. Even before the Japanese military situation began to deteriorate, however, there were problems with the perceived effectiveness of these broadcasts. Initially, Tsuneishi and his staff had little concept of the difference between domestic and overseas propaganda. Under pressure from extremist elements in the government, which insisted that the broadcasts contain the same concepts of "mystical nationalism" promoted in domestic programmes, broadcasts included references to the "holy war" being fought by the "sacred soldiers of Japan." Indeed, Tsuneishi and his team even considered assembling a group of actors who would recite Shinto prayers on the overseas transmission. (Duus,

1979:66) This displayed a remarkable lack of understanding regarding both the enemy audience, and the techniques necessary to wage a successful propaganda campaign.

A further problem confronted by this team was that there were few native English speakers to write scripts. Many of the news items broadcast, had first to be translated into Japanese to be compiled into news and commentary scripts, as they came from Dōmei, the Army and Navy Information Bureaux, the Foreign Ministry, the German DNB News Agency, and Italy's Stefani News Service. After this the scripts were passed on for translation into the language for broadcast. Hence, the version for broadcast was often very different from the original. In addition, the lack of fluent English writers resulted in many "howlers" being noted by enemy monitors. A report in Autumn 1943 said, "With the exception of one dead, all on the exchange ship were in the best of spirits." Even in the Summer of 1944, reports stated that "The confounded enemy at Chittagong is awaiting the arrival of reinforcements." (Meo, 1968:265) Futhermore, there were equally few fluent English speakers to present the programmes, and many of the announcers were untrained in presentation. Hence, problems over pronunciation also occurred regularly, and Australian monitors noted "imitation" being read for "intimidation," defied" for "deified," and even "slumbering" for "submarine." It is little wonder that "most Allied soldiers regarded the wartime Japanese news broadcasts as a big joke." (Duus, 1979:68-7) It was under these conditions that it was decided to recruit Allied prisoners-of-war with experience in broadcasting to produce a better quality of programme for the enemy soldiers.

In 1942, Charles Cousens, Wallace Ince and Norman Reyes, who had been captured in Singapore and Corregidor were brought to work on Japanese broadcasts. Although at first the prisoners merely corrected the grammar and syntax of Japanese-prepared scripts, the huge numbers of mistakes prompted them to suggest that they write the scripts, and they were allowed to do this. In 1943, new technology allowed the Japanese army to monitor American medium-wave transmissions, so listening-posts could detect news of local disasters. As a result of these two developments, plans were made to transmit the programme "Zero Hour." It began on 1 March 1943, and its aim was to make American troops in the South Pacific homesick and demoralised. Tsuneishi's team hoped that the insertion of accurate, but bad, news from home, which the troops were unlikely to hear from other sources, would discourage them, and lower their morale. However, the light entertainment and jazz slots, which were interspersed with news, were intended to encourage listening. In addition, the timing of the programme was carefully planned, so that it would come on air as the troops were relaxing after their evening meal. (Duus, 1979:77)

The new programme format was highly successful and quickly generated a following among the American troops in the South Pacific. Only four months after it had begun the *New York Times* quoted an American news report from Guadalcanal that, "Tokyo has been beaming a program called 'the Zero Hour' direct to the Russell Islands and Guadalcanal. The fellows like it very much . . ." (*op cit.* Duus, 1979:77)

The three prisoners-of-war involved in the broadcast were in a position to try to sabotage the Japanese material. Their aim was that as a cheerful entertainment programme, "Zero Hour," would boost the morale of its listeners, rather than lower it. Hence, when plans for expansion were discussed in November 1943, and it was decided to include increasing amounts of demoralising propaganda, Cousens persuaded the staff to allow him to choose the new announcer. In his testimony on 15 August 1949 he said he chose Iva Toguri,

> *With the idea that I had in mind of making a complete burlesque of the program, [her voice] was just what I wanted - rough, . . . a voice that I have described as a gin fog voice. It was . . . anything but a femininely seductive voice . . . a comedy voice that I needed for this particular job. (Duus, 1979:80-1)*

The voice and patter of "Orphan Ann" was very distinctive when compared with the voices of Radio Tokyo's other female presenters, and the popularity of "Zero Hour" among the American troops in the South Pacific increased further. (Duus, 1979:81) The seeming success of "Zero Hour" gave rise to other programmes written and performed by the Allied prisoners at *Bunka* Camp, such as "*Hi no Maru* Hour," later "Humanity Calls," and "Postman Calls."

After the war, Iva Toguri gave an interview to two reporters, Clark Lee and Harry Bunbridge, from *Cosmopolitan* magazine. She signed their contract for an exclusive interview which stated that she was the only "Tokyo Rose." In return she was promised $2,000 plus any money which might arise from other publications or from film rights. (Duus, 1979:22-3)

Despite declaring, "There is no Tokyo Rose; the name is strictly a GI invention," (Howe, 1990:65) the United States Government pursued her after the end of the war in a witch-hunt for "Tokyo Rose." The vigour with which it did so would suggest that the Japanese radio propaganda campaign had been highly successful in demoralising American troops. The trial cost the government over half-a-million dollars (Duus, 1979:1) and Iva Toguri spent over six years in prison and a further twenty years as a stateless person. She was finally released in January 1956, and was pardoned in 1976, re-gaining her American citizenship. (Duus, 1979:225-33)

The evidence, however, does not seem to support the supposition that the campaign was successful. Such was the popularity of the "Zero Hour" programme with the troops, that after Iva had claimed to be "Tokyo Rose," even her official questioning by the Eighth Army Counter-Intelligence Corps (CIC) was disrupted by "an endless stream of [American] soldiers and officers of all ranks" who "began to parade in and out of the room asking for Iva's autograph." (Duus, 1979:30) In fact, the interrogation was even interrupted by Lieutenant General Robert Eichelberger, commander of the Eighth Army, who called Iva to his office in order to meet her and have a souvenir photograph taken with her. In fact, during the war Eichelberger had ordered a B-29 bomber to drop a package of the latest hit records addressed to Tokyo Rose, in a bombing run over Tokyo. Iva Toguri knew nothing of this, but it is an indication of the popularity of the broadcasts. (Duus, 1979:30)

"Zero Hour" producer, Oki Kenichi, envied Iva's celebrity status as his wife had also been a presenter on Radio Tokyo. According to the trial testamony of Filipe d'Aquino, Iva's husband, Oki said to him at a press conference for all the Allied correspondents on 4 September 1945, "I should have told them my wife's name instead of yours." (*op cit.* Duus, 1979:29) This celebrity status would not commonly be expected for a messenger delivering enemy propaganda. The "Zero Hour" programmes did, in fact, seem to have the opposite effect from what was intended, and generally their value as entertainment for bored and war-weary soldiers was considerable. They seemed, then, to have played a role in keeping the morale of these soldiers up, rather than lowering it. It would appear that the prisoners' greater experience in broadcasting to westerners, particularly that of Cousens, ensured that they controlled the output of the programme with considerable success.

To denounce "Zero Hour" as a complete propaganda failure by the Japanese would, however, be somewhat unfair. In terms of our definition of propaganda effectiveness, that is a correct verdict. However, it became one of the few Japanese overseas radio broadcasts which succeeded in appealing widely to its target audience. Even before the outbreak of war, few outside the Japanese community listened to NHK's broadcasts to North America. In Europe, Japan's radio agreements with Germany and Italy allowed for the relay of regular exchange broadcasts on the domestic networks, but there is little to suggest that the broadcasts were particularly popular. In addition, according to the monitors' notes in the BBC's *Summary of World Broadcasts,* Japan's European transmissions often seemed plagued by a lack of power, and sections were often inaudible. The prisoner letters were a popular enticement to Australians, but they were less a shaped programme than insertions between news reports.

"Zero Hour" was, then, the first Japanese overseas programme that was truly popular amongst its target audience, because it succeeded as an American-style programme. Since the start of overseas broadcasting in 1935, Japanese programme producers had frequently realised that the type of programme needed for western listeners differed enormously from the programmes which featured in the domestic schedules, and several efforts had been made to increase the amount of jazz music broadcast. In "Zero Hour," Radio Tokyo finally seemed to have achieved success in this respect, creating a programme which appealed to the American troops it targeted, because it was a programme so like those at home. However, in allowing the prisoners the freedom to create the kind of programme which appealed so completely, the Japanese also allowed them to dilute much of the propaganda element of the programme. In the end "Zero

Hour," despite its achievements, failed in precisely that task it was established to perform.

5. HOW EFFECTIVE WAS JAPANESE WARTIME OVERSEAS RADIO PROPAGANDA?

Radio propaganda was considered of the utmost importance by all the belligerent nations during World War Two. As the scope of warfare differed from previous wars, and exposed millions of civilians to unprecedented bombings, so the battle for the civilian mind became as important as the one for that of the combatant. Japan was no exception in developing overseas radio for propaganda use. In fact, as Japan had been involved in an undeclared war in China since 1937, the role of radio in the battle to win the minds of those involved in the war, and in justifying the Japanese position to non-belligerents, had been developing prior to the start of World War Two.

Before the outbreak of the Pacific War in 1941, some forms of propaganda towards Asia seemed to meet with success. The leaders of the Burmese independence movement turned to Japan for assistance in overthrowing British rule, in exactly the manner that the Japanese and INA broadcasters appealed for Indians to do in 1942. Like IIL leaders, Aung San and Hla Myaing (Yan Aung) travelled to Japan. In 1940, they met Japanese army representatives, and the following year established the Burma Independence Army (BIA) which entered Burma alongside the Japanese in December 1941. This was described as "an occasion of great pride and joy to the Burmese, who felt that at last their national honour had been vindicated." (Aung, 1991:16) However, this cannot be attributed to radio propaganda. The desire for freedom from British rule was well established before the independence movement turned to Japan for assistance, and there was a clear division amongst its members, even after Aung San had visited Japan, over co-operation with the Japanese. In fact even Aung San was not overly enamoured of the Japanese, admiring the "patriotism, cleanliness and self-denial of the Japanese people," but disliking the "'barbarity' of some of their militarist views" and finding "their attitude towards women" shocking. (*op cit.* Aung, 1991:14)

Aung San's was a pragmatic view: that the independence movement should accept help from wherever it was offered, and monitor the situation as it developed. Aung San's turning towards Japan, was not, therefore, the result of a radio propaganda campaign by the Japanese, but the result of the perceived growing strength of Japan in Asia. However, a propaganda campaign is rarely conducted through a single medium in isolation. The radio broadcasts of Japan must have contributed to the development this perception of Japan as an Asian ally with sufficient power to overthrow Britain, but it was accompanied by newspaper and eyewitness reports from China, and the position of Japan in world politics.

In Japanese occupied Indonesia where the dissemination rate of radio sets was only 0.15% even following a drive to re-distribute captured sets formerly owed by Dutch households (Kurasawa, 1988:367) the Japanese erected radio speakers on towers or in treetops to ensure that the radio message was heard by the population at large. This is an indication of the importance attached to radio propaganda, not only in influencing the future actions of a nation, but also in controlling the actions of the population once occupation by the Japanese had begun. Such radio towers, erected in public places such as markets, railway stations, large streets, parks and squares, had been used successfully within Japan itself in the dissemination of information and opinions. They were also widely used in Asia where literacy rates were low. In Indonesia, however the "singing trees" were popular principally for the broadcast of music and frequently,

> *When the Japanese broadcast music in Java, many people would listen, but when propaganda commenced, some walked away, saying: "Nihong-Bohong" (Nippon-Lies). (Kurasawa, 1988:368)*

As only "some walked away," presumably some stayed to listen, but there is little evidence regarding its effect. The Japanese utilised films, plays, traditional Indonesian performing arts, songs and *kamishibai* (picture story shows) as well as radio to carry out their campaign of persuasion in Indonesia. The effect of this assault through all the available media was greatest amongst the uneducated and the younger generation. However, the Japanese faced considerable language problems in Indonesia, as most people spoke local dialects rather than Bahasa Indonesia. It may be assumed, therefore, that the radio campaign, which relied solely on language, was less effective than other media, which were more visual. (Kurasawa, 1988:376-8)

Broadcasts to Latin America were generally dominated by condemnation of United States' actions and attitudes. These were intended to dissuade the countries of South America from following the United States into declaring war on Japan. Each Latin American declaration of war was treated with pseudo-sympathy, and blamed not on that country, but on United States' pressure. Hence declarations of war by Brazil and Uruguay were described in August 1942 as being made "through economic necessity."[274] Argentina was held up as an example to the rest of South America for "remaining strictly neutral despite American bribes"[275] whilst the other countries of Latin America were warned of American economic imperialism.[276] In the short-term these propaganda themes would seem to have had little general effect, despite the large Japanese communities, in Brazil in particular. Within weeks of Pearl Harbor all the countries of South America except for Argentina and Chile broke off relations with Japan. However, it is probable that one effect of the stream of Japanese propaganda to South America was to heighten United States' fears regarding the position of South American countries. A possible result of this was to stimulate United States' economic aid to the region in order to prevent its alignment with Japan. If this were the case, the propaganda would seem to have had a greater effect on the United States than on its target audience.

The effect of Japanese radio propaganda on the main Allied powers is somewhat easier to analyse, as data collected by them remains in a more complete state. However, here too, it would be difficult to isolate the propaganda disseminated by radio from other factors. In enemy countries there were, naturally, few other media which Japan could utilise to present her viewpoint in the same way as in the occupied territories. The world situation, however, was seen by listeners to either confirm or deny Japanese claims. In the first six months of the war the enormous Japanese military successes were sufficient in themselves to convince the foreign audience of Japan's military strength. The radio reports made were often exaggerated, but the listener would be impressed as radio propaganda was confirmed by events. The credibility of these broadcasts so concerned the Australian government that its sub-committee on enemy propaganda was charged with finding a way to prevent the public from tuning in. It accepted that listeners were principally concerned with obtaining news about captured relatives and friends, but wished to find a means of reassuring them of their well-being without exposing them to Japanese propaganda. The source of the propaganda was, then, perceived as credible. Concern that the thought processes and behaviour of listeners would be modified under the suggestion of this source was sufficient to warrant a government survey of listening habits, and the establishment of a system of transcribing and sending the prisoners' radio letters to their families.

Later in the war, the situation began to turn against Japan. The continued exaggerated radio claims of Japanese successes became less credible, as the reports made by Japanese radio stations strayed further from what the listener perceived to be the reality of the war situation. In 1942, when the anti-British demonstrations in India were at their peak, the BBC monitoring reports, which were distributed among the relevant departments of the British government, reported Japanese broadcasts to India in considerable detail. However, despite the arrival of Subhas Chandra Bose from Germany in June 1943, and his increased activity to promote Indian independence, later monitoring reports mentioned broadcasts to India less and less frequently. Generally, the full text of a Bose speech or a particularly interesting commentary would appear, but the monitors no longer reported more general news. This would have been at the request of the government which received the reports. Presumably by this time, the British government's concern over the situation in India had lessened. The worst of the demonstrations were over and its fear of impending internal crisis had passed. In addition, the Japanese army had received several setbacks in the Pacific and was perceived as having to fight to maintain its current positions. The possibility of a Japanese invasion of India appeared less likely, so the credibility of the radio propaganda was reduced, resulting in the British government's diminished concern over it.

In order to assess the effectiveness of Japanese radio propaganda during World War Two, it is necessary to return to our definition of a successful propaganda. Firstly, it is necessary for the target audience to be in a position of receiving the message. In radio broadcasts the Japanese utilised the only media which could reach an enemy audience, and they devised methods of rendering Japanese stations appealing, in order to encourage listening. Hence, the light entertainment of "Zero Hour" appealed most to American troops isolated on the islands of the South Pacific, and letters from Allied prisoners-of-war was an effective method of encouraging listeners to tune in from Australia. In Japanese-occupied territories, radio propaganda was employed alongside other forms of propaganda, so that there would be a greater chance that the audience would encounter the message in at least one form. This is the more common method for co-ordinating a propaganda or advertising campaign. It is usual for an advertiser, for example, to promote a product simultaneously through advertisements placed on the television, radio and billboards, in newspapers and magazines, and even through direct mail, or public distribution of samples.

In territories where it was considered the audience for radio broadcasting was too small, such as in Indonesia, methods were devised for public listening, to increase the numbers of people encountering the radio broadcasts. Japan also signed "radio pacts" with her major allies, including Germany, Italy, and Thailand. These allowed for the regular relay of Japanese programmes on the domestic network of these nations, and the relay of their programmes on the Japanese network, ensuring that the audience in the countries allied to Japan also regularly heard Japanese broadcasts. In this respect, then, Japan's preparations to ensure that her radio propaganda was heard were very thorough.

The second consideration is that successful propaganda is related to the prevailing mood of the time, and to the beliefs, values and personalities of the audience. This proved to be the principal problem for Japanese propaganda. In wartime, broadcasts from the enemy are unlikely to conform to the beliefs and values of the majority of the audience. There may be an element, which is opposed to the war, or supports the enemy but it is unlikely to be large or powerful. It is also highly probable that such an element, or a group which is perceived as such, will be strongly controlled by the government, as Japanese Americans were during World War Two. Hence, the broadcaster begins at a disadvantage. Japan's disadvantage was compounded by the fact that Japan was perceived as having started the war by making the first unprovoked strike against the United States at Pearl Harbor. All the Japanese stations continually asserted that the economic sanctions placed on Japan during the 1930s and early 1940s had, in fact, been the provocation for the war, leaving Japan no other option and some United States planners preparing for the post-war period would have partly concurred in this. However, the Pearl Harbor attack was a psychological barrier in the minds of the enemy audience and it could never be completely surmounted by Japanese propagandists.

As important as the pre-conceived beliefs of the audience in the development of a propaganda campaign is its perception of the situation at a particular time. A propaganda campaign which is perceived as anachronistic, is unlikely to be as successful as one which is closely attuned to the time in which it is conducted. Thus, old television advertisements which may have very been successful in the 1950s, seem irrelevant and boring to an audience in the 21st century. Often, the only support a radio propagandist has in relating to an enemy audience is the reality of the war situation, as there is no other medium under his control through which his claims will be confirmed. Hence, at the beginning of the Pacific War the claims of Japanese stations that the old order in Asia had ended were confirmed by the rapid expansion of Japanese control and the seeming inability of both the British and the Americans to halt it. Japanese reports erred on the side of exaggeration even then, but their claims were generally credible. It is unsurprising, then, that the Australian government was concerned that Australians should not be exposed to arguments which might convince them that a Japanese invasion of Australia was inevitable. There was little military evidence to suggest otherwise. In addition, the Australian government's periodic warnings about invasion by Japan may have indirectly helped the Japanese radio propaganda.

In the same way, the British government's concern over the unrest in India in 1942 was related to the reality of the situation at that time. Once the serious threat of revolt and revolution had passed, broadcasts from Japanese-controlled stations urging Indian uprisings were not deemed sufficiently threatening for the government to consider them regularly, and monitors' reports on them became infrequent.

For an audience which does not have access to other versions of the situation, relating the propaganda to the true situation is less of a concern to the propagandist. Hence, in Japanese-controlled territories, where short-wave receivers were banned, there were few other means of learning a version of the situation different from that of the Japanese version. Here "news" of the "true situation" was manipulated so that it "confirmed" the propaganda. It can also be assumed that this was the case in the presentation of the Pacific War by Japan's allies. Hence, Axis listeners to Japanese stations were less likely to perceive a conflict between the version of events portrayed by Japanese radio and what they perceived as the "true situation," than listeners in Allied or neutral countries.

The model stated, however, that the success of a propaganda campaign must finally be measured by whether the changes desired by the propagandist can be perceived in changes in behaviour in the target audience. This is not a simple consideration, for the short-wave radio activity of the Japanese during the Pacific War cannot be viewed as a single campaign. There were different campaigns at different times and to different audiences. The campaign to Asia before the outbreak of war in the Pacific probably contributed to the initial favourable attitude of many Burmese towards Japan. Possibly the most successful of Japanese propaganda campaigns was that of the prisoner letters used to attract Australian listeners to Japanese broadcasts. However, once the Australian government had developed a system for circumventing the need to listen, listener numbers dropped rapidly. Other Japanese radio campaigns were less successful in changing the behaviour of the target audience. Radio sets in India were few, and accompanied by Gandhi's public denunciation of Japan's actions in China, the threat of a successful invasion of India by the Japanese and Indian National Armies was perceived as more serious by London than New Delhi. In addition, the "Zero Hour" and other broadcasts written by prisoners for Allied troops, failed wholly in altering the thinking of their audience, instead boosting its morale.

Despite advances in technology and developments in the use of radio propaganda, it would appear then that Japanese radio propaganda was doomed to follow the same path as Japanese military fortunes in the Pacific War - initial successes were later followed by valiant but ineffective campaigns.

CHAPTER 9 *CONCLUSIONS*

In both popular and academic circles, the Japanese war effort has often been considered as somewhat "primitive" or "pre-modern" when compared to those of Germany, Britain and the United States. This is in part because Japanese wartime propaganda often created an image of pre-modernity, by making frequent references to pre-modern ideas such as *Bushidō*. Perhaps unsurprisingly, the Pacific War as a whole has been of less interest to European scholars than to their American counterparts, but even in North America, studies of propaganda have tended largely to ignore Japan's efforts as less important and less skilful than those of the other belligerents.

It is true that the Japanese wartime government contained no individual comparable to Josef Goebbels in Nazi Germany. As the Nazi party's second most famous speaker after Adolf Hitler from 1932, Goebbels was a central figure in the German administration and as Minister for Propaganda, personally directed German propaganda in all its forms. Such a figure did not exist in Japan where there were no charismatic figures of the kind that comprised the leadership of Nazi Germany. In Tokyo, the Minister for Communications headed a workforce of civil servants who controlled the various propaganda activities of the Japanese government. Different Divisions and Sections were responsible for different areas of the operation, and none of the Ministry's campaigns became the personal responsibility of the Minister. Naturally, Goebbels did not work alone and had groups of propagandists which produced much of the Nazi material. However, he was clearly recognised as the person in charge of propaganda in Germany, and for him "radio was . . . the most important instrument of propaganda." Hence, he personally appointed all the directors of radio during the war, and required that he be consulted before news be released by radio. From 1941 he also insisted that radio commentators and news editors attend his ministerial conferences to ensure they understood his views. (Herzstein, 1979:176-9)

The Japanese system of propaganda control was spread further by the existence of several bodies external to the Ministry of Communications which were responsible for selected areas of information and propaganda. Both the Army and Navy Ministries had their own Information Departments, which issued communiqués and statements regarding military matters, independently of the Ministry of Communications. In addition, in 1936 the Cabinet Information Committee, later the Cabinet Information Bureau, was established. This body controlled many of the areas relating to censorship. Comprising representatives of each of the Ministries and the media, and reporting directly to the cabinet, its role was to relieve the pressure of censorship from the Ministries by allowing for easy discussion between the representatives of all the Ministries which needed to be consulted over a given issue.

This system would be expected to create conflicts in propaganda, as the large number of individuals involved meant that there was more scope for differences in interpretation than in the German system. However, this does not appear to have been the case. The Ministry of Communications had representatives on the CIB and consequently was aware of all CIB decisions. In addition, the daily meetings of the CIB included the Prime Minister, a serving military officer, and representatives of the Army and Navy Ministries. Hence, it was also aware of military propaganda policy. There was, therefore, less likelihood of a divergence between the propaganda line of the Ministry of Communications and that of the other Ministries than would first appear.

In fact, it would seem that the Japan's system of propaganda control was closer to the systems employed by both Britain and America than that of Germany. Here, too, it was the *bodies* in charge of propaganda, which were important rather than an individual. In Britain, the Ministry of Information and the Political Warfare Executive (PWE), established in 1941, formulated propaganda campaigns, and in the United States, the Office of War Information (OWI) controlled the propaganda output of the American media. In all of these cases, although distinguished individuals may have served on the bodies, they did not formulate policies alone, and it was the organisation which accepted responsibility.

Broadcasting was probably more important than other media in disseminating Japanese propaganda overseas, as it did not require the physical export of film reels or newsprint in order to reach its audience. In Japanese-occupied territories short-wave broadcasting was secondary to other media, including local broadcasting. However, broadcasting remained the only means of reaching a potential audience in an enemy country, and the only practicable way of maintaining frequent contact with the audience of an ally given the transport problems inevitable in wartime.

Overseas broadcasting in Japan began later than in most European countries. However, when it began its output power was 50kw, which was second only to that of the BBC's Empire Service. Over the decade that followed, the number of transmitters and their output power were further boosted as the operation expanded. It was only in February 1945, that the first contraction of NHK's overseas radio operation occurred. This ensured that the Japanese transmissions remained some of the most powerful in the world, ranking with German, British and American stations throughout the war. Technologically, therefore, one cannot justify dismissing Japanese overseas radio propaganda as unimportant, for it's output was as strong and its transmissions as far-ranging as those of the other major belligerent powers during World War Two.

The lack of research into the propaganda produced by Japanese broadcasters belies the fact that much of the propaganda was very sophisticated. Despite its late beginning, Japanese overseas broadcasting displayed a sophistication common to all the major belligerents. Japanese propagandists were aware that different peoples reacted differently to material and presentation styles, and attempted to adapt broadcasts to the culture of each target country. Hence, from the beginning of broadcasting in 1935, English was used in broadcasts along with Japanese. Within a year French and German had been added to the schedules of the European transmission, and Radio Tokyo maintained a policy of broadcasting news bulletins in several local languages on each transmission throughout its period of operation. At its height in November 1944, Radio Tokyo broadcast daily in twenty languages to fifteen transmission regions. This awareness of the potential of radio to reach the peoples of the world was one which Japan shared with Nazi Germany, the United States and the Soviet Union, all of which used foreign language broadcasts in their overseas schedules to propagate their own ideology. It was Britain which initially seemed unconcerned by this potential, and which maintained a policy of only broadcasting in English for five years after the start of the BBC's Empire Service.

It is conceivable that Britain was aware of the potential of foreign language broadcasting, but continued to broadcast only to British nationals and educated foreigners because it felt that the stability of its Empire was secure. Italian broadcasts to the Middle East in 1937 threatened this assumption, and the Arabic Service was inaugurated to counter Italian propaganda. Japan's Empire, as it existed in 1935, was not as extensive or as well established as that of Britain, and the assumption that broadcasting in foreign languages was unnecessary was not made. Radio Tokyo sought to justify the Japanese position and to detail Japanese views to the world, in languages which the world would understand. These were important features of Japanese overseas broadcasting, as they were in Nazi, American and Soviet broadcasting.

So, how far did the flexibility of content and style of Japanese broadcasts appeal to overseas listeners? Early Japanese broadcasts followed a pattern similar to Japanese domestic broadcasts, which tended to consist of newscasts, political speeches and commentaries by prominent political figures. Music tended to be martial in nature, and after the outbreak of fighting in China this tendency increased, especially as American and British music were prohibited. It remains unclear whether classical composers from the Allied nations were actually banned, but in reality their music was virtually always overlooked in preference to music by German or Italian composers.

Japanese broadcasters became increasingly aware from their surveys of listeners in overseas countries, that this was not popular amongst overseas listeners, and broadcasts were adapted to suit the tastes of the target country. The clearest example is that of broadcasts to the United States. NHK sought to employ *nisei*, as their use of idiomatic American English was considered important in attracting the American audience. The most noticeable feature of the American transmissions, however, was NHK's frequent attempts to imitate American "DJ-style" programmes. The first suggestion that Japanese broadcasting was not sufficiently entertaining to attract American listeners was made in 1936 and this self-criticism was made several times over the ten years of Radio Tokyo's operations. Jazz and swing music, considered the worst examples of Western musical decadence, were completely prohibited in Japan. Goebbels and Himmler also banned them from German broadcasts for the same reason. (Herzstein, 1979:181) However, Japanese overseas broadcasts to America and American troops in particular broadcast jazz programmes throughout the war. Each time it was suggested that broadcasts were unappealing to Westerners, jazz broadcasting was deemed to be the answer. In 1941, a Japanese jazz band, the New Order Rhythm Orchestra was even established at NHK to record live performances for the American transmissions.

It was in the programme, "Zero Hour," that NHK finally produced a programme of the "DJ-style" type, which successfully imitated the style of the popular American broadcasts it had been attempting to recreate. The fast, idiomatic, slang English used by the prisoners to confuse the censor, and the upbeat music and banter of the "Orphan Ann" spot closely resembled the type of programmes broadcast by many American domestic stations. This is reflected in its popularity amongst the American troops in the South Pacific, who were unable to pick up their favourite home stations. "Zero Hour" was written and performed by prisoners, and Iva Toguri, a *nisei*. It would appear that the difference in style was too great for Japanese writers to completely comprehend, and that this kind of programme could, in the end, only be produced by those who were entirely familiar with American tastes, and who had listened to this kind of programme over long periods.

However, the failure of Japanese scriptwriters and presenters to produce an entirely successful broadcast of this nature should not detract from previous Japanese attempts to produce a "DJ-style" jazz programme. Japanese broadcasters and propagandists understood that a different style of broadcasting was essential to attract American listeners to Japanese broadcasts, and that the same was true of other audiences. Consequently, they attempted to recreate broadcasts which would appeal to local tastes. Hence, Japanese broadcasts contained celebrations of local festivals in transmissions to South America and South East Asia, where Japan portrayed itself as respectful of local customs. To the predominantly Catholic South American communities Japanese broadcasts also stressed respect for the Vatican and Japanese criticism of British bombing raids that damaged churches, a theme which rarely appeared in broadcasts to other regions. This ability to adapt the programmes and themes, along with the use of local languages in transmissions, is a clear indication of the sophisticated nature of Japanese overseas broadcasting.

Japanese broadcasting did not have the strong ideological standpoint of stations such as Radio Moscow, which had been established in 1929 partly to promote world revolution in the Soviet style. Nor did it have the superior attitude of British broadcasting, which even when it began to broadcast in foreign languages, continued to do so in the style of British broadcasts, with little adaptation to the tastes of local audiences. With neither ideological constraints nor inflexibility, Japanese broadcasts showed a sophisticated and flexible approach to propaganda similar to that of Germany. This would seem to contradict the perceived role of Japanese radio propaganda as insignificant, as indicated by its absence in research by Western scholars.

Ulitmately, the BBC's refusal to bend to outside pressure to reshape its broadcasts helped to ensure that its propaganda was successful, because many listeners perceived it to be the impartial truth. In response to Foreign Office complaints it even asserted, "The omission of unwelcome facts of news and the . . . suppression of truth runs counter to the corporation's policy." (Hickman, 1995:19) Radio Tokyo did not have the same reputation for impartiality and truth. However, it is important to note that many minor reports in news bulletins were based on truth, although these were reported as secondary to the exaggerated military claims, which emanated from the Army and Navy Ministries' Information Sections.

It is useful to examine items other than those referring to military matters, which made up much of the news bulletins. These were selected by programme producers at NHK and not by military advisors. Naturally, all the scripts were approved by the CIB before they could be broadcast, and presented the Japanese viewpoint, but it is interesting to note that in many cases Radio Tokyo broadcasts which were less than favourable to the Allies contained many probable "truths." One of the clearest examples is the treatment of Japanese internment camps in the United States by Japanese broadcasts. Perhaps predictably, the camps were denounced as inhuman. However, the facts used to illustrate the point were undeniable: that Japanese interned in the camps were put to work on farms and that a riot had occurred during a protest at Manzanar camp near Los Angeles in 1942. The conclusion that Americans were "inhuman" may be an exaggerated one. However, one must agree with the Japanese broadcasters that American officials had been at best "heavy handed" in dealing with this section of their own public for such a riot to occur. The use of tanks to quell the riot could be viewed similarly. This was not something that would have been widely reported by the Allies, but the factual reporting, and the subsequent conclusion made by Japanese radio, would have appeared at least plausible to a listener already suspicious of American intentions.

Factual material regarding some statements made in Japanese broadcasts would have been unobtainable to Japanese script-writers, but often their statements were astute assumptions made after observing relationships between the Allies. Japanese broadcasters mentioned, from time to time, that there were problems in the capitalist-communist alliance of the Allies, both between Churchill and Roosevelt and Stalin, and between Chiang Kai-shek and Mao Tse-tung. These included accusations that Chinese Communists hampered Nationalist operations in China to sway the domestic balance of power in their direction, and that the dropping of atomic bombs by the United States on Japan, was principally to intimidate the Soviet Union. Hard evidence for such claims would have been unobtainable. However, with the benefit of hindsight, it is clear that the alliances between capitalist or nationalist regimes and communists presented some serious conflicts of ideology, which would remain unresolved throughout the war. Indeed, post-war events confirmed that these Japanese assumptions were largely true, and that wartime alliances were temporary ones between ideological enemies, who would become bitter rivals in different circumstances.

Other favourite topics of Japanese news items included Britain's concerns over the British Empire and her apparent lack of concern towards its members. Early in the Pacific War, Japanese claims that only one quarter of "British" troops in Malaya comprised British nationals, are borne out by post-war figures. The Japanese could gather accurate figures of prisoners in Malaya. However, they made assumptions based on these figures and applied them to British actions elsewhere. Hence, similar accusations, that Britain was content to let people from other countries do her fighting for her, were made concerning front line troops in Africa and later mainland Europe.

A further area of propaganda where Japanese broadcasts probably contained a good proportion of truth was in the reporting of achievements in the rebuilding of the Greater East Asia Co-Prosperity Sphere, although this is impossible to verify. Often, particularly as the war situation deteriorated, these reports provided the "good news" element in Japanese broadcasts. Many of the reported achievements were fairly unimportant other than to the local population, and it is doubtful whether the average target listener overseas would really be interested, for example, in the building of a hydro-electric plant in Surabaya.[277] The propaganda value of such reports was in conveying an image of well being and normality within the Co-Prosperity Sphere. It is probable, therefore, that the developments described in reports did occur, for they would have held so little interest for overseas listeners that to invent lies regarding them would have probably amounted to wasted effort.

With the exception of broadcasts which merely repeated the military information supplied by the Army and Navy Ministries' Information Sections, broadcasts which reported this kind of "selective truth" were probably more common in Japanese overseas broadcasts than those which lied directly. Reports on the situation in America, such as those regarding the Japanese internment camps, were often gleaned from Japanese returnees and foreign press reports, and then presented as the "truth" from a Japanese perspective. Similarly, broadcasts regarding the situation in Japan and the Greater East Asia Co-

Prosperity Sphere probably reported a "truth" which would present the Japanese in a favourable light. Naturally, the selection of news items was important, and any reports which could have been construed as damaging to Japan or the image of Japan, were rejected. In essence it was the "truth" that was reported, but not the "whole truth."

This reporting of the "selective truth" was not exclusive to Japanese wartime broadcasters. It was common to all the belligerents during the war and to any closed society since which has wished to present an image of peace and well being to the outside world. During the war, the BBC gained the reputation for "truthful" reporting and in 1941 the Danish Nazi newspaper, *Feadrelandet*, claimed "Many people have more faith in bulletins from London than in the words of the Bible." (Hickman, 1995:127) It was, in fact, a BBC plan to report more damaging "truth" than other belligerents, with the result that "if there is a disaster, we broadcast it before the Germans claim it . . . And when the tide turns and the victories are ours, we'll be believed." (Hickman, 1995:106) The Japanese broadcasts were less "truthful" than the BBC's would appear to be from this statement, in that reports of failures were never admitted. However, aside from the reports of military operations, which were not generated by NHK, the reporting of direct lies was limited and less obvious than those of the Nazi propaganda machine.

Goebbels was contemptuous of those for whom his propaganda was devised, declaring "propaganda has nothing to do with truth, but everything to do with victory." (Herzstein, 1979:74) Goebbels made statements which directly opposed previous claims. He would, in regard to Hitler's tactical alliance with the Nationalists, "speak of the unified 'National Opposition' as if he had never attacked the reactionaries, just as he had praised Hitler after 1926 as if he had never attacked him as a 'petit bourgeois betrayer of socialism.'" (Herzstein, 1979:53) It must be assumed that if he made two diametrically opposed statements, at least one of them had to be a lie. By way of contrast, Japanese statements issued through the CIB and NHK seem to have been more consistent, and were in many cases probably truthful, even if the conclusions were over-exaggerated.

The false claims of the Japanese Army and Navy Ministries, however, should not be ignored as inconsequential. Despite the probable "truth" of most non-military broadcasts, descriptions of the military situation in the Pacific War constituted much of the broadcast time in Japanese short-wave programmes. All broadcasts contained news segments which invariably reported on the latest war developments. These were exaggerated unnecessarily even while the Japanese forces were inflicting huge defeats on Britain and the United States. Thus:

> *Not content with the success of their sneak attack [on Pearl Harbor] Japanese propagandists exultantly announced that the U.S. Pacific Fleet had been virtually annihilated. And at least once a month thereafter, with monotonous regularity, Tokyo reduced the United States to 'the rank of a third-class sea power'. Thus every time a major naval engagement took place in the Pacific, Japan's zealous propagandists were compelled to refloat Uncle Sam's fleet so that it could again be sent to the bottom by the fabulous Japanese Navy. (Rolo, 1943:173)*

Rolo was a Briton writing in 1944, before the end of World War Two, so the tone of the language he used about the Japanese is understandable. His obvious bias notwithstanding, Rolo's claims regarding broadcasts seem to be born out by monitoring reports of Japanese broadcasts in the first months of the war. The rapid victories of an Asian power at Pearl Harbor, on the Malay Peninsula, in Hong Kong, Singapore, the Philippines and Indonesia were scarcely believable to the reeling world powers. That, in itself, was excellent propaganda. However, the Japanese habit of exaggerating even these victories, by claiming to have destroyed greater amounts of shipping and aircraft than was the case, left Japanese propagandists with the need to justify further battles, both in domestic and overseas propaganda. If the United States fleet had been virtually annihilated at Pearl Harbor, where did it obtain sufficient ships to warrant further attacks by the Japanese?

After the Battle of Midway in mid-1942, as the military situation began to turn against Japan, this propaganda error became increasingly difficult to sustain or to overcome. Not only did it become clear that much of the American fleet remained intact, but the victories which had allowed the Army and Navy ministries to sustain this line were reversed and the supposed "third rank" navy of the United States began to inflict defeats on the Japanese. Domestic broadcasts could conceal this while American bombers were still out of range of Japan, as information was not available to the Japanese people from outside, and short-wave receivers were illegal. In overseas broadcasts, however, the denials of American victories, and the portrayals of Japanese defeats as victories, such as the claim that the Battle for the Solomon Islands resulted in "the wholesale destruction of the Anglo-American fleet," (Rolo, 1943:174) succeeded only in alienating the foreign audience, which had alternative sources of news to compare with Radio Tokyo's statements.

The military communiqués of the Army and Navy Ministries were probably the least sophisticated propaganda used by NHK in its overseas broadcasts. Programmes written by professional broadcasters, despite being censored, showed an understanding of the need for credibility in appealing to an audience. Many of the early attempts at programmes which appealed to foreign tastes were not particularly successful, for a variety of reasons. These included a lack of writers and announcers with the necessary language skills, and a failure to appreciate fully the differences in programming styles between different countries. However, the fact that these differences existed and that they had to be accommodated in the broadcasting schedules, was recognised, and new programmes were continually developed to this end. Hence, the prisoner broadcasts, "Zero Hour" and "*Hi no Maru* Hour," were developed along with the broadcasting of prisoner letters. Regular musical exchanges were made with Germany, Italy and the countries of Greater East Asia, and local festivals and saints days were celebrated in broadcasts to South America. All of these were established in order to attract each audience and to convey a message of empathy to it. In turn, the audience was expected to accept the credibility of Japanese news reports and listen to propaganda speeches with at least a less than suspicious mind. The propaganda of the Army and Navy ministries undermined the positive effect of these broadcasts. Their over-exaggeration at the beginning of the war meant that the propaganda line soon became unsustainable. The portrayal of setbacks (no belligerent ever admits to a defeat) as victories comparable to Japan's initial victories, served only to undermine any successes achieved by other programmes and to alienate potential listeners.

One perhaps surprising feature of Japanese broadcasts was the accurate prophecy of events and tendencies made from time to time. During the course of presenting propaganda Japanese radio made several claims regarding the post-war world, which eventually proved broadly accurate. Radio Tokyo claimed that the British Empire would be broken forever by the war and that America's policy was to take over the governing of British colonial territories after the war. In the years after World War Two, Britain no longer had the power or wealth to sustain a world-wide empire, and although it retained Hong Kong until 1997, the majority of the former colonies gradually achieved their independence over the next twenty years. Yet they did not become colonial possessions of the United States. However, in much of the world, particularly the Middle East, the United States replaced the weakened Britain as the most influential Western power, and American cultural influence spread throughout most of the world.

After the dropping of the atomic bomb Radio Tokyo accused the American government of using the bomb in order to intimidate it's future enemy, the Soviet Union,[278] not to end the war with Japan. This is a theory which has been widely discussed by some historians in the post-war era. That the Soviet Union and the capitalist nations would be enemies when released from their uneasy wartime alliance was perhaps clear to many in 1945. However, until suspicion of government motives became prevalent in the 1970s it was inconceivable in people's minds that the United States might have sought to display its technological superiority by dropping atomic bombs unnecessarily. Perhaps only a wartime enemy would dare make such an accusation in the 1940s.

A frequent Japanese plea to Australia was that it belonged to Asia and would ultimately be abandoned by Britain. In the early 1940s it was far from clear that British power would diminish. However, with the loss of its empire in the post-war years Britain saw Europe as increasingly important, and in 1973 entered the European Economic Community, damaging many of its trade ties with Commonwealth countries. As a result Australian trade links within Asia, particularly with Japan, were developed. Now Australia has become a Pacific Rim rather than a colonial economy. To listeners in the 1940s the idea of such events may have seemed ridiculous propaganda, but on occasion Japanese propagandists perhaps unwittingly foretold the long-term future with considerable accuracy.

The output of Radio Tokyo was generally sophisticated and showed a clear understanding by broadcasters of the potential for overseas radio propaganda. They recognised the need to appeal to an audience, and to be perceived as credible by it. Even before the outbreak of war the role of overseas radio was to explain the Japanese standpoint to the world, particularly after Japan left the League of Nations in 1933 over her invasion of Manchuria two years previously. Japan's development of overseas broadcasting was wide-ranging and after the outbreak of war, the fears of other governments towards it suggested that it was potentially a very effective propaganda tool. Originally NHK hoped to emulate the BBC, but it was forced out of BBC-style colonial isolationism at the outset. However, it continued to follow a path between that of the BBC's "truth" and the blatant exaggerations and lies of Nazi stations. Unfortunately, it was also forced to transmit un-amended military propaganda issued by the Information Sections of the Army and Navy Ministries, which showed little understanding of the complexities of propaganda.

A further obstruction to the success of Japanese overseas radio propaganda was the lack of listeners amongst groups who may have been expected to tune in. In Asia the number of short-wave receivers was not high, although most of Asia was within range of local and Greater East Asia medium-wave broadcasting. An undated list of broadcast audiences in the BBC's files lists the number of receivers in Asia in Figure 9. The document is among others from 1946 so it is probable that it was a list drawn up by the Allies at the end of the war.

Amongst the same documents is a report on the popularity of British broadcasts to Japanese troops declaring that this was difficult to ascertain "owing to the impossibility of obtaining detailed information concerning audiences." However, it would suggest that the short-wave audience was small.

		Estimated number of short-wave receivers	Estimated number of medium-wave receivers
China		500	25,000
Siam		10,000	20,000
British Territories	Hong Kong	50	5,000
	Malaya	100	1,000
	Burma	100	1,000
Foreign Colonial Territories	Indo-China	600	150
	Indonesia	500	45,000
	Philippines	500	20,000

Figure 9: Broadcast audiences East of India

BBC Written Archives: File E2/233: *Far Eastern Service 1944-54*

Atmospheric conditions frequently rendered radio signals to Europe unreliable and Japan did not have a system of relay stations across the world as Britain did. Although stations in Greater East Asia, particularly the Singapore station, relayed broadcasts, the extent of Japanese occupied territory was not as conveniently situated as that of British territory, being entirely within Asia, and this limited the range of even relayed broadcasts. Germany relayed Japanese broadcasts across the German domestic network according to broadcasting agreements between the two countries, but there was no German co-operation in relaying broadcasts across Europe. Hence, the number of listeners in Europe, even amongst those who wished to listen regularly, was low. The American policy of interning Japanese Americans also had an adverse effect on Radio Tokyo's potential for success as internment limited access to radio receivers. German Americans, unlike the Japanese community in America, were not interned and radio transmissions from Nazi Germany had a considerable following amongst the German American community, which could listen in freely. Pre-war evidence suggests that if Japanese Americans had been able to tune in, many would have listened to Japanese broadcasts. However, the policy of internment was to deny Radio Tokyo its largest potential audience in an enemy country by denying Japanese Americans access to short-wave radio receivers.

A broader issue which cannot be left unconsidered, is the extent to which Japanese wartime overseas radio propaganda had any lasting influence on post-war international thinking. This is difficult to determine. For many who lived through the war, it was the Allied image of the Japanese which remained, and many continue to hate Japan for its treatment of prisoners-of-war and for Japanese ferocity in combat. It is possible that this may be due in part to Japanese portrayals of themselves as a warrior people, but it has much more to do with information learnt about Japanese camps at the end of the war. The occasional reference to race issues in the United States in broadcasts to American troops in particular, showed an awareness of the divisions in American society. It is unlikely, however, that Japanese radio broadcasts had much to do with growing awareness of them within America. However, it is probable that Japanese attacks on white superiority influenced the colonial peoples of Asia who gained their independence in the years after the war. In addition, NHK staff were sent throughout the Greater East Asia Co-Prosperity Sphere to train Asian staff and develop Asian broadcasting. It is probable that this training produced a group of experienced radio broadcasters in some Asian countries who were able to produce high-class programmes in the years following the war.

Despite the growing understanding and sophistication of propaganda techniques at NHK, Radio Tokyo failed to achieve its potential as a successful propaganda station. It was hampered by factors both within Japan and externally. The lack of foreign experience of many of its early programme producers and a shortage of announcers with foreign language skills meant that NHK needed time to develop broadcasts which would appeal to different audiences around the world. In the long term this experience gained during the war placed Japan in a position of leadership amongst post-war broadcasters in Asia, and ensured that overseas radio was redeveloped quickly at the end of the occupation period. The lack of Japanese-controlled areas in which to build relay stations and the American policy of internment ensured that the audience was small in most regions outside the Greater East Asia Co-Prosperity Sphere which was not considered "overseas" in terms of broadcasting. Ultimately, however, Radio Tokyo was caught up in the rivalry between the Army and Navy which eventually undermined much of Japan's war effort. In the end, the defiant language of military propaganda served to ensure that it was perceived as incredible, and was therefore largely ignored, both by general wartime audiences, and by later scholars.

Appendix 1
Archive Material

Besides the Kitayama work and other secondary sources, the material for this research has come from several notable sources. Much of the detail of actual broadcasts was from the BBC's Monitoring Reports,[279] daily records of all foreign broadcasts picked up by the monitoring station, now at Caversham near Reading, and dating back to 1939. During the war these reports were distributed daily to the Foreign Office, the Ministry of Information, and other government agencies interested in foreign propaganda or involved in countering it. These are notes in English made by the monitor regarding the important items in a broadcast. Sometimes the full text of a speech or news report was included, but more usually the reports consist of notes regarding, presumably, what those receiving the reports had specified as important topics. As a source for the historian, the reports are, therefore, not flawless. Whilst most of what is written is probably a fairly accurate summary of what was said (and occasionally there are even notes as to the tone or presentation of the announcer), often there are large sections of the broadcast which are missing. Presumably, these were considered unimportant by the agencies which received the report. However, it does mean that the *Summary of World Broadcasts* does not give a full picture of the radio propaganda reaching Britain. It is, hence, impossible to tell how long a given Japanese propaganda campaign, for example, continued, as once it became considered unimportant or ineffectual by the British propaganda agencies, items from that campaign ceased to be included in the monitoring reports.

In addition, there is also a problem of subjective bias in the monitoring reports. They were written by monitors, who listened to the broadcasts in the languages in which they were transmitted, and compiled summaries in English. Naturally, a translated version of a report will often differ slightly from the original, owing to different linguistic nuances in the two languages. In addition, it was the responsibility of the individual monitor to summarise the broadcast, and in some of the reports it is possible to detect which summaries were compiled by the same monitor, through similarities in style. This means that there is some subjective bias in the reports unwittingly added by the monitor, and that in some cases the summary is fairly detailed, and in others less so. Despite these limitations, however, the *Summary of World Broadcasts* offers a daily account of short-wave broadcasting, which is unique, and of immense value.

Besides the *Summary of World Broadcasts*, the BBC Written Archive holds files of letters and other documents relating to the BBC's contacts with Japan. Whilst these are not extensive, particularly for the pre-war and war period, their contents are of interest. The files contain brief letters between the BBC and NHK, and memos between the BBC in London and its station in New Delhi, regarding Tokyo broadcasts. Most of these seem to have been made fairly irregularly, and often the files contain no further correspondence on a given subject. However, probably the most interesting documents in these files are a series of communications between NHK and the BBC regarding preparations for the BBC's participation in the celebrations to commemorate the opening of a new broadcasting complex in Tokyo in 1939. They include telegrams confirming the schedule and even the Japanese translation of the BBC's greetings, hand written by the Japanese Press Attaché in London.

The second major source of material for this research was the United States' National Archives in Washington DC. The material relating to wartime radio monitoring is not housed in the main archive but at a smaller holding store at Suitland, Maryland. The volume of material relating to wartime radio broadcasting which still remains in the United States, is vast. The National Archives contain special reports written for different departments at various stages of the war, and separate lists of prisoner broadcasts besides the general daily, weekly, monthly and quarterly transcripts and summaries. There is a comprehensive guide to the contents of the archive and for those wishing to find something specific there are indexes to the transcripts and the sound recordings.

However, the material is not without its flaws. As it does not appear in one daily report, it is difficult to follow a chronological path through the war period. Often a series of reports which seems to have been discontinued at an arbitrary date will merely have been renamed and later reports bearing the new name will reappear under a different heading. These changes of name, and perhaps distribution, occurred during the war, and usually the last few reports of a series often announced the coming changes. However, the guide to the archives does not explain that one section is a continuation of the reports in an earlier section, under a different heading. It would, thus, be relatively easy for a researcher, to miss the second half of a series of reports by assuming that the later reports no longer exist.

A further difficulty with the daily and weekly reports is that they are concise summaries. Unlike the *Summaries of World Broadcasts,* the reports contain analysis of the broadcasts, consisting of the "highlights" of overseas broadcasts with some detail in a later section. They do not state when in the running order of a programme an item appeared, and tend to draw themes of Japanese broadcasts together, not always clarifying which Japanese-controlled stations made a claim or in which order a statement was made from stations in the Far East. The researcher, therefore, must work from analysis produced with the intention of providing counter-propaganda, rather than analysing the contents of a broadcast itself. These limitations, however, are offset by the value of the quantity of material, which has been preserved by the National Archive. Given sufficient time to navigate one's way around the collections of files, there is a vast amount of material relating to not only Japanese wartime overseas radio broadcasting, but that of the rest of the world, too.

The archive which contains least material pertaining to Japanese overseas broadcasting in the 1930s and 40s is that of NHK itself. This is not as surprising as it first appears, for much official documentation from the war was destroyed by the Japanese in August 1945 during the period between the surrender and the arrival of the American occupation forces. As overseas radio was the most important overseas propaganda tool, much documentation relating to programmes and policies was destroyed in this period. In addition, since most of the material which does remain, is in pre-1945 Japanese it presents a huge language barrier to the Western researcher. The American occupation government in its revision of education simplified the Japanese language and writing system. Most Japanese can read pre-1945 Japanese fluently but it sounds very antiquated to them. Most non-native Japanese speakers, however, will have not studied pre-1945 Japanese, and will, therefore, have some considerable problems in translating parts of the material. Generally, the linguistic rules governing many of the differences which appear in pre-1945 Japanese, will not appear in modern grammar books, and there is little aid to be sought in producing a translation. For these reasons the material which does remain is also very interesting.

Much of the material pertaining to actual broadcasts is related to the attack on Pearl Harbor in December 1941. There is a list of news reports and one of commentaries from December 1941. Generally, both lists give titles of items without further explanation or elaboration, but often there is a section entitled "Special News" in the former list which does report some of the details attached to a few of the headlines. These lists, however, do not continue beyond December 1941. The reason for this is unknown, but it must be assumed that records were still kept from 1942, and that they were destroyed or taken to the United States at the end of the war.

Other material at the NHK archive is in the form of magazines published by NHK, rather than that of material directly relating to the broadcasts themselves. Issues of the official domestic NHK magazine, *Hōsō* [*Broadcasting*], remain from July 1937 to September 1941, as do the issues of its replacement, *Hōsō Kenkyū* [*Broadcasting Research*] from October 1941 to December 1943. These were the serious public magazines published by NHK, and they contained articles relating to both the technical and programming sides of NHK, both in domestic and overseas broadcasting. Naturally, as they were not popular magazines, not only were they written in pre-1945 Japanese, but they were written for the educated classes and so the language is more sophisticated, rendering translation harder. The final set of magazines held by NHK are the programme schedules produced for distribution amongst the overseas audience. Published monthly, each edition often had three versions, one in English for North America, one in English, French and German for Europe, and one in Spanish for South America. The magazines contained articles about special broadcasts to be aired during the month and letters from listeners, along with a full programme schedule and a list of frequencies. The NHK archives contains those from January 1940 (Number 43) to February 1941, and two odd examples from August 1943 and May 1944. They do not contain all the editions for each month.

The final major source of primary material for this study was Mr. Kitayama Setsurō, author of *Rajio Tōkyō*. In an interview, he indicated the scale of material held by the NHK archive, and the best way to approach much of it. He also kindly provided copies of material from his private collection of broadcasting memorabilia, acquired from people he had interviewed during the course of his own research.

One major source of material not consulted directly in this study, were the monitoring reports of the Melbourne Listening Post in Australia. These formed the basis of the only major work in English on Japanese overseas broadcasting, L.D. Meo's *Japan's Radio War on Australia*, (Meo, 1968) which concentrated on one area of the operation. The consultation of this work has proved to be sufficiently detailed to provide the overview of short-wave broadcasting contained in this present study.

Appendix 2
Target Regions of Japanese-Controlled Overseas Broadcasting

Target area	Stations broadcasting
Australia	Tokyo, Batavia, Makasar, Saigon, Shanghai's East Asian station, Shonan, Taipei
Chungking China	Tokyo, Amoy, Canton, Hsinking, Kalgan, Peking (which also broadcast specifically for the Chinese Communists) Rangoon, Shanghai, Shonan, Taipei
Enemy troops in the South Pacific	Tokyo, Manila, Shonan
Europe	Tokyo, Hsinking, Shonan
India	Tokyo, Bangkok, Batavia, Rangoon, Saigon, Shonan, Taipei
Middle East	Tokyo, Shonan
North America	Tokyo, Batavia, Hsinking, Manila,
Russia	Tokyo, Chongjin, Hsinking, Kalgan
South America	Tokyo

Kitayama, 1988c:124

Appendix 3
Modern and World War Two Names for People and Places

Many of the names of places have changed since World War Two. Of these many were changed when countries achieved independence, the former colonial names being replaced with local names. Places occupied by the Japanese were often given a Japanese name, which was not used after the end of the war. In addition, in recent years the Pinyin system for transliterating Chinese into Roman letters has replaced the former Wade system in the People's Republic of China. Below is a list of the World War Two names as they appear in this study, and their modern equivalent.

China	Amoy	Xiamen
	Canton (city)	Guangzhou
	Canton (province)	Guangdong
	Chungking	Chongqing
	Dairen	Dalian
	Hankow	Hankou
	Hsinking	Changchun
	Kalgan	Zhangjiakou
	Manchuria	Dongbei

	Mao Tse Tung	Mao Zedong
	Mukden	Shenyang
	Nanking	Nanjing
	Peking	Beijing
	Sian	Xian
	Tientsin	Tianjin
	Taichung	Taizhong
Ethiopia	Abyssinia	Ethiopia
Indonesia	Batavia	Jakarta
	Celebes	Sulawesi
	Makasar/Macassar	Ujung Pandang
	Netherlands/Dutch East Indies	Indonesia
Myanmar	Burma	Myanmar
	Moulmein	Maulamyaing
	Rangoon	Yangon
Taiwan	Formosa	Taiwan
Singapore	Shonan	Singapore
Russia	Karafuto	Sakhalin
	Stalingrad	Volgograd
Vietnam	Saigon	Ho Chi Min City

NOTES

1. Also around this time the *Kokusai Bunka Shinkōkai* (International Cultural Friendship Society) was established with similar aims of promoting Japanese culture abroad.
2. In the same speech Iwahara also announced that a domestic schools service would be established to celebrate the anniversary. It began broadcasting on 15 April 1935. (Kitayama, 1988a:109)
3. BBC Written Archive: File E1/1035: Countries: Japan. Short-wave Transmission File 1 1935-
4. Kitayama writes that transmissions to the Eastern United States and South America began on 21 June, broadcasting on Tuesdays and Fridays. (Kitayama, 1988a:111) However, NHK's official history records that they began on 25 June (NHK 1977a:99) It is unclear whether this is the date when it was decided to make it a daily service, or whether there is some confusion regarding the start date.
5. Once the incident had started rebel troops did consider overrunning NHK, but by this time it had become too heavily guarded.
6. Ben-Ami Shillony's Revolt in Japan, which deals with the 26 February Incident does not make any mention of the role of broadcasting during the incident.
7. Believing that the domestic communist oppostion had to be eradicated before the Chinese army could resist Japan, Chiang Kai-Shek fled to Chang Hsueh-liang's (Zhang Xueliang's) headquarters in Sian to urge more active fighting against the communists. As commander of the Manchurian army which had been driven out by the Japanese, Chang's army was sympathetic to communist proposals to end the civil war and unite against Japan. On 12 December 1936, Chang arrested Chiang Kai-shek and presented him with eight demands, which included the termination of the civil war. On 14th Chang and the communist armies announced the formation of a united anti-Japanese command. Chiang Kai-shek apparently accepted the demands in principle and was released

on 25 December. He fled back to Nanking with Chang, who had surrendered to him for punishment.

8. Imperial War Museum Film Section: Film Summary Leaflet JYY 058; Daughter of the Samurai
9. Kitayama uses the term *Shinago* for "Chinese" in his description of the start of Chinese broadcasts. *Shina* was the derogatory term for China used by the Japanese during the 1930s and 40s instead of the more usual *Chūgoku*. Kitayama does not specify, but as short-wave broadcasts in various Chinese dialects began later, it is probably safe to assume that *Shinago* here means Mandarin Chinese (*Putonghua*).
10. These were attended by members of the broadcasting censors, and representatives of the regular Japanese Army, the Kwantung Army and the army in Korea.
11. Dienst was a Dutch Buddhist Priest who went to Japan from Java long before the war, and who was notorious for being very anti-European. He was described by Peter Mendelsson in 1944 as "a renegade well known to the Dutch authorities." (Mendelsson 1944:39)
12. All the telegrams and letters mentioned here are in the BBC File E1/1026: *Countries: Japan; Japan Broadcasting Corporation File 1, 1939-40*, at the BBC Archive in Caversham Park.
13. *Hakkō-Ichiu* is usually translated the "Eight Corners of the World under One Roof." It was a Japanese propaganda slogan used to imply universal Asian brotherhood.
14. Tokyo in German and English for Europe, 3 & 7 May 1940. BBC: *Summary of World Broadcasts* Numbers 290 & 294, 4 & 8 May 1940
15. See for example: Tokyo in French for Europe, 2 March 1941, and Tokyo in German for Germany, 19 April and 8 May 1941 . BBC: *Summary of World Broadcasts* Numbers 593, 641 and 660, 3 March, 20 April and 9 May 1941
16. Tokyo in German for Germany, 25 March 1941. BBC: *Summary of World Broadcasts* number 616, 26 March 1941
17. Tokyo in English for England, 7 December 1941. BBC: *Summary of World Broadcasts*, Number 873, 8 December 1941.
18. United States Records of the Foreign Broadcast Intelligence Service (FBIS): *Daily Report, Official Radio Broadcasts*, 5 December 1941 pp F4-F5
19. Tokyo in English for the United States, 14 January 1942. B.B.C.: *Summary of World Broadcasts*, Number 911, 15 January 1942

20. Tokyo in English for Europe, 9 January 1942. B.B.C.: *Summary of World Broadcasts*, Number 907, 11 January 1942.
21. United States Records of the FBIS: *Daily Report, Official Radio Broadcasts*, 6 December 1941 p F3
22. In January 1942, Prime Minister Tōjō declared that Burmese and Philippine independence within the Greater East Asia Co-Prosperity Sphere were Japanese aims. Tokyo in German for Germany, 23 January 1942. B.B.C. *Summary of World Broadcasts*, Number 920, 24 January 1942
23. United States Records of the FBIS: *Daily Report, Official Radio Broadcasts*, 23 December 1941 p H4
24. United States Records of the FBIS: *Daily Report, Official Radio Broadcasts* 10 December 1941 p F2
25. United States Records of the FBIS: *Daily Report, Official Radio Broadcasts* 20 December 1941 p H5
26. United States Records of the FBIS: *Daily Report, Official Radio Broadcasts* 22 December 1941 p H2
27. These were Japanese, English, French, German, Italian, Spanish, Portuguese, Dutch, Burmese, Vietnamese, Thai, Malay, Peking Chinese, Fukien Chinese, Cantonese, Arabic and Tagalog.
28. United States Records of the FBIS: *Daily Report, Official Radio Broadcasts*, 12 December 1941 p G6; and Tokyo in English for the United States and Europe, 4 February 1942. B.B.C. *Summary of World Broadcasts* Number 933 5 February 1942
29. The most common adjectives used to describe Americans in broadcasts to Australia were: "Synonyms of 'mercenary,' 'immoral,' 'unscrupulous,' 'vainglorious,' 'arrogant,' 'luxury-loving,' 'soft,' 'nauseating,' 'superficial,' 'decadent,' intolerant,' 'uncivilised,' 'barbarous,' 'satanic,' and 'diabolical.'". L.D. Meo: *Japan's Radio War on Australia* p 111
30. Tokyo in Italian for Italy, 11 February 1942. B.B.C. *Summary of World Broadcasts* Number 940, 12 February 1942
31. See also United States Records of the FBIS: *Daily Report, Official Radio Broadcasts* 12 December 1941 p G6
32. According to official British records, Britain's total losses (primarily as prisoners) during the campaign from 8 December 1941 to 31 January 1942 were 138,708. These comprised 38,496 British, 18,490 Australians, 67,340 Indians and 14,382 Volunteer troops. (Louis Allen: *Singapore*

1941-1945 p 270) It is not clear what nationality the volunteer troops were, but it is possible that they were Malays and Chinese as many British officers refused to recruit Malays into the regular army as they were not considered a martial race, and Chinese as they were afraid of unwittingly arming the Communist Chinese army. (Louis Allen: *Singapore 1941-1945* pp185-6) Britons thus comprised 27.75% of the total losses during the Malaya campaign. It is probable that as British soldiers tended to comprise the higher ranks their casualty rate may have been slightly lower than that of some of the other groups, but if one assumes that the number of losses is a true reflection of the number of combat troops, it would appear that British troops comprised a little over one quarter of those fighting on the British side in Malaya.

33. United States Records of the FBIS: *Daily Report, Official Radio Broadcasts*, 17 February 1942, p A4
34. Tokyo in English for Europe, 17 February 1942. B.B.C. *Summary of World Broadcasts* Number 946, 18 February 1942
35. A further broadcast to Italy claimed that Chungking was unhappy about Communist activities.. Tokyo in Italian for Italy, 22 May 1942. B.B.C. *Summary of World Broadcasts* Number 1040 23 May 1942.
36. BBC Written Archive: File E1/475/1: Burma 1940-46
37. Although the English sounds a bit odd, this was the title the Japanese gave the programme.
38. There are two types of propaganda. The first is "white propaganda," whereby the source is recognised and attempts to persuade one by means of the logic of his / her argument or by causing doubts about the respectability of one's own side. The second, "black propaganda," was developed by all sides during World War Two. Under this type of propaganda the "enemy" conceals his / her identity and purports to on be one's own side. The information from this "friendly" source is not subject to the listeners' or readers' suspicion and may, hence, be perceived as more credible. The use of "black propaganda" was common to most of the belligerent nations in World War Two. Britain and Germany in particular engaged in "black propaganda" campaigns by radio.
39. Bandoeng in English for Australian Listeners, 5 June 1942. B.B.C.: *Summary of World Broadcasts* No. 1054, 6 June 1942
40. Batavia in English for Australia, 14 June 1942. B.B.C.: *Summary of World Broadcasts* No. 1063, 15 June 1942

41. United States Records of the FBIS: *Daily Report, Official Radio Broadcasts*, 1 January 1942 p B1
42. United States Records of the FBIS: *Lists and Reports Pertaining to American Prisoners of War*, 27 October 1944.
43. The gap in the report (-----) presumably indicates a few inaudible words were broadcast. From the tone of the letter it can probably be assumed that the missing words are "a good". United States Records of the FBIS: *Lists and Reports Pertaining to American Prisoners of War*, 29 October 1944
44. Tokyo in Italian for Italy, 25 March 1942. B.B.C.: *Summary of World Broadcasts* No. 982, 26 March 1942
45. Tokyo in Italian for Italy, 29 March 1942. B.B.C.: *Summary of World Broadcasts* No. 986, 30 March 1942
46. Tokyo in Italian for Italy, 16 April 1942. B.B.C.: *Summary of World Broadcasts* No. 1004, 17 April 1942
47. The 'planes flew from the aircraft carrier *USS Hornet*. 13 bombed Tokyo and one of the remaining three bombed each of the other cities.
48. Tokyo in English for the United States and Europe, 18 April 1942. B.B.C.: *Summary of World Broadcasts* No. 1006, 19 April 1942.
49. United States Records of the FBIS: *Daily Report, Official Radio Broadcasts*, 21 October 1942, Highlights p C2
50. United States Records of the FBIS: *Daily Report, Official Radio Broadcasts*, October 22 1942, Highlights p C2
51. Tokyo in German for Europe, 2 May 1942. B.B.C: *Summary of World Broadcasts* No. 1020 3 May 1942.
52. Tokyo in English for China and Australia, 7 May 1942. B.B.C.: *Summary of World Broadcasts* No. 1025 8 May 1942.
53. Tokyo in German, Italian, French etc. for the World, 8 May 1942. B.B.C.: *Summary of World Broadcasts* No. 1026 9 May 1942.
54. A news report of Prime Minister Tojo's Diet Speech. Tokyo in English for Europe, 27 May 1942. B.B.C.: *Summary of World Broadcasts* No. 1045, 28 May 1942.
55. Tokyo in English for Europe, 17 May 1942. B.B.C.: *Summary of World Broadcasts* No. 1035, 18 May 1942
56. Tokyo in German and English for Europe, 3 May 1942. B.B.C.: *Summary of World Broadcasts* No. 1021, 4 May 1942

57. Tokyo in English for the Far East, 5 June 1942. B.B.C.: *Summary of World Broadcasts* No. 1054, 6 June 1942
58. Tokyo in English for Europe, 10 June 1942. B.B.C.: *Summary of World Broadcasts* No. 1059, 11 June 1942
59. Tokyo in English for the United States, 12 June 1942. B.B.C.: *Summary of World Broadcasts* No. 1061, 13 June 1942
60. Tokyo in English for Australia and New Zealand, 13 June 1942. B.B.C.: *Summary of World Broadcasts* No. 1062, 14 June 1942
61. United States Records of the FBIS: *Daily Report, Official Radio Broadcasts* 15 June 1942, Highlights, p 1
62. Tokyo in German for Germany, 28 June 1942. B.B.C.: *Summary of World Broadcasts* No. 1077, 29 June 1942
63. Tokyo in English for Europe, 22 June 1942. B.B.C.: *Summary of World Broadcasts* No. 1071, 23 June 1942
64. Tokyo in English for Europe, 25 June 1942. BBC: *Summary of World Broadcasts*, Number 1074 26 June 1942
65. Tokyo in German for Europe, 22 June 1942. BBC: *Summary of World Broadcasts*, Number 1071, 23 June 1942
66. Tokyo in English for Europe, 26 June 1942. BBC: *Summary of World Broadcasts*, Number 1075, 27 June 1942
67. United States Records of the FBIS: *Special Reports* #40. "The Japanese Propaganda Commitment in the Solomon Islands," 7 January 1943
68. Tokyo in English for Europe, 7 December 1942. BBC: *Summary of World Broadcasts*, Number 1239, 8 December 1942
69. Tokyo in Italian For Europe Broadcast, 8 December 1942. BBC: *Summary of World Broadcasts*, Number 1240, 9 December 1942.
70. Although usually translated as "Honourable Defeat" the term "*gyokusai*" implies that the defenders were all killed before the island could be taken, an implication absent in the English term.
71. Tokyo in English for Europe, 30 May 1943. BBC: *Summary of World Broadcasts*, Number 1413, 31 May 1943
72. United States Records of the FBIS: *Special Reports* #82, "Radio Tokyo and the Attu Attack", 19 May 1943
73. Tokyo in Italian for Europe, 25 August 1943. BBC: *Summary of World Broadcasts*, Number 1500, 26 August 1943

74. Japanese Overseas Service in German, 20 December 1943 . BBC: *Summary of World Broadcasts*, Number 1617, 21 December 1943
75. Japanese Overseas Service in German, 6 January 1944. BBC: *Summary of World Broadcasts*, Number 1634, 7 January 1944
76. Japanese Overseas Service in Italian, 9 January 1944. BBC: *Summary of World Broadcasts*, Number 1637 10 January 1944
77. Japanese Overseas Service, 19 January 1944. BBC: *Summary of World Broadcasts*, Number 1647, 19 January 1944
78. Japanese Overseas Service in English for the United Kingdom, 13 January 1944. BBC: *Summary of World Broadcasts*, Number 1641, 14 January 1944
79. Manchuria in German, 18 February 1944. BBC: *Summary of World Broadcasts*, Number 1677, 19 February 1944
80. Japanese Overseas Service in German, 28 February 1944. BBC: *Summary of World Broadcasts*, Number 1687, 29 February 1944
81. Japanese Overseas Service in English, 23 March 1944. BBC: *Summary of World Broadcasts*, Number 1711, 24 March 1944
82. Shonan in Arabic, 10 April 1944. BBC: *Summary of World Broadcasts*, Number 1729, 11 April 1944
83. Japanese Overseas Service in German, 22 June 1944. BBC: *Summary of World Broadcasts*, Number 1802, 23 June 1944
84. Japanese Overseas Service in German for Europe, 3 July 1944 . BBC: *Summary of World Broadcasts*, Number 1813, 4 July 1944
85. Japanese European Service in German, 20 July 1944. BBC: *Summary of World Broadcasts*, Number 1830, 21 July 1944
86. Japanese European Service in German, 20 July 1944. BBC: *Summary of World Broadcasts*, Number 1830, 21 July 1944
87. Japanese European Service in German, 21 July 1944. BBC: *Summary of World Broadcasts*, Number 1831, 22 July 1944.
88. Tokyo in English for Australia and China, 26 January 1943. BBC: *Summary of World Broadcasts*, Number 1289, 27 January 1943
89. Japanese Overseas Service in German, 9 June 1944. BBC: *Summary of World Broadcasts*, Number 1789, 10 June 1944
90. Japanese Overseas Service in German, 14 June 1944. BBC: *Summary of World Broadcasts*, Number 1794, 15 June 1944
91. Tokyo German for Germans in Europe, 27 January 1943 . BBC: *Summary of World Broadcasts*, Number 1290, 28 January 1943

92. Tokyo in English for Australia and China, 29 January 1943,. BBC: *Summary of World Broadcasts*, Number 1292, 30 January 1943
93. A regular feature on Radio Tokyo entitled "Pat to Charlie" (it's Japanese title was *Beijin Yori Beijin E* - "One American to Another") consisted of "a dialogue in which the naïve questions of Charlie [give] Pat chance to put [the Japanese] line across.". United States Records of the FBIS: *Special Reports* #90, "Radio Tokyo commentators and Features," 16 August 1943
94. Hsinking in English, 20 December 1943. BBC: *Summary of World Broadcasts*, Number 1617, 21 December 1943
95. Japanese Overseas Service in English for the United Kingdom, 21 December 1943. BBC: *Summary of World Broadcasts*, Number 1618 22 December 1943
96. Japanese Overseas Service in German, 5 November 1943. BBC: *Summary of World Broadcasts*, Number 1572, 6 November 1943
97. Japanese Overseas Service in German, 7 November 1943. BBC: *Summary of World Broadcasts*, Number 1574, 8 November 1943
98. Japanese Overseas Service in English, 8 November 1943. BBC: *Summary of World Broadcasts*, Number 1575, 9 November 1943
99. Arabic, Bengali, Burmese, Cantonese, Dutch, English, French, Fukien Dialect Chinese, German, Hindi, Italian, Japanese, Malay, Mandarin Chinese, Persian, Portuguese, Russian, Spanish, Tagalog, Tamil, Thai, Turkish and Urdu.
100. Tokyo in German For Europe, 7 July 1942. BBC: *Summary of World Broadcasts*, Number 1086, 8 July 1942.
101. Batavia in English for Australia, 1 December 1942.. BBC: *Summary of World Broadcasts*, Number 1233, 2 December 1942
102. Batavia in English for Australia, 21 December 1942. BBC: *Summary of World Broadcasts*, Number 1253, 22 December 1942
103. Batavia in English for Australia, 22 December 1942. BBC: *Summary of World Broadcasts*, Number 1254, 23 December 1942
104. Tokyo in German for Europe, 23 & 24 March 1943 & English for Europe, 25 March 1943. BBC: *Summary of World Broadcasts*, Numbers 1345, 1346 & 1347, 24 25 & 26 March 1943
105. Tokyo in Russian for Russia 31 March 1943 . BBC: *Summary of World Broadcasts*, Numbers 1354, 2 April 1943

106. Tokyo in English for Europe, 2 August 1943 & Italian for Europe, 4 August 1943. BBC: *Summary of World Broadcasts*, Numbers 1477, 3 August 1943 & 1479, 5 August 1943
107. For example: a commentary by Abdul Wahid declared "Burma is Free - India Must Follow," Batavia in English for India, 1 August 1943. BBC: *Summary of World Broadcasts*, Number 1476, 2 August 1943
108. Japanese Overseas Service in German for Europe, 23 October 1943. BBC: *Summary of World Broadcasts*, Number 1559, 24 October 1943
109. Japanese Overseas Service in English, 8 November 1943. BBC: *Summary of World Broadcasts*, Number 1575, 9 November 1943
110. Japanese Overseas Service in German, 11 December 1943. BBC: *Summary of World Broadcasts*, Number 1608, 12 December 1943
111. Japanese Overseas Service in German, 4 January 1944. BBC: *Summary of World Broadcasts*, Number 1632, 5 January 1944
112. Hsinking in German, 5 January 1944. BBC: *Summary of World Broadcasts*, Number 1633, 6 January 1944
113. Tokyo in English to Europe on 18 October 1942. BBC: *Summary of World Broadcasts*, Number 1189, 19 October 1942
114. Tokyo in English for Australia and New Zealand, 8 October 1942. BBC: *Summary of World Broadcasts*, Number 1179, 9 October 1942
115. Tokyo in English for Europe, 11 October 1942. BBC: *Summary of World Broadcasts*, Number 1182, 12 October 1942
116. United States Records of the FBIS: *Special Reports* #82, "Radio Tokyo and the Attu Attack"
117. Japanese Overseas Service in Italian for Europe, 7 January 1944. BBC: *Summary of World Broadcasts*, Number 1666, 8 January 1944
118. United States Records of the FBIS: *Special Reports* #113 "Japanese Atrocities Against War Prisoners.
119. United States Records of the Foreign Broadcast Intelligence Service (FBIS): *Special Reports #90*, Radio Tokyo Commentators and Features."
120. The title of the song here seems to be a mistake. There are two melodies, which seem to have been confused, "In a Persian Market" and "In a Monastery Garden."
121. There is some confusion about when "Postman Calls" was started. Ikeda recalls in *Hi no Maru Awâ* that it began on 1st April 1944, the same day that "*Hi no Maru* Hour" was renamed "Humanity Calls." However, Kitayama, whilst acknowledging that this is how Ikeda remembers the

programmes, states that the records show it actually started on 18 September.

122. United States Records of the FBIS: *Lists and Reports Pertaining to American Prisoners of War 1944-45*, 13 October 1944

123. United States Records of the FBIS: *Lists and Reports Pertaining to American Prisoners of War 1944-45*, 13 November 1944

124. The query after "keg" is in the original.. United States Records of the FBIS: *Lists and Reports Pertaining to American Prisoners of War 1944-45*, 24 December 1944

125. United States Records of the FBIS: *Special Report #90*, "Radio Tokyo Commentators and Features," 16 August 1943

126. English for Australia and New Zealand, 6 December 1942. BBC: *Summary of World Broadcasts*, Number 1238, 7 December 1942

127. English for Australia, 7th December 1942. BBC: *Summary of World Broadcasts*, Number 1239, 8 December 1942. There were of course also critics of Roosevelt's actions in the United States, who blamed him for starting the war.

128. English for Australia and New Zealand, 17 December 1942. BBC: *Summary of World Broadcasts*, Number 1249, 18 December 1942

129. English for Australia and China, 23 December 1942. BBC: *Summary of World Broadcasts*, Number 1255, 24 December 1942

130. English for Australia and China, 3 February 1943. BBC: *Summary of World Broadcasts*, Number 1297, 4 February 1943

131. English for Australia and China, 26 December 1942. BBC: *Summary of World Broadcasts*, Number 1258, 27 December 1942

132. English for China and Australia, 22 January 1943. BBC: *Summary of World Broadcasts*, Number 1285, 23 January 1943

133. English for Australia and China, 13 January 1943. BBC: *Summary of World Broadcasts*, Number 1276, 14 January 1943

134. United States Records of the FBIS: *Special Report #90*, "Radio Tokyo Commentators and Features," 16 August 1943

135. English for Australia, 5 March 1943. BBC: *Summary of World Broadcasts*, Number 1327, 6 March 1943

136. United States Records of the FBIS: *Special Report #90*, "Radio Tokyo Commentators and Features," 16 August 1943

137. Japanese Overseas Service in German, 1 October 1944 . BBC: *Summary of World Broadcasts*, Number 1903, 2 October 1944

138. Japanese Overseas Service in Japanese for Australia and the South Pacific, 3 February 1945. BBC: *Summary of World Broadcasts*, Number 2028, 4 February 1945
139. Japanese Overseas Service in German, 4 February 1945. BBC: *Summary of World Broadcasts*, Number 2029, 5 February 1945
140. Japanese Overseas Service in German and in Japanese for Australia and the South Pacific, 20 February 1945. BBC: *Summary of World Broadcasts*, Number 2045, 21 February 1945
141. Japanese Overseas Service in English, 24 February 1945. BBC: *Summary of World Broadcasts*, Number 2049, 25 February 1945
142. Japanese for the Japanese Empire, 13 March 1945. BBC: *Summary of World Broadcasts*, Number 2065, 14 March 1945
143. Japanese European Service in Italian, 3 April 1945. BBC: *Summary of World Broadcasts*, Number 2087, 4 April 1945
144. Japanese Overseas Service in English, 19 and 24 March 1945. BBC: *Summary of World Broadcasts*, Numbers 2072 and 2077, 20 and 25 March 1945
145. Italian for Europe, 22 March 1945 . BBC: *Summary of World Broadcasts*, Number 2075, 23 March 1945
146. Japanese Overseas Service in English, 13 May 1945 . BBC: *Summary of World Broadcasts* No. 2127, 14 May 1945
147. Japanese Overseas Service in English, 26 June 1945. BBC: *Summary of World Broadcasts* No. 2171, 27 June 1945
148. Japanese Overseas Service in English, 1 May 1945,. BBC: *Summary of World Broadcasts* No. 2115, 2 May 1945
149. Japanese Overseas Service in Italian, 2 May 1945. BBC: *Summary of World Broadcasts* No. 2116, 3 May 1945
150. Japanese Overseas Service in Italian, 5 May 1945, . BBC: *Summary of World Broadcasts* No. 2119, 6 May 1945
151. Japanese Overseas Service in Italian, 14 February 1943. BBC: *Summary of World Broadcasts*, Number 2039, 15 February 1945
152. Japanese Overseas Service in Italian for Europe, 13 February 1945. BBC: *Summary of World Broadcasts*, Number 2038, 14 February 1945
153. Japanese Overseas Service in German, 14 February 1945. BBC: *Summary of World Broadcasts*, Number 2039, 15 February 1945
154. Japanese Overseas Service in Japanese for China, 10 April 1945. BBC: *Summary of World Broadcasts*, Number 2094, 11 April 1945

155. Japanese European Service in Italian, 9 April 1945, . BBC: *Summary of World Broadcasts*, Number 2093, 10 April 1945
156. German for Europe, 13tApril 1945. BBC: *Summary of World Broadcasts*, Number 2097, 14 April 1945
157. Provisional Government of Free India (Shonan) in English for India, 13 April 1945. BBC: *Summary of World Broadcasts* No. 2097, 14 April 1945
158. Tokyo in English, 27 July 1945. BBC: *Summary of World Broadcasts* No. 2202, 28 July 1945
159. See Singapore in English for Australia, 28 July 1945. BBC: *Summary of World Broadcasts* No. 2203, 29 July 1945
160. United States Records of the FBIS: *Daily Reports of Foreign Radio Broadcasts*, 28 July 1945, p A1
161. Japanese Overseas Service in German, 14 October 1944. BBC: *Summary of World Broadcasts* No. 1916, 15 October 1944
162. Tokyo in German, 27 May 1945 . BBC: *Summary of World Broadcasts* No. 2141, 28 May 1945
163. See Tokyo in Italian, 28 May 1945. BBC: *Summary of World Broadcasts* No. 2142, 29 May 1945
164. It was this station which was noted as Radio Batavia by British monitors, and which broadcast the Australian prisoner messages in the Australian Home News Hour
165. Japanese Overseas Service in German, 6 August 1944. BBC: *Summary of World Broadcasts*, Number 1847, 7 August 1944
166. Japanese Overseas Service in German, 9 August 1944. BBC: *Summary of World Broadcasts*, Number 1850, 10 August 1944
167. Japanese Overseas Service in German, 11 August 1944. BBC: *Summary of World Broadcasts*, Number 1852, 12 August 1944
168. Japanese Overseas Service in German, 6 August 1944. BBC: *Summary of World Broadcasts*, Number 1847, 7 August 1944
169. Japanese Overseas Service in German, 9 August 1944. BBC: *Summary of World Broadcasts*, Number 1850, 10 August 1944
170. Japanese Overseas Service in German, 5 October 1944. BBC: *Summary of World Broadcasts*, Number 1907, 6 October 1944
171. United States Records of the FBIS: *Lists and Reports Pertaining to American Prisoners of War 1944-5*, 24 January 1945

172. 26 May in the United States. Throughout this section I give the date in Japan, which is one day later than in the United States. However, in his book Zacharias lists them as per the date in Washington.
173. The underlining is in the original
174. The underlining and the note form of the language are from the original
175. Tokyo in French, 7 August 1945. BBC: *Summary of World Broadcasts* Number 2213, 8 August 1945
176. Tokyo in French, 8 August 1945. BBC: *Summary of World Broadcasts* Number 2214, 9 August 1945
177. Tokyo in German, 8 August 1945. BBC: *Summary of World Broadcasts* Number 2214, 9 August 1945
178. Batavia in English, 9 August 1945. BBC: *Summary of World Broadcasts* Number 2215, 10 August 1945
179. Singapore in English, 9 August 1945. BBC: *Summary of World Broadcasts* Number 2215, 10 August 1945
180. Tokyo in English for Europe, 10 August 1945. BBC: *Summary of World Broadcasts* Number 2216, 11 August 1945
181. Tokyo in English, 10 August 1945. BBC: *Summary of World Broadcasts* Number 2216, 11 August 1945
182. Tokyo in English, 12 August 1945. BBC: *Summary of World Broadcasts* Number 2218, 13 August 1945
183. Domei in French and English for Europe, 10 August 1945. BBC: *Summary of World Broadcasts* Number 2216, 11 August 1945
184. Batavia in English for North America, 19 August 1945. BBC: *Summary of World Broadcasts* Number 2226, 21 August 1945
185. Singapore in English, 18 August 1945. BBC: *Summary of World Broadcasts* Number 2224, 19 August 1945
186. Singapore in English for British forces, 25 August 1945. BBC: *Summary of World Broadcasts* Number 2231, 26 August 1945
187. Saigon in English, 25 August 1945. BBC: *Summary of World Broadcasts* Number 2231, 26 August 1945
188. Tokyo in English for North America, 20 and 25 September 1945. BBC: *Summary of World Broadcasts* Numbers 2257 and 2262, 21 and 26 September 1945
189. Tokyo in Japanese, 7 September 1945. BBC: *Summary of World Broadcasts*, No. 2244, 8 September 1945

190. Tokyo in Japanese for Europe, 19 September 1945. BBC: *Summary of World Broadcasts*, No. 2256, 20 September 1945
191. The NHK official history acknowledges that the instructions were then modified to allow short-wave broadcasts to Korea, Taiwan and China for overseas Japanese. NHK: *50 Years of Japanese Broadcasting* p 137
192. Tokyo in German for Germany, 13 May 1941. BBC: *Summary of World Broadcasts* Number 665, 14 May 1941
193. For example, the monitoring reports in the BBC's *Summary of World Broadcasts* for the first week of 1942 (numbers 897-903) show that 64% of news items listed in the reports concerned the war.
194. Tokyo in English for Europe, 6 April 1942. BBC: *Summary of World Broadcasts* Number 994, 7 April 1942 (- ? -) indicates that the word was inaudible to the monitor.
195. Singapore in English, 30 July 1945. BBC: *Summary of World Broadcasts* Number 2205, 31 July 1945
196. Tokyo in English, 8 September 1939. BBC: *Summary of World Broadcasts* Number 23, 9 September 1939
197. Tokyo in German for Europe, 10 April 1940. BBC: *Summary of World Broadcasts* Number 267, 10-11 April 1940
198. Tokyo in English for Australia and New Zealand, 30 September 1942. BBC: *Summary of World Broadcasts* Number 1171, 1 October 1942 (? word) indicates a word supplied by the monitor as the original was inaudible.
199. Tokyo in German for Europe, 16 September 1943. BBC: *Summary of World Broadcasts* Number 1522, 17 September 1943
200. See Tokyo in English for Europe, 15 September 1943. BBC: *Summary of World Broadcasts* Number 1521, 16 September 1943
201. Japanese Overseas Service in German, 9 June 1944. BBC: *Summary of World Broadcasts* Number 1789, 10 June 1944
202. Radio Shonan in English for South West Asia, 7 June 1944. BBC: *Summary of World Broadcasts* Number 1787, 8 June 1944
203. Japanese Overseas Service in German, 8 June 1944. BBC: *Summary of World Broadcasts* Number 1788, 9 June 1944
204. Japanese Overseas Service in German, 15 June 1944. BBC: *Summary of World Broadcasts* Number 1795, 16 June 1944
205. Japanese European Service in Italian, 5 May 1945. BBC: *Summary of World Broadcasts* Number 2119, 6 May 1945

206. Japanese Overseas Service in Italian, 2 May 1945. BBC: *Summary of World Broadcasts* Number 2116, 3 May 1945
207. Singapore in English for British troops in India and Burma, 7 June 1945. BBC: *Summary of World Broadcasts* Number 2152, 8 June 1945
208. Tokyo in German for Germany, 23 August 1941. BBC: *Summary of World Broadcasts* Number 767, 24 August 1941
209. United States Records of the FBIS: *Daily Report; Official Radio Broadcasts*, 13 December 1941, pp H1-2
210. Tokyo in English for England, 1 April 1942. BBC: *Summary of World Broadcasts* Number 989, 2 April 1942 (?agape) indicates that the word supplied by the monitor as the original was inaudible
211. Tokyo in English for Europe, 29 May 1942. BBC: *Summary of World Broadcasts* Number 1047, 30 May 1942
212. Batavia in English for India, 23 March 1943. BBC: *Summary of World Broadcasts* Number 1345, 24 March 1943
213. United States Records of the FBIS: *Daily Report, Official Radio Broadcasts*, 5 December 1941, p F4
214. United States Records of the FBIS: *Daily Report, Official Radio Broadcasts*, 5 December 1941, p F4
215. Tokyo in English for Europe, 15 February 1942. BBC: *Summary of World Broadcasts* Number 944, 16 February 1943
216. Tokyo in German for Germany, 23 January 1942. BBC: *Summary of World Broadcasts* Number 920, 24 January 1942
217. United States Records of the FBIS: *Daily Report, Official Radio Broadcasts*, 6 December 1941, p A3
218. Tokyo in German for Europe, 3 May 1942. BBC: *Summary of World Broadcasts* Number 1021, 4 May 1942
219. Japanese Overseas Service in English, 8 November 1943. BBC: *Summary of World Broadcasts* Number 1575, 9 November 1943
220. Tokyo in German for Europe, 4 July 1945. BBC: *Summary of World Broadcasts* Number 2179, 5 July 1945
221. Batavia in English for India, 29 August 1942. BBC: *Summary of World Broadcasts* Number 1139, 30 August 1942
222. Singapore in English for India, 25 June 1945. BBC: *Summary of World Broadcasts* Number 2170, 26 June 1945
223. Singapore in English, 18 August 1945. BBC: *Summary of World Broadcasts* Number 2224, 19 August 1945

224. Tokyo in English for Europe, 19 April 1942. BBC: *Summary of World Broadcasts* Number 1007, 20 April 1942
225. Tokyo in English for Europe, 24 June 1942. BBC: *Summary of World Broadcasts* Number 1073, 25 June 1942
226. Japanese Overseas Service in English for Britain, 14 November 1943. BBC: *Summary of World Broadcasts* Number 1581, 15 November 1943
227. Tokyo in Japanese for the Japanese Empire, 26 July 1945. BBC: *Summary of World Broadcasts* Number 2201, 27 July 1945
228. Tokyo in English for Australia, 29 November 1942, BBC: *Summary of World Broadcasts* Number 1231, 30 November 1942
229. Tokyo in English for Europe, 23 October 1942. BBC: *Summary of World Broadcasts* Number 1194, 24 October 1942
230. Tokyo in Italian for Europe, 17 April 1943. BBC: *Summary of World Broadcasts* Number 1370, 18 April 1943
231. United States Records of the FBIS: *Daily Report, Official Radio Broadcasts*, 18 January 1944, p AA2
232. United States Records of the FBIS: *Daily Report, Official Radio Broadcasts*, 19 January 1944, p AA2
233. United States Records of the FBIS: *Daily Report, Official Radio Broadcasts*, 19 January 1944, p AA2
234. United States Records of the FBIS: *Daily Report, Official Radio Broadcasts*, 24 January 1944, p AA1
235. United States Records of the FBIS: *Daily Report, Official Radio Broadcasts*, 2 August 1943, P A2
236. Japanese Overseas Service in German, 28 September 1943. BBC: *Summary of World Broadcasts* Number 1534, 29 September 1943
237. Tokyo in Italian for Europe, 25 August 1942. BBC: *Summary of World Broadcasts* Number 1135, 26 August 1942
238. Tokyo in German for Germany, 3 January 1943. BBC: *Summary of World Broadcasts* Number 1266, 4 January 1943
239. United States Records of the FBIS: *Daily Report; Official Radio Broadcasts*, 5 December 1941, p F3
240. Japanese Overseas Service in English, 12 December 1943 . BBC: *Summary of World Broadcasts* Number 1609, 13 December 1943
241. Tokyo in English for Europe, 8 January 1942. BBC: *Summary of World Broadcasts* Number 906, 10 January 1942

242. Tokyo in German for Europe, 1 June 1942. BBC: *Summary of World Broadcasts* Number 1050, 2 June 1942
243. Batavia in English for India, 13 March 1943. BBC: *Summary of World Broadcasts* Number 1336, 15 March 1943
244. United States Records of the FBIS: *Daily Report; Official Radio Broadcasts*, 12 December 1941, p G6
245. United States Records of the FBIS: *Daily Report; Official Radio Broadcasts*, 13 December 1941, p H4
246. Tokyo in Italian for Italy, 11 February 1942. BBC: *Summary of World Broadcasts* Number 940, 12 February 1942
247. Tokyo in English for Europe, 15 January 1942. BBC: *Summary of World Broadcasts* Number 913, 17 January 1942
248. Japanese Overseas Service in English, 3 February 1944. BBC: *Summary of World Broadcasts* Number 1662, 4 February 1944
249. Japanese Overseas Service in Italian, 4 February 1944. BBC: *Summary of World Broadcasts* Number 1663, 5 February 1944
250. Tokyo in English for the United States and Europe, 18 April 1942. BBC: *Summary of World Broadcasts* Number 1006, 19 April 1942
251. Tokyo in Italian for Italy, 20 April 1942. BBC: *Summary of World Broadcasts* Number 1008, 21 April 1942
252. Tokyo in English for Australia and New Zealand, 19 October 1942. BBC: *Summary of World Broadcasts* Number 1190, 20 October 1942
253. Tokyo in Italian for Europe, 21 July 1943. BBC: *Summary of World Broadcasts* Number 1465, 22 July 1943
254. Tokyo in English for Europe, 21 July 1943. BBC: *Summary of World Broadcasts* Number 1465, 22 July 1943
255. Tokyo in English for Europe, 11 February 1944. BBC: *Summary of World Broadcasts* Number 1671, 13 February 1944
256. Tokyo in English for the United States and Europe, 6 March 1942. BBC: *Summary of World Broadcasts* Number 963, 7 March 1942
257. Tokyo in English for China and Australia, 27 March 1943. BBC: *Summary of World Broadcasts* Number 1349, 28 March 1943
258. Japanese Overseas Service in German, 9 August 1944. BBC: *Summary of World Broadcasts* Number 1850, 10 August 1944
259. Japanese Overseas Service in German, 6 August 1944. BBC: *Summary of World Broadcasts* Number 1847, 7 August

260. Tokyo in French, 8 August 1945. BBC: *Summary of World Broadcasts* Number 2214, 9 August 1945
261. Shanghai in Russian for Russia, 27 February 1942. BBC: *Summary of World Broadcasts* Number 956, 28 February 1942
262. Tokyo in English for Europe, 11 March 1942. BBC: *Summary of World Broadcasts* Number 968, 12 March 1942
263. Tokyo in English for (?America), 17 April 1942.BBC: *Summary of World Broadcasts* Number 1005, 18 April 1942
264. Batavia in English for Australia and New Zealand, 21 June 1942. BBC: *Summary of World Broadcasts* Number 1070, 22 June 1942
265. Tokyo in Italian for Europe: 25 June 1942. BBC: *Summary of World Broadcasts* Number 1074, 26 June 1942
266. United States Records of the FBIS: *Special Reports* #113, "Japanese Atrocities Against War Prisoners."
267. Tokyo in English for The United States and Europe, 30 January 1942. BBC: *Summary of World Broadcasts* Number 927, 31 January 1942
268. Batavia in English for India, 25 March 1943. BBC: *Summary of World Broadcasts* Number 1347, 26 March 1943
269. Batavia in English for India, 28 December 1942. BBC: *Summary of World Broadcasts* Number 1260, 29 December 1942
270. Batavia in English for India, 21 April 1943. BBC: *Summary of World Broadcasts* Number 1374, 22 April 1943
271. Australian Self-Interest, Fear, Gratitude to Japan, Pride and Vanity, Prejudice, Jealousy and Anger, War Weariness and Nostalgia, and the Forming of Trade and Political Circles.
272. Provisional Government of Free India (Shonan) in English for India, 18 June 1945. BBC *Summary of World Broadcasts* No. 2163, 19 June 1945
273. Singapore in English for India, 25 June 1945. BBC *Summary of World Broadcasts* No. 2170, 26 June 1945
274. United States' Record of the FBIS: *Daily Analyses of Propaganda Concerning Latin America*, 22-24 August 1942
275. United States' Record of the FBIS: *Daily Analyses of Propaganda Concerning Latin America*, 6 October 1942
276. See for example, "The United States wants South America as a Colonial Possession" and "Japan is liberating Greater East Asia but the United States wants slaves," United States' Record of the FBIS: *Daily Analyses of Propaganda Concerning Latin America*, 8 and 21 October 1942, and

"Wallace's recent speech shows the true extent of American exploitation in degrading Bolivia," *Weekly Analyses of Shortwave News and Propaganda Concerning Latin America*, 25 May 1943

277. Tokyo in English for Europe, 18 June 1942. BBC: *Summary of World Broadcasts*, No. 1067, 19 June 1942
278. Tokyo in English, 12 August 1945. BBC: *Summary of World Broadcasts* Number 2218, 13 August 1945
279. There are three full sets of these monitoring reports of which I am aware. One at the BBC's Written Archives also at Caversham, one in the Imperial War Museum in London, and one at the London School of Economics' Egham Depository Library in Egham, Surrey. I consulted copies in the two former. In the text of this study I have used the term *Summary of World Broadcasts*, in reference to the monitoring reports, as this how they are termed by the BBC. However, at the other locations the reports are known merely as the BBC's Monitoring Reports.

BIBLIOGRAPHY

1. PRIMARY MATERIAL:

Asahi Shinbun 1 January 1941-30 September 1945 (University of Sheffield Library)

BBC: File E1/475/1 *Countries: Burma* 1940-46

File E1/1024 *Countries: Japan; Foreign Language Broadcasts A-Z*; 1940- 1944

File E1/1026 *Countries: Japan; Japan Broadcasting Corporation Files 1 and 2*; 1939-1940 and 1947-1954

File E1/1027 *Countries: Japan; Japan Broadcasting Corporation A-Z*; 1940-1953

File E1/1029/2 *Countries: Japan; Japan Service File 2a*; 1943-June 1945

File E1/1030 *Countries: Japan; Japan Service Monitoring File*; 1943-1945

File E1/1031 *Countries: Japan; Monitoring A-Z*; 1941-1949

File E1/1032 *Countries: Japan; Propaganda File 1*; 1940-1944

File E1/1035 *Countries: Japan; Short-wave Transmissions File 1*; 1935-1938

File E1/1036 *Countries: Japan; Technical A-Z*; 1938-1943

File E1/1060 *Countries Malaya* 1932-54

File E2/233 *Far Eastern Service* 1944-54

(BBC Written Archives, Caversham, Reading,)

BBC Monitoring Reports: *Summary of World Broadcasts*; 31st August 1939 to 30th September 1945, (BBC Written Archives, Caversham, Reading and Imperial War Museum, London)

Hongkong News, 14 January 1942-14 August 1945, (Hong Kong Public Records Office, Central, Hong Kong)

Hong Kong Public Records Office:

File PRO/REF/44 *The Battle for Hong Kong*

File PRO/REF/45 *Japanese Occupation and Surrender of Hong Kong, 1941-45*

File PRO/REF/55 *Radio Hong Kong*

(Hong Kong Public Records Office, Central, Hong Kong)

Imperial War Museum Film Section: Film Summary Leaflet JYY 058 *Daughter of the Samurai* (Imperial War Museum, London).

Japan Times: 1 July 1937 - 30 September 1945. (University of Sheffield Library)

(The *Japan Times* had several different titles during this period. It was called the *Japan Times and Mail* until 10 November 1940. From then until 1 January 1943, it was called the *Japan Times and Advertiser*, and for the rest of the war it was known as the *Nippon Times*.)

NHK: *Hōsō* [*Broadcasting*], July 1937-September 1941, (NHK Museum of Broadcasting Library, Tokyo).

NHK: *Hōsō Kenkyū* [*Broadcasting Research*], October 1941-December 1943, (NHK Museum of Broadcasting Library, Tokyo).

N.H.K: *Radio Tokyo* (Overseas broadcasting schedules) January-December 1940, January 1941 Great Asia edition, February 1941 America and Hawaii edition, August 1943, May 1944, (NHK Museum of Broadcasting Library, Tokyo).

(*Radio Tokyo* went through several name changes during this period. It was called *Overseas Broadcasts* and divided into three magazines, one for North America, China and the South Seas, one for Latin

America and one for Europe, until October 1940, although Southwestern Asia was added to the North American magazine in July 1940. In November and December 1940 the magazines had no titles other than *Overseas Broadcasts for Europe* (November 1940), *Overseas Broadcasts for Near East and Europe* (December 1940), *Radioemision a La America Latina*, and *Overseas Broadcasts for North America, Hawaii, China, the South Seas and Southwestern Asia*. In January 1941 it became *Radio Tokyo* and was divided into four magazines, Greater Asia, North America and Hawaii, Latin America and Europe. By August 1943 *Radio Tokyo* had changed to *Rajio Tōkyō* and had become a single publication listing all the radio schedules)

NHK Kokusai-kyoku [NHK International Bureau]: *Kaigai Hōsō Senden Kiroku* [*Overseas Broadcasting Propaganda Records*], December 1941, (NHK Museum of Broadcasting Library, Tokyo).

NHK Kokusai-kyoku Hensei-bu [NHK International Bureau, Editing Department: *Kaigai Hōsō Bangumi* [*Programmes for Broadcast Overseas*],

1 February 1944

1 April 1944

1 August 1944

5 November 1944

5 April 1945

(NHK Museum of Broadcasting Library, Tokyo).

United States Office of Strategic Service Part One: *Japan and its Occupied Territories during World War Two* (University of Sheffield Library)

Social Conditions and Propaganda in Burma, 6 April 1942

Social Conditions and Propaganda in Malaya, 7 April 1942

Social Conditions and Propaganda in Thailand, 19 June 1942

Japanese Administration in Burma, 10 July 1942

Japanese Attempts to Infiltrate the Muslims, 14 May 1943

Intrigue in Indo-China, Thailand, Burma and India, 28 June 1943

Psychological Warfare in Burma, 12 November 1943

Indians in Japanese Occupied Territory, 1944

Japanese Films, 30 March 1944

Degrees of Japanese Control in Indo-China, 1 May 1944

Japanese Administration in Malaya, 8 June 1944

Programmes of the Japanese in the Philippines, 29tJuly 1944

Japanese Attempts to Infiltrate the Muslims, August 1944

Singapore, 8 August 1944

Programmes of the Japanese in the Philippines, 1 September 1944

Black Propaganda, 5 October 1944

Programmes of the Japanese in Java and Bali, 1945

Programmes and Administation of the Japanese in Sumatra, 1945

Programmes of the Japanese in the Chinese Central Government,

20 January 1945

Programmes of the Japanese in Korea, 10 February 1945

The Indoctrination of the Youth in the Far East, 28 March 1945

Programmes of the Japanese in Manchuria, 30 April 1945

Indo-China, 31 August 1945

United States Records of the Foreign Broadcast Intelligence Service (National Archives, Washington D.C.):

Transcripts of Monitored Foreign Broadcasts: 1940-45

Daily Reports of Foreign Radio Broadcasts: September 1941-September 1945.

Quarterly Review: ca March 1942.

Special Releases January 1943-January 1944

Indexes to the Far Eastern Section of the Daily Report: January - September 1945

Daily Digests of Official Shortwave Broadcasts Beamed to North America: September-November 1941

Daily Digests of Official Shortwave Broadcasts Beamed to Latin America: September-November 1941

Daily Analyses of Propaganda concerning Latin America: August 1942-May1943

Weekly Analyses of Shortwave News and Propaganda Concerning Latin America: May-August 1943

Weekly Analyses of Propaganda Pressures on the United States: August-October 1942

Radio Reports on the Far East: August 1942-September 1945

Exposés of Enemy Radio Blunders: August-October 1942

Special Reports: Series I; July1941-February1942
Series II; April 1942-October 1944

Names and Places in the News: March 1943-February 1943

Shortwave Reception Notes October 1943-September 1945

Lists and Reports Pertaining to American Prosoners of War: 1944-5

Script of *From One American to Another*, 9th August 1945

Ward, Robert S.: *Hong Kong Under Japanese Occupation: A Case Study in the Enemy's Techniques of Control*

A report by the American Consul for the Far East Unit of the Bureau of Foreign and Domestic Commerce in the Department of Commerce, Washington D.C., 1943

(Hong Kong Public Records Office, Central, Hong Kong)

2. SECONDARY MATERIAL:

2.1 Japanese Language:

Fujiwara Ahihisa (1970), *Taiheiyō Sensō* [*The Pacific War*], No. 23 in the *Kokumin no Rekishii* Series Tokyo: Semin Buneitō

Hara Kōjirō (1978), *NHK: Kōkyō Hōsō no Rekishi to Kadai* [*NHK: The History and Problems of Public Broadcasting*] Tokyo: Kyuikusha

Ikeda Norizone (1979), *Hi no Maru Awâ* [*Hi no Maru Hour*] Tokyo: Chūōkōron-sha

Ikeda Norizone(1981), *Puropaganda Senshi* [*A History of Wartime Propaganda*] Tokyo: Chūōkōron-sha

Kitayama Setsurō (1982), *'Kaigai Hōsō Shōshi (Ichi)'* ['A Brief History of Overseas Broadcasting'] in Kaigai Hōsō Kenkyū Gurupu [Overseas Broadcasting Research Group] (ed.), NHK *Senji Kaigai Hōsō* [*NHK's Wartime Overseas Broadcasting*] Tokyo: Hara

Kitayama Setsurō (1988a), *Rajio Tōkyō: Shinju Wan e no Michi* [*Radio Tokyo: The Road to Pearl Harbour*]: Tokyo: Tabata Shōten

Kitayama Setsurō (1988b), *Rajio Tōkyō: "Daitōa" e no Michi* [*Radio Tokyo: The Road to "Greater East Asia"*]: Tokyo Tabata: Shōten

Kitayama Setsurō (1988c), *Rajio Tōkyō: Haiboku e no Michi* [*Radio Tokyo: The Road to Defeat*]: Tokyo: Tabata Shōten

Kitayama Setsurō (1995a) "Shūsen to Taigai Hōsō - Piisu Tōku to Atoroshitizu" [Overseas Broadcasting at the End of the War - Peace Talks and Atrocities], in *Media-shi Kenkyū - Media History* Vol. 2, February

Kitayama Setsurō (1995b), *Eiyaku Shūsen Shōsho* [*The English Translation of the Imperial Edict Ending the War*]: Author's personal notes, 17th June 1995

NHK (1977a), *Hōsō Gojū Nen-shi* [*50 Years of Broadcasting*] Volume 1, Tokyo: NHK

NHK (1977b), *Hōsō Gojū Nen-shi* [*50 Years of Broadcasting*] Volume 2, Tokyo: NHK

Ono Toshiro (1982), 'Sekai no Dempa Hōsō-sen' ['The World Radio War'] in Kaigai Hōsō Kenkyū Gurupu [Overseas Broadcasting Research Group] (ed.): *NHK Senji Kaigai Hōsō* [*NHK's Wartime Overseas Broadcasting*] Tokyo: Hara

Senzenki Kanryōsei Kenkyūkai [Pre-War Bureaucracy Research Group] (ed.) (1981), *Senzenki Nihon Kanryōsei no Seido . Soshiki .*

Junji [*The Organization, Structure and Personnel of the Japanese Pre-War Bureacracy*] Tokyo: Tokyo University Press

Uchida Yoshimi (ed.) (1973a), *Masu Media Tōsei* [*Mass Media Control*] Volume 1 (Volume 40 in *Gendai-shi Shiryō* Series), Tokyo: Misuzu Shōbo

Uchida Yoshimi (ed.) (1973b), *Masu Media Tōsei* [*Mass Media Control*] Volume 2 (Volume 41 in *Gendai-shi Shiryō* Series), Tokyo: Misuzu Shōbo

Yamamoto Fumio (ed.) (1973, *Nihon Masu Komyūnikêshon-shi* [*The History of Mass Communication in Japan*] Tokyo: Tokai Daigaku Shuppankai

2.2 English Language:

Adams, Michael C.C (1994), *The Best War Ever: America and World War II,* Baltimore: John Hopkins University Press

Aldrich, Richard J. (1993), *The Key to the South: Britain, the United States and Thailand during the Approach of the Pacific War*,Oxford: Oxford University Press

Allen, Louis (1977), *Singapore 1941-1945,* London: Davis-Poynter

Aung San Suu Kyi (1991), *Freedom from Fear and Other Writings,* New York: Penguin Books

Ba Maw (1968): *Breakthrough in Burma: Memoirs of a Revolution 1939-1946,* New Haven and London: Yale University Press

Baptiste, Joseph C. (1985), *The Enemy Among Us: World War Two Prisoners of War,* Ann Arbor, Michigan: University Microfilms International

Balfour, Michael (1979), *Propaganda in War, 1939-1945: Organisations, Policies and Publics in Britain and Germany*, London: Routledge & Kegan Paul

Bartlett, F.C. (1954), "The Aims of Political Propaganda" in Daniel Katz (ed.), *Public Opinion and Propaganda: A Book of Readings,* New York: Holt, Reinhart and Winston

Beasley, W. G. (1963), *The Modern History of Japan*, London: Wiedenfeld and Nicolson

Berelson, B. and De Grazia, S (1947), "Detecting Collaboration in Propaganda," in *Public Opinion Quarterly* 11.2

Best, Antony (1995), *Japan, Britain and Pearl Harbor: Avoiding War in East Asia 1936-41,* London: Routledge

Bhargava, Moti Lal (1982) *Netaji Subhas Chandra Bose in South East Asia and India's Liberation War 1943-45,* Kerala, India: Vishwavidya

Bischof, Günter and Dupont, Robert L. (eds) (1997) *The Pacific War Revisited*, Baton Rouge, Louisiana: Eisenhower Center, University of New Orleans

Boyer, Paul S., Clark, Clifford E. Jr., Kett, Joseph F., Salisbury, Neal, Sitkoff, Harvard, and Woloch, Nancy (1993) *The Enduring Vision: A History of the American People* Lexington, Mass.: D.C. Heath and Company

Boyle, Joseph Michael (1986), *British Foreign Policy During the Tientsin Crisis, 1939-1941*, Ann Arbor, Michigan: University Microfilms International

Briggs, Asa (1965a), *The History of Broadcasting in the United Kingdom: Volume 1: The Birth of Broadcasting,* London: Oxford University Press

Briggs, Asa (1965b), *The History of Broadcasting in the United Kingdom* Volume 2: *The Golden Age of Wireless,* London: Oxford University Press

Briggs, Asa (1985), *The BBC: The First Fifty Years,* Oxford & London: Oxford University Press

Buchanan, A. Russell (1964), *The United States and World War II, Volume 1,* New York: Harper & Row

Butow, Robert J. C. (1978), *Japan's Decision to Surrender*, Stanford, California: Stanford University Press

Cairns, John: (1992), *The BBC - Seventy Years of Broadcasting,* London: BBC

Calvocoressi, Peter, Wint, Guy and Prichard, John (1989), *Total War: The Causes and Courses of the Second World War* London: Penguin

Childs, Harwood L. and Whitton, John B. (eds.) (1942), *Propaganda by Shortwave,* Princeton: Princeton University Press

Crick, Bernard (1980), *George Orwell: A Life,* London: Martin Secker and Warburg Ltd.

Daniels, Gordon (1983), "Japanese Domestic Radio and Cinema Propaganda, 1937-45" in K.R.M. Short (ed.), *Film and Radio Propaganda in World War Two,* London: Croom Helm

De Mendelsson, Peter (1944), *Japan's Political Warfare,* London: George Allen and Unwin Ltd.

Dear, Ian C. B. (ed.) (1995), *The Oxford Companion to the Second World War,* Oxford: Oxford University Press

Doherty, Martin (1993), "Black Propaganda in the Second World War: The Concordia Broadcasts to Britain 1940-1," a paper given at the Institute of Contemporary British History's 6th Annual Summer School, *Britain and the Mass Media in the Twentieth Century*, 14-07-93.

Doob, Leonard W. (1948), *Public Opinion and Propaganda,* New York: Henry Holt and Co.

Doob, Leonard W. (1954), "Goebbels' Principles of Propaganda" in Daniel Katz, (ed.) *Public Opinion and Propaganda: A Book of Readings,* New York: Holt, Reinhart and Winston

Duus, Masayo (1979), *Tokyo Rose: The Orphan of the Pacific,* Kodansha International Ltd.

Elphick, Peter (1997) *Far East Asia File: The Intelligence War in the Far East 1930-45,* London: Hodder & Stoughton

Fussell, Paul (1989), *Wartime: Understanding and Behaviour in the Second World War,* New York: Oxford University Press

Gailey, Harry A (1995)., *The War in the Pacific: From Pearl Harbour to Tokyo Bay*, Presidio Press: Novato, California,

Hale, Julian (1975), *Radio Power: Propaganda and International Broadcasting*, Philadelphia: Temple University Press

Hall, John Whitney (1987), *Japan from Prehistory to Modern Time,* Tokyo: Charles E. Tuttle

Hart, Liddell (1992), *History of the Second World War*, London and Basingstoke: Macmillan Papermac

Hawthorn, Jeremy (ed.) (1987), *Propaganda, Persuasion and Polemic,* London: Edward Arnold

Hayashi, Ann Koto (1995), *Face of the Enemy, Heart of a Patriot: Japanese-American Internment Narratives,* New York & London: Garland Publishing Inc.

Herzstein, Robert Edwin (1979), *The War that Hitler Won: The Most Infamous Propaganda Campaign in History,* London: Hamish Hamilton

Hess, Gary R. (1986), *The United States at War 1941-1945,* Arlington Heights, Illinois: Harlan Davidson, Inc.

Hickman, Tom (1995), *What did you do in the War, Auntie? The BBC at War 1939-45,* London: BBC Books

Howe, Russell Warren (1990), *The Hunt for "Tokyo Rose"* Maryland and London: Madison Books

Hoyland, Carl I. And Weiss, Walter (1954), "The Influence of Source Credibility on Communication Effectiveness" in Daniel Katz, (ed.) *Public Opinion and Propaganda: A Book of Readings,* New York: Holt, Reinhart and Winston

Hunter, Janet (1989), *The Emergence of Modern Japan: An Introductory History Since 1853,* New York: Longman

Ienaga Saburo (1978), *The Pacific War: World War II and the Japanese 1931-1945*, New York, Pantheon Books

Iriye Akira (1981), *Power and Culture: The Japanese-American War, 1941-1945,* Cambridge, Massachusetts & London: Harvard University Press

Jowett, Garth S. and O'Donnell, Victoria (1986), *Propaganda and Persuasion,* Beverly Hills: (Sage Publications

Kasza, Gregory J. (1988), *The State and Mass Media in Japan, 1918-1945*, Berkley and Los Angeles: University of California Press

Kato, Masuo (1946), *The Lost War: A Japanese Reporter's Inside Story*, New York: Alfred A Knopf

Kitchen, Martin (1995), *Nazi Germany at War,* London: Longman

Kris, Ernst and Speier, Hans (1944), *German Radio Propaganda*, London and Oxford: Oxford University Press

Kurasawa Aiko (1988), *Mobilisation and Control: A Study of Social Change in Rural Java, 1942-1945*, Ann Arbor, Michigan: University Microfilms International

Kokusai Eiga Kyokai [International Cinema Association of Japan] (1938), *Cinema Yearbook of Japan 1938,* Tokyo: Kokusai Bunka Shinkokai

Large, Stephen S. (1992), *Emperor Hirohito and Showa Japan. A Political Biography,* London: Routledge

Lee, Loyd E. (ed) (1998), *World War II in Asia and the Pacific and the War's Aftermath, with General Themes: A Handbook of Literature and Research*, Westport, Connecticut and London: Greenwood Press

Levine, Alan T. (1995), *The Pacific War: Japan versus the Allies*, Westport, Connecticut: Praeger Publishers

Lyons, Michael J. (1999), *World War II: A Short History* 3rd Edition, Upper Saddle River, New Jersey: Prentice Hall

Mance, Osborne (1944), *International Telecommunications,* London: Oxford University Press

Masani, Zareer (1987), *Indian Tales of the Raj,* London: BBC Books

Mack Smith, Denis (1969), *Italy: A Modern History,* Ann Arbour: University of Michigan Press

Macksey, Kenneth (1987), *Military Errors of World War Two,* Poole, UK: Arms and Armour Press

Meo, L.D. (1968), *Japan's Radio War on Australia*, Melbourne: Melbourne University Press

Morris, John (1943), *Traveller From Tokyo,* London: Penguin Books Ltd.

Nair, A. M. (1985), *An Indian Freedom Fighter in Japan,* New Dehli: Vikas Publishing House

Nish, Ian H.(1985), "Japanese Reports on Indonesian Independence in 1945" in *International Studies* 85.2

Nish, Ian H. (1996), *Preparing for Peace and Survival: the Japanese Experience 1943-46,* Liddell Hart Centre for Military Archives Annual Lecture, 04-11-96

NHK Radio and Television Cultural Research Institute, History Compilation Room (1967), *The History of Broadcasting in Japan,* Tokyo: NHK

NHK Radio and Television Cultural Research Institute, History Compilation Room (1977c), *50 Years of Japanese Broadcasting,* Tokyo: N.H.K

Nobutaka Ike (ed.) (1967), *Japan's Decision For War: Records of the 1941 Policy Conferences,* Stanford, California: Stanford University Press

Owen, David (1993): *The Radio War*. Part 3 of BBC Radio Four's *Dirty Tricks* Series, broadcast 19.20 14-10-93

Pandy, B. N. (1969), *The Break-up of British India,* London: Macmillan

Porter, Bernard (1984), *The Lion's Share. A Short History of British Imperialism 1850 – 1983,* Harlow, UK: Longman

Purdy, Roger W. (1992), "Nationalism and News: 'Information Imperialism' and Japan, 1910-1936," in *The Journal of American-East Asian Relations* 1.3

Pronay, Nicholas & Taylor, Philip (1984), "An Improper Use of Broadcasting: The British Government and Clandestine Radio Operations against Germany during the Munich Crisis and After" in *Journal of Contemporary History* 19.3

Reynolds, E. Bruce & Kamchoo, Chiawa (1988) *Thai-Japanese Relations in Historical Perspective,* Bangkok: Inomedia Co. Ltd.

Reynolds, E. Bruce (1994), *Thailand and Japan's Southern Advance 1940*-45 Basingstoke: MacMillan

Robbins, Jane M. J. (1995), "Freedom Under Britain or Freedom Under Japan: The Radio Battle for India, December 1941-September 1945" in *Japan Forum* 7.2

Robbins, Jane M. J. (1996), "Japanese Overseas Broadcasting: The Manchuria Crisis and After (1931-1937)" in *Papers of the British Association for Korean Studies* 6

Robbins, Jane M. J. (2001), "Presenting Japan: the Role of Overseas Broadcasting by Japan during the Manchurian Incident (1931-1937)" in *Japan Forum* 13.1

Rolo, Charles (1943) *Radio Goes to War*, London: Faber and Faber

Rothermund, Dietmar (1993), *An Economic History of India From Pre-colonial Times to 1991,* London: Routledge

Sainsbury, Keith (1994), *Churchill and Roosevelt at War: The War they Fought and the Peace they Hoped to Make,* New York: New York University Press

Sheldon, Michael (1991), *Orwell: The Authorised Biography,* London: William Heinmann Ltd.

Shillony, Ben-Ami (1973), *Revolt in Japan: The Young Officers and the February 16 1936 Incident,* Princeton: Princeton University Press

Shillony, Ben-Ami (1981), *Politics and Culture in Wartime Japan,* Oxford: Clarendon Press

Sivram, M. (1966), *The Road to Dehli*, Tokyo: Charles Tuttle and Co.

Smith, Bradley F. (1996), *Sharing Secrets with Stalin: How the Allies Tracked Intelligence 1941-45*, Lawrence, Kansas: University Press of Kansas.

Spear, Percival (1983), *A History of India. Volume Two,* Harmondsworth, UK: Penguin Books Ltd.

Stembridge, Jasper H. (1945), *The Oxford War Atlas: The First Two Years,* London: Oxford University Press

Stephan, John J. (1984), *Hawaii Under the Rising Sun. Japan's Plans For Conquest After Pearl Harbor*, Honolulu: University of Hawaii Press

Storry, Richard (1965), *A History of Modern Japan,* Harmondsworth, UK: Penguin Books Ltd.

Taylor, Philip M. (1983), "Propaganda in International Politics" in K.R.M.Short (ed.), *Film and Radio Propaganda in World War Two,* London: Croom Helm

Taylor, Philip M. (1990), *Munitions of the Mind: War Propaganda from the Ancient World to the Nuclear Age,* Wellingborough, U.K: Patrick Stephens

Thorne, Christopher (1978), *Allies of a Kind: The United States, Britain and the War Against Japan,* London: Hamish Hamilton

Thorne, Christopher (1980), *Racial Aspects of the Far Eastern War 1941-1945 - Raleigh Lecture on History 1980*, Proceedings of the British Academy, LXVI, London: Oxford University Press

Thorne, Christopher (1986), *The Far Eastern War: States and Societies 1941-45,* London: Counterpoint, Unwin Paperbacks

Thorpe, Elliott R. (1969), *East Wind, Rain; The Intimate Account of and Intelligence Officer in the Pacific 1939-49,* Boston: Gambit Inc.

Tindall, George Brown and Shi, David E. (1993), *America: A Narrative History,* New York and London: W.W. Norton and Company

Trotter, Ann (1975), *Britain and East Asia 1933-1937,* London: Cambridge University Press

Turkell, Studs (1984), *The Good War: An Oral History of World War II*, New York: The New Press

Van Waterford (1994), *Prisoners of the Japanese in World War II: Statistical History, Personal Narratives and Memorials Concerning POWs in Camps and on Hellships, Civilian Internees, Asian Slave Laborers and Others Captured in the Pacific Theater,* Jefferson, North Carolina: McFarland & Co. Inc.

Varley, H. Paul (1973), *Japanese Culture,* Rutland, Vermont and Tokyo: Charles E. Tuttle Company Inc.

Walker, Andrew (1992), *A Skyful of Freedom: 60 Years of the BBC World Service,* London: BBC Books

Walters, F. P.(1960), *A History of the League of Nations,* London: Oxford University Press

Wasserstein, Bernard (1988), *The Secret Lives of Trebitsch Lincoln,* New Haven: Yale University Press

Welch, David (ed.) (1983), *Nazi Propaganda: The Power and the Limitations*, London Croom Helm

West, W.J. (ed.) (1985), *Orwell: The War Commentaries,* London: Dulkworth and Co. and BBC

West, W.J. (ed.) (1987), *Orwell: The War Broadcasts,* London: Penguin Books Ltd

Wetzler, Peter (1998), *Hirohito and War: Imperial Tradition and Miliary Decision Making in Prewar Japan*, Honolulu: University of Hawaii Press

Wilson, Dick (1983), *When Tigers Fight: The Story of the Sino-Japanese War, 1937-1945,* Harmondsworth, U.K.: Penguin Books Ltd.

Willmott, HP (1992), *The Great Crusade; A New Complete History of the Second World War,* London: Pimlico

Wood, James (1992), *History of International Broadcasting,* London: Peter Peregrinus Ltd.

Yoon, Won Zoon (1978), *Japan's Occupation of Burma 1941-1945,* Ann Arbor, Michigan: University Microfilms International

Zacharias, Ellis M., Capt, USN (1946), *Secret Missions: The Story of an Intelligence Officer,* New York: GP Putnam's Sons

2.3 German Language:

Boelke, Willi A. (1977): *Die Macht des Radios: Weltpolitik und Auslandsrundfunk 1924-1976* [*The Power of Radio: World Politics and Overseas Radio 1924-1976*], Berlin: Ullstein

INDEX

Printed in Italy by

LCM, Milano

and In UK and USA by Ligthning Source

www.ingramcontent.com/pod-product-compliance
Ingram Content Group UK Ltd.
Pitfield, Milton Keynes, MK11 3LW, UK
UKHW041843190726
13854UKWH00002B/693